MILITARIZATION AND VIOLEN
WOMEN IN CONFLICT ZONES
MIDDLE EAST

This book examines and discusses the ordeals that women face as violence is perpetrated against them in politically conflicted and militarized areas. In conflict zones, every act is affected by, dependent on, and mobilized by militaristic values. The militarization of both the private and public space and the use of the gendered bodies increase the vulnerability of both men and women, and further masculinizes the patriarchal hegemonic powers. Through the stories and ordeals of women in politically conflicted areas and war zones, and by sharing voices of Palestinian women from the Occupied Territories, it is shown that claims based on 'security reasoning', fear from 'terrorism', nationalism, preservation of 'cultural authenticity', and preservation of the land can turn women's bodies and lives into boundary markers and thus sites of violence, contestation, and resistance.

DR NADERA SHALHOUB-KEVORKIAN is a senior lecturer at the Hebrew University of Jerusalem Faculty of Law's Institute of Criminology.

CAMBRIDGE STUDIES IN LAW AND SOCIETY

Cambridge Studies in Law and Society aims to publish the best scholarly work on legal discourse and practice in its social and institutional contexts, combining theoretical insights and empirical research.

The fields that it covers are: studies of law in action; the sociology of law; the anthropology of law; cultural studies of law, including the role of legal discourses in social formations; law and economics; law and politics; and studies of governance. The books consider all forms of legal discourse across societies, rather than being limited to lawyers' discourses alone.

The series editors come from a range of disciplines: academic law; socio-legal studies; sociology; and anthropology. All have been actively involved in teaching and writing about law in context.

Series editors

Chris Arup
Monash University, Victoria
Martin Chanock
La Trobe University, Melbourne
Pat O'Malley
University of Sydney
Sally Engle Merry
New York University
Susan Silbey
Massachusetts Institute of Technology

Books in the Series

Diseases of the Will
Mariana Valverde

The Politics of Truth and Reconciliation in South Africa
Legitimizing the Post-Apartheid State
Richard A. Wilson

Modernism and the Grounds of Law
Peter Fitzpatrick

Unemployment and Government
Genealogies of the Social
William Walters

Autonomy and Ethnicity
Negotiating Competing Claims in Multi-Ethnic States
Yash Ghai

Constituting Democracy
Law, Globalism and South Africa's Political Reconstruction
Heinz Klug

The Ritual of Rights in Japan
Law, Society, and Health Policy
Eric A. Feldman

The Invention of the Passport
Surveillance, Citizenship and the State
John Torpey

Governing Morals
A Social History of Moral Regulation
Alan Hunt

The Colonies of Law
Colonialism, Zionism and Law in Early Mandate Palestine
Ronen Shamir

Law and Nature
David Delaney

Social Citizenship and Workfare in the United States and Western Europe
The Paradox of Inclusion
Joel F. Handler

Law, Anthropology and the Constitution of the Social
Making Persons and Things
Edited by Alain Pottage and Martha Mundy

Judicial Review and Bureaucratic Impact
International and Interdisciplinary Perspectives
Edited by Marc Hertogh and Simon Halliday

Immigrants at the Margins
Law, Race, and Exclusion in Southern Europe
Kitty Calavita

Lawyers and Regulation
The Politics of the Administrative Process
Patrick Schmidt

Law and Globalization from Below
Toward a Cosmopolitan Legality
Edited by Boaventura de Sousa Santos and Cesar A. Rodriguez-Garavito

Public Accountability
Designs, Dilemmas and Experiences
Edited by Michael W. Dowdle

Law, Violence and Sovereignty among West Bank Palestinians
Tobias Kelly

Legal Reform and Administrative Detention Powers in China
Sarah Biddulph

The Practice of Human Rights
Tracking Law Between the Global and the Local
Edited by Mark Goodale and Sally Engle Merry

Judges Beyond Politics in Democracy and Dictatorship
Lessons from Chile
Lisa Hilbink

Paths to International Justice
Social and Legal Perspectives
Edited by Marie-Bénédicte Dembour and Tobias Kelly

Law and Society in Vietnam
The Transition from Socialism in Comparative Perspective
Mark Sidel

Constitutionalizing Economic Globalization
Investment Rules and Democracy's Promise
David Schneiderman

The New World Trade Organization Agreements: 2nd Edition
Globalizing Law Through Intellectual Property and Services (2nd Edition)
Christopher Arup

Justice and Reconciliation in Post-Apartheid South Africa
Edited by François du Bois, Antje du Bois-Pedain

Militarization and Violence against Women in Conflict Zones in
the Middle East
A Palestinian Case-Study
Nadera Shalhoub-Kevorkian

Child Pornography and Sexual Grooming
Legal and Societal Responses
Suzanne Ost

MILITARIZATION AND VIOLENCE AGAINST WOMEN IN CONFLICT ZONES IN THE MIDDLE EAST

A Palestinian Case-Study

Nadera Shalhoub-Kevorkian

CAMBRIDGE
UNIVERSITY PRESS

CAMBRIDGE
UNIVERSITY PRESS

University Printing House, Cambridge CB2 8BS, United Kingdom

Published in the United States of America by Cambridge University Press, New York

Cambridge University Press is part of the University of Cambridge.

It furthers the University's mission by disseminating knowledge in the pursuit of education, learning and research at the highest international levels of excellence.

www.cambridge.org
Information on this title: www.cambridge.org/9780521708791

© Nadera Shalhoub-Kevorkian 2009

First published 2009, 2011
Second Edition 2012
Reprinted 2013

A catalogue record for this publication is available from the British Library

ISBN 978-0-521-88222-4 Hardback
ISBN 978-0-521-70879-1 Paperback

To all Palestinian women

If you can see only what light reveals and hear only what
    sound announces,
Then in truth you do not see nor do you hear.

(Gibran 1995: 57)

CONTENTS

FIGURES

ACKNOWLEDGEMENTS

I want to begin by thanking all women who participated in this book project and whose voices shaped my analyses. This book would not have been possible without the generosity, trust, and openness of many Palestinian women. I want to thank them for their patience in replying to all my queries and for their continuous support in analysing and understanding the ordeals of Palestinian women facing militarization and the ongoing occupation. When in doubt, I always went to them, whether in Jerusalem, Gaza, Jenin, Nablus, Ramalah, or Hebron. They are the ones who gave me the benefit of their analyses and helped me theorize by involving me in their daily lives and telling me their life stories, their histories, fears, worries, challenges, and more. They taught me how to search for the unseen and hear the unheard, question the unquestioned, and understand their voices and languages. They showed me different ways to approach their resistance, agency, and struggle and the need for persistence in order to accomplish goals.

I also wish to thank those individuals who could not be with me while producing this book but whose contributions are reflected herein. I especially acknowledge the love of my father Jamil Shalhoub and my grandmother Wardeh Salloum, whose struggles created the foundation that nurtured my thinking, especially when I became discouraged. I also want to thank my family, for they were the most essential in the book's completion. For three years, my biological mom Evelyn Shalhoub, my mother-in-law Mary Kevorkian, my husband Gaby Kevorkian, and my daughters Maro, Tamar, and Salpy lived with my uncertainties, my challenges and struggles, while writing this book. They lived through my absences from home, but despite such absences we all became a closer, stronger, and more supportive family. My youngest sister Yasmin Shalhoub and my brother-in-law Jule Awwad were always willing to share with me their insights and offered their warm home, which reminded me that Palestinian families, close or far, together or apart, always know how to create a place filled with warmth, the smells of wonderful food, and much love.

A special thank you goes to a family member by choice, Michael B. Preston, a professor of political science at the University of Southern California, and a man who is more than a friend and partner, a man to whom I am indebted. Professor Preston shared with me the ordeals of his people, the Blacks in America. He made me re-read Fanon, discussed bell hooks with me for hours on end, explained Derrida, Foucault, and Agamben; together, we explored ideas. One cannot ask for a better mentor to organize ideas and develop them into a book project.

I owe my friends and colleagues at the Women's Studies Center, the Family Defense Society, and the Women's Center for Legal Aid and Counseling a special debt for their insights and materials and for supporting my various research projects. Special thanks goes to my colleagues and friends Maha Abu-Dayyeh, Fatmeh Al Muaqat, Suraida Hussein, Rana Salfiti, Halimeh Abu Sulb, Hanan Bakri, and Sama Aweidah for the long discussions and their wonderful insights. To director Natasha Khalidi and staff Zahra, Odeit, Mariam, Sheren, Duha, and Samar at the Jerusalem Center for Women I owe a big 'thank you'. They facilitated much of my fieldwork over the last three years and their assistance allowed me to be in the field and so meet the wonderful Palestinian women who have suffered from the loss of their beloved ones – losses due to violence or incarceration – and from the loss and demolitions of their homes. A special thank you goes to World Vision-Jerusalem, especially to Allyn and Holly Dhynes, Charles Clayton, and Dan Simmons, for funding my project on the effect of the Israeli Separation Wall on children in Jerusalem.

Special thanks goes to Professor Sherene Razack of the Ontario Institute for Studies in Education, University of Toronto, who through the many talks and deep discussions we have had and her countless reading recommendations, led me to look in depth into issues facing women in conflict-ridden areas. Many thanks go to my friends Nan Stein at Wellesley College and Sally Merry at New York University; without their encouragement and constant guidance, I could not have finished this book.

Special thanks goes to Aaron Back, Rosemary Sayigh, Eileen Kuttab, Rita Giacaman, Cynthia Enloe, Daphna Golan-Agnon, Zaheera Kamal, Fadia Daibes, Aida Touma-Suliman, Himmat Zu'bi, Einas Odeh Haj, Areej Sabbagh, Nabil Elsaleh, Michael Karayanni, Raef Zreik, Manar Hasan, David Myers, Nomi Stolzenberg, and Areen Hawari. Through various discussions and brain-storming meetings, they all helped me to complete the writing of this book, as well as challenging it. My friends and colleagues Prof. Nahla Abdo, Prof. Leslie Sebba, Prof. Simha Landau, and Prof. Dorit Roer-Strier were always there to meet and talk about my ideas and to ask me good questions in order to help me think through my problems, whether philosophical, analytical, or methodological. Dorit made the School of Social Work at the Hebrew University a wonderful workplace and home for the past three years.

In addition, a big thank you goes to my colleagues at the Hebrew University, the University of California, Los Angeles, and the University of Southern California who listened to partial articulations of ideas, read earlier drafts, and offered much encouragement and intellectual stimulation. Special thanks goes to Prof. Chris Littleton from the UCLA Law School, who not only spent many nights sharpening the ideas but also offered her office, so much chocolate, and much more to create a safe haven for me so that I could finish the book.

I am especially indebted to Mada al-Carmel (the Arab Center for Applied Social Research) in Haifa. Through its insightful seminars, its academic activities, and above all through its openness and willingness to be there for me when I needed work through theoretical or methodological challenges, I was able to complete this book. A special thank you goes to Prof. Nadim Rouhana, Mada's director, who constantly encouraged me to discuss with him my ideas and concerns and who offered new and very insightful venues of thinking. Nadim pushed me towards finishing the book.

I am deeply grateful to my two editors Dr Shantanu Duttaahmed and Stephan Dobson, without whom the book would not be in its current shape. They both were extremely helpful in shaping my argument and correcting my language. I am also greatly indebted to many teachers and colleagues in the past: Ahmad Baker, Ibrahim Abu-Lughod, Mili Mass, and Stan Cohen for introducing me to new theories, concepts, and analytical lines.

During the course of this work, I was supported in part by Ford Foundation, UNIFEM, World Vision, Kvina Tel Kvina, Institute of Criminology-Hebrew University, and Women for Women's Human Rights research grants.

Finally, Tamar Berenblum, Sana Khsheiboun, and Tal Grietzer, three special persons, participated in virtually every phase of this book. As a research assistant, Tamar read and handled the many queries of my editors, checked every single line of the book, and spent many weekends in my house in the old city of Jerusalem, pushing me towards finishing the manuscript. Sana, my PhD student and friend, was always ready not only to read, spend hours listening to my ideas, collecting new data, finding missing references, and offering new interpretations, but was also there to offer her place with the wonderful food Kamilia prepared – a space for peace of mind for body and soul. Tal, from the UCLA law school, never turned down any of my requests for help when looking for a reference, when searching for new material, and when needing him to help out in faxing, photocopying, or looking for new books and articles.

Nadera Shalhoub-Kevorkian
Old City Jerusalem

CHAPTER 1

INTRODUCTION

Fahimeh, a woman called Um Riad by her neighbours in the Jenin refugee camp, was sitting on her balcony, half of which had been destroyed during the Israeli invasion in 2002. She was talking to me while making food for her children, the ones who were still with her, as one had been killed and two others had been imprisoned. She keeps a piece of paper in her brassiere – the *Kushan* that establishes her ownership of her house in Haifa, which she has owned since 1948 but which she has been unable to visit due to her displacement and exile. She said (the translations are mine): '*Kataluna Bi Dun Rahmeh*' – 'they killed us without any mercy'. She added: 'We were tortured, humiliated, invaded [she paused for a couple of seconds] … how history repeats itself, history repeat itself'. She stopped talking momentarily while gazing around her at the destruction of her home and the neighbouring houses and then continued: 'In their crimes they strengthened our history … with our resistance we will build our future; let me finish cooking for those who are still with us'.

Um Riad's ordeal points to the three main issues that this book addresses. First, it shares and thereby reveals women's suffering in war zones. Second, it shows the way in which women in war zones and under military occupation become warriors and resisters, what I call frontliners. As with Um Riad, with her few possessions, with her wrecked balcony, her hidden *Kushan*, and her survival strategies, the contribution of women frontliners to resistance is usually invisible to outsiders and for the most part goes mostly unnoticed, but it exhibits a great deal of power and resilience. Fighting with whatever resources they can muster,

1

women such as Um Riad – with her destroyed balcony that symbolizes her losses but simultaneously also signifies her history, legacy, and activism – reflect the hidden energies within women who are confronting political violence. Her voice, as with many other women's voices in this book – and indeed in other conflict areas across the globe – speaks truth to power through her daily resistance against the settler-colonial project and its gendered violence in all of its geo-political, bio-political, economic, and psychological forms. As such, a major theme of this book is how Palestinian women's resistance, agency, and victimization, as with all women in conflict zones and under occupation and as exemplified by Um Riad's resilience, is an inescapably analytical feminist location that should be acknowledged and acted upon.

The third issue addressed by this book is the complex way in which hegemonic economic, political, and patriarchal powers, including the mass media, ostracize Palestinian women and reproduce oppressive gender politics. If someone looks at Um Riad through the hegemonic lens, he or she might construct an image of this Palestinian woman based upon the popular discourses, such as the US media's portrayal of Palestinian women as 'bad' mothers who 'couldn't care less' for any of their losses, or who encourage 'terrorism', support extremism, and generally promote violence. Too often, their suffering, pain, and voices are camouflaged by the physics of the authority of Empire and the politics of representation that are a-historicized and de-contextualized. As an Orientalist perspective, this discourse transforms men and women into faceless, voiceless, and a-historical subjects who lack agency and who are in need of 'modernization' to raise them up from their 'uncivilized' state. Other discourses focus only on women's victimization, their displacement, and so on without looking at the complexity of the geo-economic politics of their suffering and loss. The dramatization of women's helplessness and victimization, the demonization of their actions of resistance, and much else that falls in between will be extensively discussed in this book, all based on women's own words and experiences. In Chapters 3, 4, and 5, I discuss various discourses that are related to the complex ways local and global forces impact women while showing the way the machinery of oppression turns women's bodies, their sexuality and minds, into symbols of heroism, victimization, helplessness, and identity, and ultimately create them as boundary markers. In so doing, I show the way in which colonialist military power carves its strength and inscribes its boundaries on the most personal realms of individual women's lives, bodies, families, sexuality, homes, spaces, and gender relations.

Fourth, I look at the way the issues of women's 'modernization', liberty, and 'rights' can be discussed when the politics of women's resistance in a conflict zone is deeply affected by the global economy of fear. Women's rights to education, freedom of movement, freedom from violence, right to resistance, and so on are perceived as part of the general ideological war between the haves and the have-nots, the West and the rest, the 'civilized' and the 'Otherized', thereby turning women's bodies, suffering, and lives in conflict zones into ones that have no right to *right*. The rights of many women living in the global South who face political violence and continuous displacement are negotiated constantly, as are their spaces, places, locations, bodies, sexualities, lives, and futures, thereby turning women into boundary markers (see Kandiyoti 1992: 246). The use of the language of 'rights' and the language of 'modernization' and 'liberation' turns out to be very problematic, not because it is a façade – a lie – but because one's rights and liberty are defined by those in power, by the state, the occupiers, etc. As Abu-Lughod stated in her introduction to her edited volume *Remaking Women*: 'With regard to remaking women, discussion revolved around the roles as mothers, as managers of the domestic realm, as wives of men, and as citizens of nation ... with a critical eye for the way in which they might not have been purely liberatory' (1998: 8). This need to 'remake' and 'liberate' women transforms women's voices – and feminist discussions concerning these voices, discussions that wrestle between the extremes of Orientalism and fundamentalism – into what Abu-Lughod termed 'minefields' (in reference to the current imperialist obsession with 'the plight of Muslim women') that require careful scrutiny (Abu-Lughod 2002: 783). In her discussion of the project of 'modernization', Mervat Hatem posed the question of whether such a project exacerbated class and gender inequality and jeopardized working class and rural – and I would add women's – statuses in terms of violence against women in conflict areas and war zones (1993: 117–22). The fact that such feminist analyses are considered part of the global economy of fear that are also affected by the multiplicity of violent contexts in conflict zones and the global structure of power must further complicate our analyses.

Sally Merry Engle traces the links between global production and local appropriation and examines how human rights law works in practice, reminding us that even the human rights language is challenged when dealing with gender violence. As she states:

> Like colonialism, human rights discourses contain implicit assumptions about the nature of civilized and backward societies, often glossed as

modern and traditional. Concepts of civilization and savagery, rationality and passion, that were fundamental binaries of thinking during the imperialist era creep back into debates over human rights and social justice. The practice of human rights is burdened by colonialist understanding.

(2006: 226)

Many questions remain to be addressed. How can we sustain the multiplicity of women's resistance and agency, and how can we uphold a 'politics of difference', in a world that constantly homogenizes diversity? How can the voice of the subaltern be raised, heard, and sustained? How can I bring into writing representative spaces of the female subaltern Other? And how can I gather together women's voices in a way that can help me create more power to prevent silence and silencing? In drawing from my activism and research as a Palestinian woman in the field, it seems that I am always borrowing meaning from the voices of those negotiating a narrow path between moments of power, agency, and victimization; moments of dire need; moments when one needs to scream when one's words have been stolen. When the tears have yet to dry, Palestinian women continue to fight back. Perhaps the world did not hear Um Riad, maybe it missed the complex connection between victimization and agency that lies in her voice; but this book tries to unravel the complexity of the connection between women's suffering and their agency for a world in denial. In her way of sitting on her balcony, in her preservation of her *Kushan*, I heard a cry to historicize suffering; in her silences I heard echoes of the very painful present, and even more her survival and resistance. The story of Um Riad is only one reflection of the story of the suffering of the Palestinian people, my people, who were dispossessed as a result of the Zionist actions, who suffered from the settler-colonial project that resulted in the Nakba (catastrophe) of 1948, who have been persecuted in their Diaspora and exile, and who have been disregarded and denied rights by the Western Empire. But it is also the story of those who have, like Um Riad, risen with new strength from every disaster.

In listening to Palestinian women's voices as they engage in acts of resistance – whether minute or large-scaled – this project considers these women to be miraculous survivors of a sustained attack on their historical legacy as well as on their socio-economic and psychological well-being. I advocate the use of the term frontliners in referring to Palestinian women, for they always incur the first wave of violence as well as the final one. As the narratives in the ensuing chapters will reveal, whether as guerrilla fighters or protectors of the domestic sphere, the 'frontlines' that these women occupy constitute the most visible position in the field of activity in daily life within a conflict zone, positions of grave responsibility. Occupying the material space of the frontline, these women must often carry the burdens of the outcome of the fighting. These women survive both the daily assaults against their quotidian activities and the psychological warfare that is endemic to a militarized zone. By bringing the voices of these frontliners to the forefront of my work, I hope to reveal the unseen and unrecognized agency of these women.

This project has come to fruition amidst moments of such urgency, while sitting on the balcony with Um Riad, while walking with women in their daily struggles for survival. The book was written while witnessing and living the Palestinian Intifadas (uprisings), the invasions, targeted assassinations, internal violence, house demolitions, land confiscations, imprisonments, torture, and more. It is based on my observations and interventions as a feminist activist, my clinical work as a therapist, my research projects as a criminologist and victimologist, and my own personal experiences as a Palestinian woman born and raised in Haifa, a mother of three young women, and an Israeli citizen living for the past twenty-seven years in the Old City Jerusalem. Given this mix of positions and persuasions, no doubt contradictions abound in my own words and I leave those contradictions in place.

HISTORICAL OVERVIEW

> Zionism, be it right or wrong, good or bad, is rooted in age-long traditions, in present needs, in future hopes, of far greater import than the desires and prejudices of the 700,000 Arabs who now inhabit that ancient land.
> (Arthur James Balfour, 11 August 1919)

> The Palestinians must be made to understand in the deepest recesses of their consciousness that they are a defeated people.
> (Moshe Yaalon, Israeli Army Chief of Staff, August 2002)

Both the international political legacy and the Palestinian genocide, as reflected in the previous epigrams, affect and mirror the current socio-economic, geo-political, and military situation affecting gender relations in Palestine. The tragedy of Palestine and the Palestinians, the continuing occupation of the land and the resulting oppression, was best described by the late Edward Said in his explanation of how the Palestinians were rendered voiceless (1984). For a group of people who are constantly being 'summarized' by the West, I am generally resistant to providing 'short histories' of Palestine but for the purposes of this introduction, an overview is necessary.

Prior to, during, and following 1948, the Jewish colonial movement and then its state massacred thousands of Palestinians, demolished entire towns, and forced inhabitants to flee or be killed. One question that was raised by Falak, a nineteen-year-old student in Al-Najah University, was addressed to her mother. She asked, 'Why did we leave our houses in 1948?' Her mother answered: 'I wish we had died instead of leaving but they threw us out of our houses.' Why did the Palestinians leave their homes, lands, farms, animals, and belongings to the newly arrived Jewish immigrants? Why did my own mother leave, leaving behind her parents, her house, her memories, having to walk, bare-footed, carrying three children aged four months to three years, with only the clothing that she was wearing? Why, by the end of the 1949 fighting, were almost a million Palestinians forced off their land? The history of the Palestinians shows that 400 to 500 Arab villages in Palestine were taken over by the Jewish state while leaving the inhabitants refugees lacking the right to return (for more detail, see, for example, the writings of Illan Pappe 2007 and Nur Masalha 1992). In the Palestinian village of Safsaf, for example, four women were raped, four were killed, and fifty-two men were tied up with a rope, dropped into a well, and then shot, with an additional ten more killed separately. In Sa'Sa, another village, there were cases of mass murder with over 100 dead and the whole village population expelled.

Rashid Khalidi argues that: 'it was Great Britain rather than the United States that initially created the problem of Palestine. But in Palestine, as elsewhere, it has been the lot of America, Britain's successor as the Western power with undisputed hegemony over the Middle East, to contend with this problem and its seemingly unending sequels.' Khalidi continues by stating:

> The outlines of the problem can be simply stated: with the Balfour Declaration of November 2, 1917, Britain threw the weight of the greatest power of the age, one that was at that moment in the process of conquering Palestine, behind the creation of a Jewish state in what was then an overwhelmingly Arab country. Everything that has followed in that conflict-riven land has flowed inevitably from this decision.
>
> (Khalidi 2004: 118)

Jewish Israeli historians have discussed the abuses inflicted upon Palestinians by the Jewish state, defining the Nakba, the Palestinian disaster in 1948–9, as 'ethnic cleansing' or 'crimes against humanity' (Kimmerling and Migdal 2003; Morris 2001; Pappe 1994, 2007). Others, such as Norman Finkelstein (1995) and Edward Said and Hitchens (2001) have argued that, at bottom, Israel offered two limited options for the indigenous Palestinian people: either eviction and expulsion or semi-imprisonment within a 'semi-Apartheid' state. Despite the clear injustice that Palestine and the Palestinians have suffered, political powers including the US supported the Zionist state for political reasons, ignoring the human disaster that it caused. Unable to marshal a powerful lobbying group, the Palestinians have consistently failed to gain a fair hearing. Hence, the terrible memories from the Holocaust, combined with the vivid biblical narrative that justifies the Jewish 'right' to the Palestinian land, and supported by the vivid and familiar narrative of an America that leans towards supporting Israel, have together made it difficult for both Arabs and Palestinians to make an impact on the political system of Empire. Rashid Khalidi explains:

> in the wake of the murderous, suicide attacks of September 11, 2001, on New York and Washington, the convergence between the policies of the Bush administration and the government of Prime Minister Ariel Sharon has reached the point that they are virtually indistinguishable in a number of realms, notably as regards what has become their shared rhetoric on the topic of 'terrorism'. Nowadays, Palestinian militant groups like Hamas and Islamic Jihad are lumped together with al-Qai'da in the statements of the Bush administration and the Israeli government, and increasingly appear to be the object of the similar attention in US law and as a target of law enforcement agencies.
>
> (2004: 122)

In general, the attitude of Jews towards Arabs when the former reached Palestine was hostile. In 1917, the British government, in secret and without regard for the existing native majority, transmitted a promise to the Zionist Federation concerning the creation of a Jewish 'homeland' in Palestine. During the British occupation of Palestine (1918–48), Palestinian peasants, who in 1920 constituted approximately 80 per cent of the indigenous population, contributed more than any other class to the national resistance movement, yet due to lack of economic means they never led it (Sayigh 1979). The Palestinian peasants' exclusion from knowledge and decision-making

was deepened during the British occupation, an exclusion that contributed to their vulnerability and led in many cases to their eviction,
displacement, and Diaspora during the catastrophe of 1948. However,
the Arab resistance to Zionism prior to the founding of the Israeli state
was overt and explicit. Between 1936 and 1940, Palestinians conducted
a nationalist revolt against the British Mandate that expressed an
implicit resistance against Zionism that was clear to many of the
Zionist leaders, including Ben Gurion. In his book *The Fateful
Triangle*, Noam Chomsky (1984) illustrates the way in which
Palestinians viewed the Zionists as aggressors who wanted to take their
lands. In May of 1948, the state of Israel was created, and approximately
700,000 Palestinians either fled the area or were expelled.

The story of the Palestinian catastrophe is the story of people who are
paying for 'the sins of Europe and America'. Chomsky summarizes:

> The Jews of Europe suffered a disaster on a scale and of a character
> unknown in human history, following upon centuries of persecution
> and terror. Their growing national movement turned back to a homeland
> that had not been abandoned in memory of tradition. The author of the
> Balfour Declaration expressed widely-held sentiments in the industrial
> West when he wrote, in 1919, that 'Zionism, be it right or wrong, good or
> bad, is rooted in age-long tradition, in present needs, in future hopes, of
> far profound import than the desires and prejudices of 700,000 Arabs who
> now inhabit that ancient land' ... Somehow the Palestinian peasants
> mired in their prejudice, were never able to appreciate their moral
> responsibility to expiate the sins of Christian Europe. Whatever one
> may think of the conflicting claims to national and human rights in the
> former Palestine, it is difficult not to be appalled when Western politi-
> cians and intellectuals explain their backing for Israel's policies in terms
> of 'moral obligation', as if the sins of the Nazis and their predecessors, or of
> the Americans who closed the doors to refugees from Hitler's horrors,
> require the sacrifice of the Palestinians – on moral grounds. How easy it is
> to meet one's moral obligations by sacrificing someone else's life.
>
> (1991: 3)

Moreover, Hanna Arendt states:

> after the war it turned out that the Jewish question, which was considered
> the only insoluble one, was indeed solved – namely, by means of a
> colonised and then conquered territory – but this solved neither the
> problem of the minorities nor the stateless. On the contrary, like virtually
> all other events of the 20th century, the solution of the Jewish question
> merely produced a new category of refugees, the Arabs, thereby

increasing the number of stateless and rightless by another 700,000 to
800,000 people. And what happened in Palestine within the smallest
territory and in terms of hundreds of thousands was then repeated in India
on a large scale involving many millions of people.

(1951: 290)

Hanna Arendt's insight shows us that Hitlerian politics should not be
seen as exceptional but rather as exemplary of a certain way of managing
vulnerable populations. It is a policy that produced the ordeal of Um
Riad and many other Palestinians, and also the pain of expulsion and
loss of family, land, and home. Subsequently, it rationalized the expulsions of the Palestinians as 'stateless people across the borders', to gather
them in small enclaves and camps in order to render them largely
invisible to the outside world. These moves were part of a process
defined by Pappe as 'the ethnic cleansing of Palestine'. Pappe investigates the fate suffered by the indigenous population of Palestine in the
1940s at the hands of the Zionist political and military leadership. He
offers a detailed account of the events of 1947–8 that eventually led to
the biggest refugee problem in modern history. During this period,
around a million people were expelled from their own country at
gunpoint, civilians were massacred, and over 400 to 500 Palestinian
villages were deliberately destroyed. Pappe persuasively argues that the
consequent dispossession of a million native Palestinians from their
homeland and the continued denial of their right of return constitute
a violation of international human rights. He decisively links these
events to contemporary Middle East politics and the prospects for a
lasting peace in the country and, therefore, in the region (2007).

It is against this history that we need to contextualize the ongoing fear
of ethnic cleansing in Palestine, a fear that is understandable given the
reality of such crimes in the past. These crimes against the Palestinians
have been manifested in various ways, including massacres of villagers
(such as took place at Doueimah, Qibya, and Kafr Kasem), population
expulsions (such as that of 70,000 residents from Lydda and Ramle), and
displacements (as with thousands of Bedouins) (Said and Hitchens 2001).
Israeli state crimes have included, among other punitive policies against
Palestinians, deportation, assassinations, and collective punishments of
civilians, demolition of homesteads, torture, and a fatality rate maintained
at between 50 to 100 Palestinians dead for every Jewish fatality.

The onset of the First Intifada in December 1987 awakened the West
from its slumber concerning the issue of Palestine and raised awareness
of the Palestinian cause and its demands for justice. At the Oslo

conference in 1993, labelled the 'peace process', Palestinians were led to believe that Israel would withdraw from the West Bank and Gaza and would come to an agreement with it on both the status of Jerusalem and the right of return of Palestinian refugees. However, regardless of which political party was in power, Israel has continued to demolish houses, take over Arab neighbourhoods in East Jerusalem, confiscate land, imprison Palestinians, and construct new checkpoints, all the while restricting Palestinian freedom of movement by interfering with access to workplaces, hospitals, schools, and other spaces of everyday life. As Palestinian protests grew in response to these continuing oppressions, the Israeli army rocketed several Palestinian cities, destroying entire neighbourhoods and causing large casualties. By September 2000, many Palestinians realized that Israeli policy was not aimed at ending the occupation, nor was it seeking peace. Uri Avnery, an Israeli peace activist, stated on 3 February 2001 that Prime Minister Ehud Barak

> promised peace and brought war, and not by accident. While speaking about peace, he enlarged the settlements. Cut the Palestinian territories into pieces by 'by-pass' roads. Confiscated lands. Demolished homes. Uprooted trees. Paralyzed the Palestinian economy. Conducted negotiations in which he tried to dictate to the Palestinians a peace that amounts to capitulation. Was not satisfied with the fact that by accepting the Green Line, the Palestinians had already given up 78% of their historic homeland. Demanded the annexation of 'settlement blocks' and pretended that they amount to only 3% of the territory, while in fact he meant more than 20% would remain under Israeli control. Wanted to coerce the Palestinians to accept a 'state' cut off from all its neighbors and composed of several enclaves isolated from each other, each surrounded by Israeli settlers and soldiers ... Boasts publicly that he has not given back to the Palestinians one inch of territory ... When the intifada broke out, sent snipers to shoot, in cold blood from a distance, hundreds of unarmed demonstrators, adults and children. Blockaded each village and town separately, bringing them to the verge of starvation, in order to get them to surrender. Bombarded neighborhoods. Started a policy of mafia-style 'liquidations', causing an inevitable escalation of the violence.
>
> (Avnery 2001)

PALESTINIAN WOMEN ON THE FRONTLINES

Palestinian women's proactive responses to oppression, those voices and their choices made within the complex reality of occupation, were and are deeply influenced by the legacies of loss and the constant fear of ethnic cleansing, continuous displacement, and other violent politics. Their acts were and are affected by the juxtaposition of local factors (historical legacy, geopolitics, and a spatial policy of colonization; the existing context of a gender hierarchy; the politico-economic and social conditions) and global ones involving conflicts and political developments among powers (Western colonization and the policies that emerged in the late 1980s and early 1990s such as the New World Order, the Gulf War, the attack on New York City on 9/11, the 'war against terror', the war against Afghanistan, the occupation of Iraq, capitalist restructuring, and the list goes on), combined with the regional context. The evolving localized context of Palestinian women's resistance grew amid colonial Zionist and militaristic Israeli policies that continually violated Palestinian norms and morality, these together with an increase over time in the power of the Empire's denial of Palestinian suffering.

The context of political despair and the hegemonic silencing of both the Palestinian voice and cause have influenced women's resistance, including the development of an organized women's movement. Such political activism, be it on the personal level or the public level of social and political groups, was deeply affected by changes at the national Palestinian level. Reema Nazal, for example, has emphasized that the national cause and the political parties were the basis for the establishment of various developmental, social, and civil women's organizations. She explained that the main problem with women's activism was its promotion of national liberation actions while delaying social and women's liberation for a later time or stage (2005). Further, in his extensive analysis of the development of the Palestinian women's movement, Aziz Daragmmi (1991) stated that after the year 1978 it became clear that the women's and feminist movements began to realize that they could not stress national liberation while divorcing it from social liberation, and therefore these began organizing towards the raising of social and women's issues while resisting Israeli military occupation. Ebba Augustin argued against Aziz Daragmmi's analysis by stating that the Palestinian Intifada in 1987 was what motivated women and the feminist movement to organize and sharpen their feminist liberation ideology (1994), while Eileen Kuttab and Nida' Abu Awwad (2004) explained that feminist resistance against domination grew following the Oslo Agreement of 1993. I personally believe that the Oslo Agreement was turned into a lethal weapon against women's resistance and feminist frontline activism. The refusal of the Israeli military powers to stop acts of further colonization of the land, the water, the resources; the refusal of Western powers to put an end to the suffering of the Palestinians and to address the plight of refugees; and the failure of the young Palestinian quasi-state to organize itself – all of these have contributed to the further marginalization of women's voices of resistance.

The complex, multilayered suffering that this book focuses on, and the unpredictable political, social, and spatial context (in the form of constant land grabbing, restrictions on movement, military checkpoints, a racist separation wall, and so on) has changed, hindered, and in some cases sharpened women's actions and activism. Such complexity how-ever has allowed women to revisit their historical legacies and to chal-lenge their social and political roles, and in some cases this has assisted them in enduring their objectification and subordination. Palestinian women's activism began in the early 1920s. The Palestinian Women's Union led demonstrations against the Balfour Declaration and organ-ized the first General Palestinian Women's Congress in Jerusalem in 1929 (Al-Khalili 1977: 77). They played a very active role in the revolt against the Mandate between 1936 and 1939. In addition to caring for the injured, they participated in demonstrations, hid and otherwise helped rebels, signed petitions, and took up arms themselves to defend their land (Abu Ali 1974: 30–2). In 1948, Palestinian women were not only displaced and made to suffer the effects of forced eviction and exile; they also took on responsibility for their children, their families, and the nation, and adjusted their social roles in order to cope with the devas-tating effect of the Palestinian Nakba. Following the Nakba, women were fighting on two fronts: the internal domestic front, wherein they were trying to help their families and nation survive the Nakba and its consequences, and the external political one, such as in joining the various political movements, including Fatah, the Arab National Movement, the Ba'ath party, and the Jordanian Communist Party (Al-Khalili 1977). Although not usually made visible by historians and other researchers, Palestinian women were active in three locations: within the West Bank and Gaza Strip, inside Israel, and in exile. Within these three locations, Palestinian women joined the nationalist move-ment in both armed and unarmed resistance roles (Abdulhadi 2006; Moghannam 1937).

The overwhelming defeat of the Arab regimes in 1967 and the Israeli occupation of the West Bank, Gaza, and East Jerusalem was a turning point for women's activism and resistance. The defeat of the Arab nations in 1967 led to an increase in women's power and participation within the Palestine Liberation Organization (PLO) and the establishment of Palestinian guerrilla groups that called for, and at times practiced, armed struggle as the only strategy for the liberation of Palestine. There were two fronts to women's resistance: the political movement (including membership in guerrilla groups) and the not-so-visible domestic front. Such acts of resistance affected the balance of power between women and men and so disturbed gender roles. Women thus became militant frontliners and activists (Abdulhadi 1998: 655), but also were glorified icons of nation, icons that in part replied to the Israeli demographic war that called for the production of a larger Jewish population (Abdo 1991: 24). Additionally, women were signifiers of national honour (Warnock 1990) even given the Israeli sexual harassment and abuse of women (during imprisonment, interrogation, and other political oppressive methods); women are expected to give precedence to the homeland over their own honour. The nationalist slogan *al-ard qabl al-'ird*, meaning 'land before honour', became popularized after the 1967 events and was part of a (male!) trajectory within nationalist discourse intended to recast gender relations, which had begun after the Nakba. The goal was to change consciousness, so that people would not flee their land out of fear of sexual violence against women (see Hasso 2000), and as such counter violent Israeli land grabbing. However, *in its effect* it indicated to women that they were not to fear the militarized sexual abuse rampant under the Israeli occupation because national liberation was and remains more important than women's 'honour' or their victimization that follows upon sexual abuse (see Thorhill 1992: 24, 31-2). The marking of the Palestinian body and space as defining nation and honour during the early period of the Israeli military occupation and in later stages during the first and second Intifadas, and the militarized inscriptions of women's bodies, land, and life, were part of the way the military occupation operated, and therefore it was also part of women's resistance, philosophy, and activism.

Despite the severe effect of militarization and violence on women's everyday lives, their bodies and survival strategies, the documentation of women's history and frontline activities in war and conflict zones is generally lacking. This said, the history of the powerless and the process of knowledge production should not be based solely on what has been written but crucially also on those who have been denied a voice and a space in history books to date. Her-story of resistance and activism reminds me of an African proverb that states that: 'If lions were to write history, lion hunters would never be heroes.' Palestinian women's history – her-story and narrative – suffers from exclusion and denial to the degree of total cancellation. Although this book is not a history of women's frontline activities, it does closely examine the effect of political violence on women and on their frontline survival and activism while documenting historical facts when these issues are raised by the Palestinian women I spoke with. I do hope that future researchers will closely study women's history, for to me, refusing to acknowledge women's voices, their hidden transcripts of power and powerlessness, and their roles deeply affects our understanding of women's ways of survival and of the way they deal with victimization, resistance, and activism.

As Fleischmann (2003) explains, despite most historians' dismissal of Palestinian women's activities during the British Mandate period – in part through portrayal of them as 'bourgeois', 'passive', or 'politically unaware' – Palestinian women in the early 1900s organized movements that were actively involved in social, political, and national affairs, and despite the continuous dismissal of women's narratives and voices, there exist hidden transcripts and voices of Palestinian women frontliners.

The onset of the First Intifada in December 1987 provided Palestinian women with new sites and spaces of resistance. It opened up new paths for challenging the existing structures of oppression and allowed for the construction of new feminist struggles. The First Intifada gave birth to and developed new feminist skills that enabled women to speak up, network, interact, become part of the public and political scene, and challenge existing social discriminatory hierarchies. Women's sense of empowerment was translated into their participation in socio-economic and political activism. This sense of empowerment included women from cities, refugee camps, or villages, and of different socio-economic strata, ages, and educational attainments. This participation was altered and challenged by both the Israeli colonial occupation and power holders internal to Palestinian society. Thus, during the years following the onset of the First Intifada, Israel exploited the concept of honour in order to recruit Palestinians as collaborators or to create fear of sexual abuse against women. Islamic extremists set about imposing new codes of 'moral behaviour' and 'dress' that were said to be 'authentic cultural' expressions and religious practices which thereby marked women's bodies as powerful sites of contestation. The deterioration of the situation and the increase in political violence, the humiliation of Palestinian men and women, and the constant public disgrace of the male figure via challenges to his 'masculinity and virility' at the hands of occupation forces, all together deepened gender conflicts inside the domestic sphere and within Palestinian society more generally. The effect of this continuous humiliation and emasculation was reflected in the importance Palestinians gave to the issue of female sexual abuse by the Israelis and called *Isqat* – literally, the 'downfall' (Shalhoub-Kevorkian 1995). *Isqat* refers to the use of the politics of sexuality – as reflected in the violation of societal codes of women purity, honour, sexual abuses, integrity, and social respectability – for the soliciting of information that can provide the Israeli military and the Shabak (secret service) with 'security information'. Such solicitation is conducted in violation of human rights law and violates Palestinian moral codes of privacy and intimacy. It sometimes occurs through sexual solicitation of minor and young women: for example, by placing cameras in clothing change rooms and photographing women; by sexually harassing and abusing women political prisoners; through the use of collaborators; by involving young women in socially disapproved relationships in order to blackmail them into collaborating in the gathering of information on political activists; and so on. The use of the term *Isqat* was meant to show the way military powers used patriarchal perceptions of sexuality and honour to put down and 'defeat' individual women and their families personally, socially, and politically. Fear of *Isqat* turned any discussion of sexual crimes and sexual abuse into a very sensitive, heavily loaded discussion, and it increased officials' and indeed societal reluctance to address the issue and thereby help victims of such abuse.

During and following upon the First Intifada (primarily between 1988 and 1995), I was working to establish the first hotline for abused women, and in the Women's Center for Legal Aid and Counselling we dealt with twelve cases of sexual abuse against women due to *Isqat* (see Shalhoub-Kevorkian 1998a). *Isqat* created a moral and social panic in conjunction with the increase in Israeli violence, the increase in the number of incarcerated men and women, the fear of transfer (that is, forced displacement to a location outside the borders of the occupied Palestinian territories, the OPT), the continued land grabbing via the building of yet more Jewish settlements on Palestinian land, the demolition of more homes, the theft of natural resources such as water, and so on. This fear intensified following the Oslo Agreement and the creation of the Palestinian National Authority (PNA) in the West Bank and Gaza in 1994. Despite the creation of new hotline services and NGOs between 1993 and 1995 that dealt for the first time and openly with female sexual abuse, the new PNA leadership, although willing to listen to women activists and NGOs in order to construct new reforms, was hesitant to address sexual crimes in such an early stage of nation-building (Shalhoub-Kevorkian 2002). Such reluctance increased in tandem with the increase in political violence in 1998–9 and the onset of the Second Intifada in 2000 – which in turn increased religious, conservative, and patriarchal modes of resistance. When cases of sexual abuse arose (as in the case of a three-year-old child in Hebron [see Shalhoub-Kevorkian 1998b] and the case of a young five-year-old girl from Nablus in February 2000 in which the offender was sentenced to life imprisonment), both officials and society at large dealt with the cases as 'national security' matters rather than as criminal offences. The newly established PNA failed to control political violence and began flexing its power in the Palestinian streets, and therefore needed the help and support of informal (family and tribal) religious, patriarchal power holders in order to preserve its limited power. Such patriarchalization of the formal (state) system and the continual violent attacks on the nation's body not only empowered masculinistic social codes but also led to the further minimalizing of various issues, including crimes against women.

The increasing patriarchalization of the leadership (both formal and informal) and social practices marginalized women's roles and voices, questioned the acts of women activists, and resulted in the creation of additional restrictions on women's lives, activism, and mobility. Simultaneously, organizations such as Hamas (the Islamic Resistance Movement) and paramilitary bands of young men were frustrated with both the international and the PNA failure to prevent violence against the Palestinians and became very cynical about the 'Western-oriented' solutions that caused more human, political, and economic losses for Palestinians, leading in turn to a certain desperation. Such groups looked for religious and local modes for expanding their politico-economic power. In so doing, they decided to oppose any legal reforms pertaining to crimes against women (or what is termed legally as 'crimes against morality and public order', including sexual crimes), and supported the imposition of the Hijab (the wearing of the veil – primarily in Gaza and later in the rest of the Occupied Territories) (Hammami 1990), and out-Islamized and out-nationalized those who opposed them. The threat of *Isqat* added to the threat of non-compliance with the local diktats of both the extremist religious and the nationalistic and secular power holders (a situation that is exacerbated by Israel's attempts to recruit collaborators), limited women's actions, and led to women innovating new defence mechanisms in order to survive and cope with the resulting marginalization. Most women were either unable to or chose not to challenge threats to their honour and social integrity, and many ended up using culturally grounded modes of coping to ensure their survival, freedom, and ongoing activism. The modes of survival that were most apparent in my own studies were related to acquiring higher education, working outside the house, and so building economic independence, and getting married at an early age to ensure economic and social survival – and then going back to school or developing domestic job opportunities such as selling pastries, clothing, making shoes, and so on (Shalhoub-Kevorkian 2005a, 2005c).

Moreover, during the first years of the First Intifada when I was an instructor of Social Work at Bethlehem University, I witnessed many female students changing the way they dressed. I recall one of the discussions that took place between two very active political students. Yusra explained that her choice to wear the veil was based on her belief that God, by commanding that Muslim women wear the Hijab, intended a differentiation between respectful, modest Muslim women and others. Maisoon stated that she turned to wearing the veil not only for religious reasons, but also for political and social ones. She said that God's command during hard times – here meaning during the Intifada – is of focal importance and carries a divine wisdom. The command is intended to protect and secure women from sexual harassment or abuse at the hands of military forces and also allows women to participate with greater freedom in the struggle. Wearing the veil, as Maisoon and Yusra stated, made them socially respected political activists, for their fear of *Isqat*, as Maisoon said, 'turned my life upside down'. Such fear was also evident in Gaza. Abdulhadi quotes an activist from a Gaza refugee camp who discussed women's survival of *Isqat*:

> Through word of mouth, we spread the news that no one should have a drink while making a social visit. No coffee, no RC [Royal Crown Cola], nothing. 'Even while visiting your own brother, do not drink anything, except if the can is sealed!' At one point, we started saying that we were fasting; we were either making up for the days lost [while menstruating] in Ramadan or because it was a Monday or a Thursday [days during which fasting is favoured].
>
> (1998: 658)

Whether the fear of *Isqat* came as either an additional method for the protection or control of women, or both, women's bodies and their lifestyles were transformed into new sites of struggle, marking the boundaries between Palestinians and non-Palestinians and between male and female frontliners.

The marking of women's bodies, lives, and homes was exacerbated following the onset of the Second Intifada in September 2000 and increased formal and informal injustice around issues of gender relations, gender violence, and subordination. Women's desire to improve their status was constantly challenged. Their activism, the building of new women's organizations, the new NGOs that focused on tracking violations of women's rights and of violence against women, the establishment of new shelters for abused women, the constant efforts to combat the 'honour crimes', and other political and social forms of struggle opened new windows of opportunity for resistance against all manner of oppression. But at the same time, the international and regional transformations (especially following the 9/11 attacks with the rise of Islamo-fascism and Islamo-phobia) in combination with the local events of the 1987 and 2000 Intifadas added to the continuous violence and simultaneously marked the opening of new opportunities for women – but also created new constraints for them. This was apparent for example in the construction of the Israeli Separation Wall (ISW) and the addition of military checkpoints. Such spatial constraints restricted women's mobility; they also increased the feminization of poverty, and the deprivation of education, and affected women's physical and mental health. The failure of the international community to put an end to the violence and the Western attack on Muslims and Islamic movements, especially following the 9/11 events, only increased the power and credibility of Islamic forces in Palestine and elsewhere.

Islamists offered a 'safe' space and a new discourse, a discourse that was presented as 'authentic' and culturally and religiously grounded. This discourse attacked many existing programmes and activities. One clear example was apparent in the vicious criticism against the request to revise the laws to make them gender sensitive, as seen in the project of the Palestinian Model Parliament (PMP) that suggested legal reforms. I was a member of this collective effort on the part of legislators, local NGOs, activists, feminists, and members of human rights organizations; all needed to stand firm amid criticism regarding our proposed reforms and our discourses. Our language of equality, our use of 'rights' discourse, was criticized by some political and Islamist activists who felt that these represented the hegemonic power of the West and so carried with them an image of occupation and invasion. The social and political gender relations were also affected by the decline of the power of the PLO following the Oslo Agreement, and by the onset of the Second Intifada – together combining to add yet more weight on the 'woman issue'. Furthermore, the worsening economic conditions, the failure of the political negotiations between the PNA and Israel, and the serious confrontation with the Israeli military empowered the *Shabab* ('young men') and strengthened the paramilitaries. Between 1994 and 2000, feminist activists (including myself) at the Al-Aman hotline for abused women noticed that with the increase in masculinized resistance, the *Shabab* began to launch a campaign to establish a 'proper code of morality'. They created new strategies and bureaucracies that imposed new codes of dress and behaviour solely for the purpose of controlling women. Abdulhadi quotes a feminist Bir Zeit University professor:

> As the Intifada declined, an emerging laid-off army of Shabab, or young men, launched a campaign of 'social violence' against their own people … Self-assigned the role of morality police that operated in the streets of the West Bank and Gaza, the Shabab embarked on 'rooting out' what they viewed as moral decay.
>
> (1998: 660)

The onset of the Second Intifada further empowered such groups, primarily due to the inability of formal social control mechanisms, including those of the criminal justice and legal systems, to function. The socio-political changes in combination with the worsening economic situation led to a further multiplicity of women's activism and modes of struggle. The militancy of the *Shabab* created moral panic and social fear, especially following upon several incidents in which women were killed while standing accused of collaboration, misbehaviour, and dishonouring their society. (I recall the case of two fourteen- and seventeen-year-old girls from Beit Jala, and remember the discussion around the issue by various women activists at the Christmas hotel in East Arab Jerusalem in 2001.) The constant Israeli attacks and the ongoing Israeli policy of displacement added to the official Palestinian system's failure, reluctance, manipulation, or refusal to prosecute criminals, thereby constructing an insecure space for women.

Both myself and many Palestinian women I have worked with remain stunned by the way in which, despite the very vulnerable position in which Palestinian women are situated, Empire's discussions of Palestinian women's behaviour, activism, and resistance have been construed in a racist manner, all the while portraying us/them as either the 'passive victim' or the 'terrorist Other'. Both constructions serve a

need to turn the Palestinian Other into a dangerous, threatening crea-
ture. Yet Palestinian women, be they those who ended up dead, injured,
or imprisoned, all tried to promote resistance according to their own
abilities and based on available resources. These include women such as
Aisheh Odeh, who has just published a book sharing with the reader her
ordeals, including her sexual abuse, in prison (2005); or others such as
Rula Abu Daho, Khawla al-Azrak, and Rabiha Diad, young women who
joined my classes and became my students at Bethlehem University and
who resisted the humiliation and oppression, offering a new way of
resistance; and many others who have not been recognized, such as
Um Riad. By applying the little power they held, women's acts of
resistance aimed at challenging domination. The main challenge that
they have faced, and we as Palestinian women continue to struggle with,
is how the dominated and oppressed can create an oppositional world
view, a consciousness, an identity, a standpoint that can exist to oppose
dehumanization and military occupation, and also create a movement
which enables resourceful self-actualization. The acts of resistance by
women frontliners – such as by Samiha Khalil, whose activism did not
divorce the social from the national, the personal from the political, the
economic from the geo-political – and the acts of the many women who
spoke truth to power in many of my research projects, including this one,
created new spaces, spaces where resistance to domination in all its
modalities remain.

In examining Palestinian women's resistance and frontline activism –
primarily while looking at the role contemporary NGOs have played – and
basing this on my own experience and my talks and encounters with the
various women that inform my book, I see that academic ideas about
resistance and freedom in many cases were far from reflecting the depth,
power, and insights of women resistors and freedom fighters. The 'non-
profit industry complex' as it is called in the book *The Revolution Will Not
Be Funded* (INCITE 2007) penetrated and in some cases damaged local
activism. The 'non-profit industry complex', the politics of funding and
funding opportunities, co-opted political movements, activists, and
careerists and affected the politics of representation of Palestinian wom-
en's activism (Qassoum 2002; Jad 2003; Carapico 2000; Hammami 2000).
In addition, teaching for almost ten years at Bethlehem University (from
1986–95) taught me that even young women's management of dissent was
violated by international donors as well as by local, well-funded NGOs.
The fact that some NGOs were informed by the values, lifestyles, and
behaviour of Empire further burdened women's activism.

The various strategies used by women frontliners to combat domination and to shield and protect themselves and those around them created oppositional frontline discourses, epistemologies, and activism. Such opposition ranged from total accommodation to total confrontation, from challenging social and political taboos to negotiating them, and from accepting subordination as a short-term strategy to fighting them by building strategies for women's future empowerment. In many ways, this opposition confronted and challenged the dominant views concerning women's ability to manoeuvre within this complex context. It prevented women's seclusion in the home while transforming every location into a frontline position. Women became frontliners not only in their homes, actions, bodies, minds and in their traumatic ordeals; they became frontliners in their locations as young pupils, as mothers, as pregnant women, as workers, and in their needs and different experiences and languages. Women's acts, their power, and at other times their powerlessness – and sometimes both simultaneously – should never be divorced from the interplay between international, regional, and local conditions, including Israeli practices. Palestinian women's voices should never be analysed without a close examination of the intersection between Israeli violence, social patriarchy, nationalist ideologies, the global denial of the Palestinian situation, and the various layers of oppression within this situation.

Women with whom I worked and from whom I learned taught me that it is only by putting aside notions of femininity and masculinity and instead concentrating on frontline activism and the hidden agency of those who are affected by global domination and local militarization that we would be able to see the unseen, hear the unheard, and acknowledge women's resistance discourses. Women's own examinations of their struggle against the marginalization efforts of the Israeli geo-political oppression, the global and Israeli economic strangulations, the violence of the military occupation, and the oppression and abuse of the Palestinian patriarchal repression is central to helping us to understand in depth women's victimization and agency. Palestinian women's state of marginality, in both local and global terms, was altered by these women into a site of transformation wherein a liberated Palestinian subjectivity could fully emerge. The individual and multiple counter-hegemonic discourses presented in this book stress the fact that women's frontline activism is a chosen marginality – a marginality that is turned into a site of resistance. Contrasted to collective Palestinian activism, an individual woman's day-to-day struggle created a new but marginal space of liberation that managed to move, disrupt, threaten, and confront power.

Despite Palestinian women's struggle and frontline activities, sexism and gender discrimination continue to be dangerous factors that silence their/our liberation. The narratives shared in this book show that women's daily struggle and activism sharpened their liberatory agenda. Women from different backgrounds, despite the various hardships and obstacles they faced, paid close attention to each and every small opportunity that presented the possibility of a new strategy for fighting against oppression, thereby transcending the boundaries while overcoming local, regional, and international socio-political and economic obstacles. But, this same difficult situation limited women's activism and struggle to the political and economic spheres all the while that women refused, negotiated, and in some cases adhered to, the changes within the social and private spheres. Women in Palestine did not speak in a single voice, but their voices were deeply affected by the long history of activism against colonization and occupation. Their legacy, when juxtaposed with their own personal history, generated a variety of activisms that carried exclusive acts of women's frontlining and brought about a variety of discourses, voices, and combativeness. The Palestinian women's history of accumulating acts of struggle not only challenged their marginalization but also created new, safe spaces within their marginalized status – new locations and new languages to act against different forms of oppression.

RESEARCH METHOD AND SOURCES OF DATA

The narratives and data discussed in this book are based on clinical and other observations including in-depth interviews, focus groups, and analyses of writings and visual data (see Shalhoub-Kevorkian 2000, 2001, 2002, 2003a, 2003b, 2004a, 2004b, 2005a, 2005c, 2006, 2007a). In addition, intervention projects with Palestinian women with whom I have worked during the past fifteen years provide an additional source of data (see, for example, Shalhoub-Kevorkian 1994, 1998a, 1999a, 1999b). The narratives analysed herein are based on five projects with four Palestinian NGOs and one international one. The first is based on my clinical work between 1994 and 2000 as the head of a hotline for abused women and as the director of various research studies with the Women's Counseling and Legal Aid Center (WCLAC) during the years 1999–2002. These projects studied the crime of femicide and analysed the disclosure of child sexual abuse and the role of the criminal justice system during political conflict. The second source of data is based on my various projects that began in 2000 and continue until the present through the Jerusalem Center for Women (JCW). The JCW's projects focused on voice therapy for mothers of martyrs and with female relatives of political prisoners, and also a current action-oriented project on the effect of house demolitions and constant displacement on women. The third body of data was gathered through the Women's Studies Center–Jerusalem (WSC) between the years 2002 and 2006, and is comprised of three studies. The first study, conducted with a group of researchers at the WSC, examined the effect of the trauma of political violence on women. The second, undertaken with Nahla Abdo, mapped and analysed the hardships facing Palestinian women in Jerusalem. The last study looked at the effect of militarization on gender and education. The fourth body of data utilized in this book are clinical analyses of cases based on the documentation and clinical work of the Family Defense Society (FDS) in Nablus between the years 1996 and 2005. The source of data is based on two projects funded by World Vision (WV). One project examined the effect of the Israeli Separation Wall on children, both male and female. The second project examined the effect of political violence on children in the Gaza Strip. In addition, the book is also based on in-depth interviews I conducted with young, middle-aged, and older women and my own clinical work and observation in the field.

The research method for this book, therefore, included action-oriented research, participatory observations, clinical examinations and interventions, focus groups, and visits to sites with women in order for them to share with me and tell me more about their conditions and the meaning of their suffering. All of these took place in various locations in the OPT of the West Bank, Gaza Strip, and Arab East Jerusalem. While some of the interviews conducted with women were forty to fifty minutes long, the majority took two to three hours. The topic of discussions varied; I never structured the interviews, but rather discussed, shared, and learned from women's own epistemologies consistent with qualitative feminist methods. The data gathered was transcribed either by a team of specially trained local Palestinian women or by myself, then translated either by myself or with the help of local activists and friends into English and thematically coded to ensure maximum accuracy following a modified grounded theory approach (on which, see Strauss and Corbin 1990).

The Palestinian women in this book ranged from university and college students to women with no formal education. Some lived in refugee camps, while others lived in villages or in urban areas. Some were married, some were engaged, and some were divorced, widowed, or single. Some were young girls, and others were older women. Some were very poor, but others were well off. However, one common denominator was that the political violence and its ramifications directly affected all. Their suffering mirrors the complexity of a very long political conflict. They all had suffered the trauma of enforced migration, displacement, or eviction. They have all either witnessed violence, have lost a loved one, or have or have had a family member in prison. They have all had to face soldiers, pass through checkpoints, and face the construction of the Israeli Separation Wall, all the while fearing the loss of their ability to study, work, meet family members, and even participate in their loved ones' special occasions, including funerals, weddings, graduations, and so forth.

The book does not include the voices of female leaders, political activists, or ministry or official party representatives. All women gave their consent to participation. Consent for young girls' participation was obtained from their parents and schools, including obtaining formal approval from the Palestinian Ministry of Education. Similarly, when I worked in courts, with the District Attorney, with police officers, and with the Center for Forensic Medicine, I also obtained formal approval from officials in both the Ministry of Judicial Affairs and the Ministry of Health. I began my actual work and field study in 1999, a year before the onset of the Second Intifada, but intensive work began with the increased violence and the onset of that uprising which I witnessed occurring around my home in the Old City Jerusalem.

Being an active member of the four above-mentioned NGOs allowed me to participate in their various activities, including training sessions, demonstrations against the military violence, and more. The fact that I was an insider, although opening me to the charge of bias, had the crucial advantage of allowing me to get to know in detail the daily ordeals of women. For example, I worked with WCLAC on a daily basis and the FDS on a weekly one and was able to follow the hardships women faced. During invasions or other forms of violence, I was either in the field working and helping out or on the phone building modes of trauma intervention and prevention of further trauma. I do not claim neutrality nor am I hiding my position as a Palestinian woman living and suffering from hardships that are similar, indeed often shared, with the women who are the subject of this book.

By working with women in the field in various locations in the West Bank and Arab East Jerusalem, I learned that the economic hardships and misery and the unpredictable and uncontrollable political violence was exceeded by internal local violence against women. Women's narratives of these hardships necessitated that I use my professional expertise as a therapist and so suggest different modes of intervention to help women cope with the traumas they faced (see for example Shalhoub-Kevorkian 2003b, 2005a). I was fortunate in that all organizations, whether local or international, joined forces in the variety of intervention and research projects aimed at learning more from women's ordeals and which planned appropriate intervention programmes. For example, while collecting the data on child sexual abuse with the WCLAC, I felt that there was a need not only to work closer with women survivors but also to train officers of the criminal justice system about the issues. WCLAC acquired funding and then organized training sessions and workshops with Palestinian judiciaries. Such meetings turned out to be very successful and also an eye-opener for me not only in terms of sharing women's hardships with the judges but also in terms of seeing them recognize their own inability to function and maintain due process under conditions of political unrest and within a stateless structure.

Following upon a visit to the Jenin refugee camp in 2002 with the director of the Women's Studies Center, we decided to take some action. I wrote a proposal that was approved by the WSC and funded by the Swedish NGO Kvinna Tel Kvinna (Women for Women) for the years 2003–5. (I was involved in the first year of the project, but it is still running and helping women who have lost a family member.) The project was an action-oriented study that was based on quantitative data analyses, the collection of narratives through focus groups, and group therapy. The study unearthed many layers of women's power and powerlessness in this politically conflicted area of Palestine (for more detail, see Abu-Baker *et al.* 2005).

In addition, my work with the JCW gave me the opportunity to learn more about the city I reside in and to personally intervene and work with women facing direct political violence. In my work with groups of women, I also promised them that I would share their ordeals with international activists and scholars and bring their voices and stories to the attention of people beyond Palestine (see Shalhoub-Kevorkian 2003b, 2005a, 2005c). I am still working, supporting, and learning from the young women at the JCW, mainly in our last focus group on the crime of house demolitions and its gendered ramifications.

The Family Defense Society (FDS) in Nablus allowed me to learn more about the northern area of the West Bank with its unique characteristics and hardships. I worked with the FDS on a weekly basis and managed to give them counselling and walk them through the daily hardship of social workers working in a severely disturbed context of both domestic abuse and military oppression. The FDS team assisted me in implementing innovative intervention programmes such as 'ABC's for Survival and Resistance', 'The Dialogue Tent', and group therapy with families that had lost members during the Second Intifada. The above-mentioned projects showed how the sexual division of labour during war and political struggle (including the Intifadas in particular) was challenged by women; the traditional picture, wherein men fight in the forefront and women provide sustenance and otherwise take care of the home front, were constantly defied. Thus, the intervention methods used helped us reveal how social boundaries in this particular violent context are daily negotiated and how gender definitions are subject to daily constraints. The fact that I shared the daily hardships, observed the daily encounters with security forces, and walked with women as they applied their coping strategies gives me special authority to speak about those experiences while revealing women's agency and their daily improvizations for defending their fathers and brothers, hiding their male neighbours, and confronting soldiers – daily activities that negotiate and challenge boundaries and transform them into sources of empowerment.

My own political involvement, feminist activism, and participation in various human rights and research organizations – including Israeli ones such as B'Tselem and Gisha and Palestinian ones in Israel such as Women Against Violence in Nazareth and Mada al-Carmel in Haifa, where I am currently directing the Gender Studies Project – when juxtaposed with the daily hardships facing me as a Palestinian woman living in the Old City of Jerusalem and also with the stories and hardships facing my daughters, my family, friends, co-workers, clients, students, and so on, made the collection and analyses of this book's material very subversive. In addition, my other identity as a senior lecturer at the Hebrew University teaching at the Faculty of Law–Institute of Criminology and School of Social Work and Public Welfare was very useful, for it allowed me to share my work, research, and activism with university colleagues, friends, and students. It helped me, in some cases, to take some distance from the chaos, to watch and listen to the analyses from the other side of the fence, but in some cases it increased my worries and increased the Otherization techniques used by each side to annihilate their respective adversaries. In an effort to create some space from my activism and research in the field, I spent almost sixteen months, in four-month intervals, at the UCLA Center for the Study of Women, its School of Law, and at the USC School of Law; at these institutions, I shared my work, taught courses on women and militarization and on violence against women, and tried to keep a bit of a distance from the reality of Palestine – of course, without divorcing myself entirely from the news from home.

In addition to my experience as outlined above, I have also relied in writing this book on publications of various Palestinian women's groups, including various research centres, grassroots organizations, activists, and voluntary charitable associations. I also drew from the writings and discussions of Palestinian women in both Arabic and English. All of the above-mentioned material, writings, and experiences are used here to help me illustrate, understand, and comprehend women frontliners' actions and ordeals and the effect of the militarized context on their bodies and lives.

It must be noted that working under occupation in such a politically insecure and physically threatening atmosphere called for watchfulness and caution in planning meetings, organizing discussions, or even being seen walking or talking in the street. In many cases I needed to help women frontliners fight back. In other cases, the atrocities and suffering almost made me end my research and leave Palestine. In one instance, an eleven-year-old boy who had lost his father and his home during the invasion of Jenin in 2002 was trying to figure out why I had come to this refugee camp. He was telling me that everything was destroyed and lost. While sharing his thoughts with myself and a young girl who accompanied me all the time in the camp, he said to us: 'All one could see is *Damar, Damar, Damar* [destruction; he said this three times] and everything smells of death ... You walk, you smell the odour of dead bodies.' The young girl tried to explain to him what I was doing, so she first told him that I was born in Haifa, and that most of the refugees in Jenin were forced to immigrate from Haifa; but then she said: '*Hay doctora ... doctoret hob* ... she is a doctor, a doctor of compassion. And she could make you love life again.' I was stunned by her conceptualization of my role, but the boy then told her while looking at me: 'So, you are a doctor, a doctor of compassion ... Do you know that you might be stepping on my father's bones? So this is what compassionate doctors do.' On this occasion, I felt the need to disappear; as we say in Arabic, I wanted the ground to crack open and suck me in. I wanted to stop my writing and my journey. But then I realized that I do not have the luxury of being depressed, and must continue the way the young boy and girl did, despite the pain and agony.

To ensure that women would feel comfortable participating in my project, I informed them that their names, addresses, and other details were to remain confidential and would not be used for any other purpose than the study. In many cases, and given the seriousness and threatening nature of the political situation, I omitted or changed details in order to avoid possible identification of women participants. No woman I approached declined participation in this study, but when we faced gunfire, invasion, or fear of loss I stopped my conversation and helped them respond to whatever needed to be done, such as carrying a baby, helping girls to pass the Wall without being harassed by soldiers, holding someone's hand, and even taking the injured to a hospital in my car. Although I sometimes used a tape recorder, in many instances I was aware of the fear caused by this practice and so either took notes or, in cases where it was inappropriate to use one of the previous methods, wrote my notes and impressions later from memory.

METHODOLOGY: THE PROBLEM

Given the many restrictive features and the imbalance in power between the observer and informant, especially in researching women's issues, feminist researchers have tried to create more appropriate research methodologies. Many of these researchers have collected data on women's experiences while attempting to overcome traditional hierarchical relations that exist in such situations between the observer and the observed. At the end of the day, as researchers we are actively engaged in the processes of history through our recording of it, and the processes of history are inflected by politics, the social, economics, and gender. If research is a quest for (some kind of) truth, it is nevertheless a 'truth' that is *made* by people and not one that functions outside ideology. Searching for the politics of these truths – through the voices of (primarily Palestinian) women in conflict areas, is the focus of my own research. What intrigues me are the truths that are constructed and mediated through the structures of culture, language, knowledge, history, political economy, psychology, and the ever-present dynamics of power.

In my previous work, I have focused on the connections between the dynamics of political conflict and the ensuing violence against women, including femicide, domestic violence, and sexual, physical, geo-political, and emotional abuse. This project builds on that previous work by specifically focusing on narratives by Palestinian women from conflict zones (by 'zone' I mean both the physical as well as the socio-political spaces of women), and it uses those narratives to analyse the dynamics of gendered violence. My work in the region has been three-fold. First, I have made an extended effort to understand the specific nature and dynamics of violence against women in Palestine. Second, I have used several forms of interactive group and individual therapy, such as the 'Dialogue Tent', to enable women to break their silence, form collaborative communities with other abused women, and to bring their multiple discourses to the fore. Third, I have advocated the creation and implementation of a collaborative and proactive research strategy that affectively disrupts the us–them, observer–observed binary in order to generate material alternatives that enable these women to create more optimistic possibilities for the future. One example of this type of action-oriented study is my research (conducted between 2000 and 2003) that focuses on the effect of the political conflict on Palestinian women's mental health. It is an analysis of their survival strategies, strategies that allow women to carve out a high degree of agency in the midst of devastation. My research has enabled me to dialogue with women suffering from the militarized social and cultural apparatus of the region and to become more cognizant of the need to further investigate the social and mental conditions of women. Such data is invaluable to the current and future reality of Palestinian society, and must be both analysed and shared.

It has always been my purpose as a scholar and researcher to advocate and promote politically progressive and liberating research method-ologies. In this instance, by political I mean a critical examination of the process of knowledge production itself with regard to colonized/oppressed people. Similarly, by liberating I refer to the fact that our research methodologies ought to empower our research subjects. Our methodologies should offer innovative methods of inquiry and con-sciously analyse and criticize the often-colonizing theoretical underpin-nings that underlie all research. By progressive, I mean that the research should aim to benefit – in material ways – those who are studied. Thus, it will come as no surprise that I consider myself an activist as much as I position myself as a researcher or scholar. Consequently, I believe we should attempt to create a politically conscious research method and hence a setting that links activism with our research. By being aware of the contextual sensitivity and also potentialities of the research, I aim to engage with women's manifold epistemologies and projects. This cannot be achieved without raising questions regarding the power and location of feminist scholars while specifically focusing on the issue of who has the right to produce and circulate knowledge in relation to colonized people.

VOICING AND FRONTLINERS

This book foregrounds the narratives, voices, and suffering of Palestinian women living under violent military occupation. My project therefore negotiates the complexities of knowledge production in a region that daily loses its material specificity while becoming ever more liminal. Working in a region that is under constant surveillance, as a result of previous colonial and Zionist policies, the neo-colonial representation as present in the ongoing occupation, the 'war against terror', and Empire's political economy, further complicates the matter. While the constant redrawing of boundaries (be they geo-political, economic, racial, or religious), the further breaking up of the landscape through Israeli land-grabbing policies, the Apartheid Wall, checkpoints, barricades, and many other means of separation, constantly reconfigures the 'map' of the region resulting in a lack of material specificity for Palestinians. These are, as I see it, exilic spaces replete with multiple displacements and refugees of many kinds. Such exilic spaces bring their own stresses to bear in the dynamics of knowledge production. The internal movements occurring repeatedly – from the 1948 Nakba to the 1967 Naksa (setback), from the First Intifada to the Second – calls for a scholarship that must negotiate multiple militarized and colonized occupations in every voice.

Studying and researching 'silence' – those voices that are present but unheard – is also a multilayered and often problematic proposition. While my privileges as a Palestinian, as a woman, activist, and academic allows me to voice these silences, my aim is not to speak for those who have been silenced, but rather to make available an alternative language that I believe is rich and critically important in what it has to offer us. It is also my aim to expose the reasons – at least as far as I can discern them – for the West's inattentiveness or refusal to hear these voices. In so doing, I am also theorizing a strategy for radical social and political understanding that in time may bring about material transformation.

Do I have the right to bring forward voices such as Um Riad's? And can Um Riad speak – or as Spivak (1985) asks, 'Can the subaltern speak?' I argue that Palestinian women's context does not raise the issue of bringing forth the voice of the subaltern, since the voices are out there; the problem lies in the politics of interpretation and representation. Spivak indicated that the subaltern's failed efforts at self-representation were due to the fact that speaking outside colonial/ patriarchal channels was not understood or supported by Empire. People's inability to reach the level of utterance or their inability to access the language of cultural imperialism created a space of difference – and made it subaltern. But speaking, speech, and voicing in this book are social and political categories of a particular significance. Therefore, my work does not aim at giving the subaltern a voice, but rather works against subalternity while clearing the space to allow it to speak. It is not a question of whether or not the subaltern can speak, the subaltern *is* speaking; the real question concerns the refusal to hear such voices. Is it on account of fear, 'security' concerns, or self-protection? How and why is it that Palestinian women – as with most women in war zones and conflict areas – are not heard?

Thus, working from Spivak's now famous question and revisioning her initial less-than-optimistic answer, I want to look at the various ways in which, along with the multiplicity of voices through which Palestinian women are speaking and making themselves heard. And since I am consciously using 'silence' as a category of analysis, it is important to look at the specific relationships (often culturally and politically overdetermined) between women and silence and what kinds of speaking such silence yields. The dynamics of the ways in which Palestinian women are claiming their own self-determination is an integral part of the silence I refer to. If we listen closely to the language of this silence, it is clear that Palestinian women are aware that it is not only their land that continues to be occupied but also their *truths* as well, truths that they feel have been held hostage as a legacy of continuing political oppression.

It is by no means a surprise that endemic to the violence that is committed against women is a corresponding move to silence what the patriarchal political and social order does not want to acknowledge: the violence enacted on women's bodies, psyches, spaces, or minds. This persistent attempt to negate the voices and narratives of women who have suffered political violence as well as patriarchal oppressions internal to their own societies is further aggravated in conflict areas where material strife, political unrest, or war foregrounds the existing tensions of a gender-biased world. The denial of systemic violence against women in conflict zones has caused both the experiences of victimization and the survival strategies of women to be largely absent from the social and political analyses of these areas. Through my specific strategies of 'voicing', I am attempting in this book to fill this void.

My analysis borrows from some 'subaltern intellectuals' – if I may call them so. For example, the influential work of Fanon has shown the harmful psychological effect of racism to the degree that it could blind black people to the subjection of the universalized white norms and alienate their consciousnesses. From Fanon I learn – and as a therapist I will demonstrate it throughout the book – how opening the space to speak, share, think, cry, be silent, fight back, react, and so on reduces the harmful effects of the political situation. Nawal, a fifteen-year-old Palestinian girl, told me that while she was sitting in painful silence watching the construction of the ISW beside her house that her grandmother told her not to feel weak when looking at it. She said: 'The Wall should remind us that they fear us, and why? Because we are *Ashab Haq* [the possessors of a just cause].' Nawal's comment made me realize that the aggressive acts on the part of the hegemonic power holders are actually not reflections of power per se but rather of fear and powerlessness, and so led me to add to Fanon's analysis; that is, that the hegemonic powers, as powerful as they can be with all the Empire's support, will always stand weak, fearful, and naked, for they cannot mute the voices of the suffering frontliners.

Fanon aimed at resisting the colonial and its hegemonic discourse that shaped cultures. In his book *The Wretched of the Earth*, Fanon states that it takes a total revolution, 'absolute violence', to be absolutely free of the past (1963: 37), and he claims that true revolution comes from the *fellaheen*. By analogy, revolution must be made by Palestinian women and men. Any activity of men without women would be insufficient, for men alone or women alone cannot remake the entire system. As the book shows, Palestinian women's relentless oppositional way of speaking, thinking, and acting against their suffering was not only confronted by the failure of the hegemonic power's ability to understand such counter-discourses but was also transformed into criminality and deviation by those who control the production of knowledge, all the while calling women 'terrorists', 'backward', or 'primitive', 'uncivilized', 'unfit mothers', and so on.

Since 9/11, the corporate media has exacerbated its stigmatization and Otherization of the East and the Empire's leaders have started using a new language – such as that of crusade, good versus evil, freedom from fear, and so on – while drawing on the distinction between Islam and the West, the civilized, and the Arab, and the liberated and the veiled women. The war against Iraq has further affected perceptions toward the Palestinian–Israeli conflict, leaving women's suffering and the violence against them unacknowledged, unseen, and unheard.

RESEARCHING WOMEN IN POLITICALLY CONFLICTED AREAS

Representation and the subject of the oppressed should not be forgotten. Therefore, the meanings of expressions, of the voices of the oppressed, will be analysed in the context of the oppressed and their critical views and with the theoretical box of tools of the intellectual. Among many other feminists, Chandra Mohanty (1991) for one has urged scholars to culturally contextualize our analyses and to concretize the effects of such analysis on women. Thus, in attempting to voice the violence against women, to bring their narratives to the surface, we must necessarily be attentive to the micro-politics of the cultural and physical space that is defined as specifically 'Palestinian' and the macro-politics of the conflict that is inseparable from any conceptualization of 'Palestine' that might obtain outside the region and the global economic and political systems which have created this conflict. While the voices of women are necessarily pluri-vocal and multiple, they are nevertheless embedded in and born out of the singular political matrix of Palestine. The experiences and stories of women globally are too often subjugated by the dominant discourse, which dictates what is considered 'truth', what constitutes victimization/resilience, and most importantly what determines the limits of whatever survival strategies can be put into place.

This book is not a historical book, but a book that documents, shares, and analyses the effect of a history of suffering. My analysis aims to provide Western and non-Western audiences with an alternative portrait of violence against women in conflict zones in general and in occupied Palestine in particular, one that will challenge the global North and its corporate media images, thereby returning women victims' humanity. It also aims to allow the local patriarchal power holder inside the Palestinian society to realize and acknowledge the way women's bodies, their spaces and lives, have been used, abused, and jeopardized throughout the conflict.

In the midst of the political crisis of Palestine itself, women were often prevented from speaking of experiences of interpersonal violence.

While they were allowed to complain of abuses committed against them by the Israeli military, they often found themselves silenced if they criticized local patriarchal powers (Shalhoub-Kevorkian 1994, 1998a). In such instances, women were viewed as disloyal and disrespectful toward national and male authority at a time when Palestinian men ostensibly needed to be uncontested as they resisted the occupiers. My aim is to present an alternative narrative of these women, through their own voices, that will illuminate the strategies, activities, and activism that inscribes their acts of survival. I hope to reflect through this project the self-assertive powers of these women frontliners without pathologizing them as either 'terrorists' or victims – or rendering them as the object of pathos.

Being a frontliner means being in a place of constant combat – both material and psychological – that enervates all the energies that one has to resist, yet these women continue not just to resist but also to re-create. The frontline for these women is many things: a place, a span of time, a place to grow, to change, to transform, and to transgress. For many if not all of these women, the house itself is a militarized and occupied space, whether directly or indirectly, but it is also a site of resistance and transgression. The frontliner can be a woman who is lining up or is humiliated at a checkpoint, a woman singing her children to sleep in the middle of night raids and incursions, one selling yogurt to make some additional money and buy food for her children, a woman giving birth at a checkpoint because she has been prevented from reaching a hospital, or one screaming and crying in court while refusing to accept the law's failure to protect her rights, and more.

The frontline in Palestine, as I see it, is constantly shifting from the locus solely defined in masculine military terms to wherever women are fighting to live their lives and creating safe havens for their families, children, and neighbours. Women's voices and narratives aim at redefining the hegemonic concept of the frontline and through such redefinitions to bring to bear new liberating epistemologies, thoughts, theories, and philosophies during their continuing fight against oppression. The difference between women or feminist frontliners and their masculine counterparts is that they do not only take orders within a hierarchical structure, as do other male formal frontliners, but they also act, think, and search for methods of survival as they prepare the food for their children.

My aim in this project is not to forward a definitive or 'correct' representation of Palestinian women. I share, along with many other scholars, the dilemmas and perhaps even the impossibility of creating definitive representations. Perhaps the best that I can hope for is to work as a translator, a medium for women's ideas, someone who can hear the silences and translate them into a language, a discourse that can be heard and disseminated. I also hope that this book will go beyond such acts of translation (which is for me also an instance of feminist activism) to show how the oppressive material realities of Palestinian women are also transformed by these women into productive energy. When we talked, shared, cried, visited, sang, ululated, and wrote our thoughts, I also felt my own energy rise and a sense of the enormous yet trapped powers within us released and liberated. The energy of young Salwa who refused to accept a marriage that would 'secure' her future; or Maha who stood in front of the soldiers and protected her family; or Samaher who argued with the *Mukhtar* (tribal head) and convinced him to testify in court in her support; or Nahla who accepted humiliation from the occupier in order to preserve her personal dignity by insisting on caring for and supporting her imprisoned loved ones. In just naming them, I feel a sense of empowerment.

It is important to note that this book does not merely present a collection of narrative data. The narratives of women are not merely literary ways to frame the material horrors of their existence, or of their losses and pain. In my previous research, the 'listening' has unearthed ways in which Palestinian women are continually shaping strategies for coping, for creating optimistic possibilities, and for community-building literally in the midst of the fire. I hope that my further research into women's voices will uncover broader patterns of survival that I can contextualize in terms of my own work as a Palestinian, a feminist activist and therapist, and legal scholar.

MILITARIZATION AND VIOLENCE AGAINST WOMEN IN WAR AND CONFLICT ZONES

Collectively, the Palestinian experience has been that of a series of occupations by colonizing powers: of being culturally and materially subjected to nineteenth-century European racial hierarchies and gender politics and of being indoctrinated into all-male Ottoman, European, and later Israeli administrative systems. The condition of women's lives, including violence against women, is closely linked to this dynamic of continuous oppression and political occupation. To use occupation as a trope is not an attempt to impose a pre-determined grid that will simplify or homogenize either the complexity or diversity of the 'occupations' in play, but rather is an effort to lay a foundation which can direct our investigation of violence against women within various contexts of war and political conflict.

In revealing the effect of political and military violence on violence against women, Chapter 2, subtitled 'Women and war', provides an overview of the 'militarized zone' and its consequences for women. This chapter simultaneously takes into account the convergence of a specific material history and the dynamics of Palestinian 'nationhood' under *and as a result of* occupation. Juxtaposed against and within these issues are women's own narratives that reflect the effects of this present and continuing history – an acute merger reflected in their narratives of time as present, past, and future – as well as foregrounding the personal losses emanating from occupation(s) and the coping strategies which the women bring to daily life. The chapter explores the effects of trauma and victimization of women in areas of political conflict as specifically revealed through the voices of mothers of martyrs in Palestine who participated in a 'voice therapy' empowerment group. The narratives of these mothers contain political and ideological implications that highlight the need to re-examine the analytical framework with which to explain the conditions and reactions of women to trauma. Such narratives reveal an analytic framework that aims to counteract the continuing Orientalizing of the region that privileges and subsumes most accounts within us–them and here–there binaries. While this chapter presents an ethnography of women surviving in a conflict zone, I am also deeply interested in going beyond a portrait of chaos and trauma in order to present the importance of building intervention programmes, programmes that first and foremost acknowledge the muted voices of women who have experienced this chaos – and also to make their voices heard. Chapter 2 introduces, in a material and specific way, two critical themes that are further developed in this book: first, the ways in which narratives and conceptualizations of 'nation' play out in the specific space of Palestine as well as in women's lives (Chapter 3 explores this very important issue theoretically); and second, the way 'history' has to be reconfigured in discussing these particular spaces.

Chapter 3, entitled 'Veiled powers', engages the relationship between women and conceptualizations of 'nation'. The issue of gender oppression and 'nation' is an extremely complicated, vexed, and contested area of contemporary feminist research, and one of the most dynamic areas in which feminist scholars are working. Conceptualizations of the 'nation' are endemic to the violence against women that I am discussing, and this chapter is an attempt to explore the link between the two. Kaplan *et al.* put it succinctly when they write in the introduction to their volume *Between Woman and Nation* that:

> we have the never ending experience of nation making, through which the vulnerability of certain citizens, some of whom are often in question, can be mapped. Often these subjects stand on the edge of contradictory boundaries – equality and liberty, property and individual self-possession, and citizenship itself – that the modern nation-state cannot resolve.
>
> (1999: 6)

It is both my goal and my hope that through comparative legal and psychological analyses and 'voicing' that we can begin the kind of mapping to which this passage refers. One of the foundational premises of modern feminism has been that the personal is political; the case study of Palestine necessarily takes such a dictum to both its logical and material extremes. It will be our challenge as feminists, through the personal narratives of Palestinian women, to enable a more optimistic reconceptualization of women's suffering.

Much of contemporary race as well as cultural studies theory have engaged in discussions and reconceptualizations of the 'nation'. Beginning with Anderson's *Imagined Communities* (1991), and continuing with the conceptualization of 'nations' under transnational capitalism, scholars have been continually questioning the ability of the term 'nation' to designate a finite and identifiable space in our contemporary global culture. Since the case of Palestine is so integrally bound up with the specifics of *material* space, the debates become even more urgent for this project. Additionally, the concept of 'nation' or 'home' or of both simultaneously becomes particularly critical as well. As the narratives of the women reveal, the 'exilic' conditions for Palestinian women within the space of 'home (-land)' and 'nation' becomes particularly important to explore.

Chapter 4, 'Women frontliners in conflict zones', elaborates on the notion of 'occupation' and how the concept plays out within the territorial space of the 'nation' and more specifically the spaces in which embodied women are located. The chapter specifically engages a textual movement from occupied 'nation' to the occupied bodies of women. The militarized social space of the region and the dominant nature of the military system has intensified, dichotomized, and made rigid the categories of 'masculine' and 'feminine' (Albanese 1996;

Goldstein 2001; Mojab 1997) and has increased the levels of violence against women. Empirical research has shown the large number of severe psychological symptoms present within Palestinian society. Symptoms of depression, anxiety, psychosomatic ailments, and post-traumatic stress disorder (PTSD) are more intense among Palestinian women than among their male counterparts. Under the violent conditions that prevail in Palestinian society, it is not surprising that the vulnerability of women and children to increased violence from both within and outside the family structure rises exponentially. Historical fears on the part of society regarding women's 'purity' and its conflation with notions of 'family honour' have been aggravated under the present political realities of Palestine. Configuring notions of women's 'purity' within the existing framework of the Israeli occupation has resulted in the conceptual interchangeability of 'land' and 'honour'. Thus a need to (ostensibly) 'protect' women increases and intensifies during heightened politico-military crises in Palestine, and indeed too often elsewhere as well. In short, Palestinians' sense of despair and Palestinian male frustration and anger resulting from ongoing oppression by the Israeli occupation is increasingly directed at Palestinian women, making them a secondary target of male retaliatory aggression. At the same time, Palestinian women continue to be systematically targeted by Israeli soldiers for verbal, physical, and sexual violence.

Building upon issues of occupation and violence against women, Chapter 4 examines the effect of what I term the weaponization of women's bodies and lives within the specific political legacies and culture of Palestine in order to study the power dynamics at play. As a way of examining the collusion and the interaction between the patriarchal systems that become activated in militarized areas with regards to sexual abuse, I want to focus on the way women's bodies are used as a weapon in the hands of patriarchal power holders. In this regard, my general objection to relativizing (and thereby dismissing) the problem of weaponization, sexual abuse, and harassment in the conflict zones by invoking 'culture' becomes even more acute: I am arguing that the cultural specificities of living in a conflict zone – while they must be accounted for – do not supersede the global politics of denial. In other words, 'culture' and 'politics' are not interchangeable. Understanding such interconnections as manifested in the practice of weaponization is the core focus of this chapter.

I deal with spatial policies in Chapter 5, 'Speaking truth to power', primarily in terms of the consequences of the Israeli Separation Wall that continues to be extended even as I write. Israeli spatial policy, land grabbing, and colonial strategies reflected in the Separation Wall are both metaphor and material practice as well. The Wall literally manifests itself as an object that separates – that marks a border or boundary that threatens consequences for unauthorized border crossings. The Wall is materially consequential as well: it not only separates, it also devastates, depletes human activities, and increases economic and social burdens for individuals (Shalhoub-Kevorkian 2006, 2007a). During my research I also found that the Wall is text, pure and simple: it writes the lives of those it divides, while they write upon it – literal inscriptions of their suffering. In this chapter, the voices and words of the young of Palestine and the photographs they have taken as part of my research project on the ISW allowed me to analyse and understand the amount of violence (whether hidden or apparent) it has caused.

While these voicings allow us to reduce the suffering of these young people in however small a measure, they also strengthen our conviction against participating in the creation of all forms of essentialist and reductive knowledge aimed at defining the other, especially the vulnerable other, by further circulating media-coded images and ideas sanctioned by the dominant culture. Such images validate the violent operations of the powerful use and misuse of knowledge. My methodology in this study stresses how irreplaceable are the first-hand testimonies that these young people provide. In my estimate, the effect and importance to gender and feminist studies of such seeing – particularly in the production of transnational feminist studies – cannot be overestimated. However, it is critical to remember that what such witnessing also reveals is not only what was actually seen but also by implication what is not seen, what we have *not been allowed* to see. Through my methodological interventions in the voicings and the photographs, I look beyond the predictable and limiting inscriptions of Western hegemony, its repeated litany of 'terrorism' and 'primitivity', and make at least a preliminary attempt to understand the struggles of the Palestinian people while once again keeping in mind that all representations are constructed. Chapter 6 is based on autobiographical ruminations. It is a deeply personal, political, and international essay.

Finally, I do hope that this project will illustrate that the production of feminist knowledge continues unabated, despite overwhelming odds. And the feminist knowledge production of which I speak refers not just to women researchers like me, but more importantly to the women whose voices and narratives I have brought forth in this study. While the history of Palestine is a long one, in some sense it is fair to say that the written history of Palestinian women is short. Yet short as it might be, it still illustrates the often-vexed connections between nationalism, racism, colonialism, and feminist aspirations for gender equality. In listening to the voices of women in this project, it is critical to keep in mind that the invocation of 'culture' in hegemonic discourse is used, as I stated earlier, as an overall Orientalized explanation of each and every issue regarding women in the Middle East. I do not posit Palestinian women as markers of cultural authenticity outside the realities of war and occupation. They are major players in the process of colonization and occupation itself and the ensuing struggles against it. Consequently, their agency and resilience is also affected by the politics of their identity as Palestinian women and the historical, spatial, and economic context of their present voices and silences.

CHAPTER 2

VIOLENT TRANSLATIONS: WOMEN, WAR, AND NARRATIVE IN CONFLICT ZONES

On 7 September 2003, Wisam called my house in Los Angeles. I was spending my sabbatical year at the University of California Los Angeles Center for the Study of Women and Faculty of Law and the University of Southern California Faculty of Law. She called to remind me of the weekly counselling meeting with my team from the Family Defense Society (FDS) in Nablus, Palestine. Knowing that Wisam always speaks clearly and with joy in her voice and was usually thrilled to share their weekly activities and work plan with me, her low and sombre voice told me that something was wrong. When I called back to check on her and the rest of the team, they informed me that they were very busy with the recent catastrophe in Nablus. The Israeli Occupation Forces had demolished one of the buildings that we used as a counselling centre for our work with fifteen families. Others began to talk to me about the incident. Some spoke of the pain, others of the horror of such a crime against young children.

But it was Ula's voice that came through the boldest and the clearest. Ula is a mother of three who lost all she had when her apartment was demolished. She said:

> I did not know what to do ... all I did is search amidst the destruction for some memories: plates, pictures, medicine, clothes. Maybe I could find the baby's cradle ... I needed to get my anger out, so I started fighting with my husband for not bringing the documents and money we had in the apartment. I screamed at him in front of his parents ... I screamed with all the power I had, and ended up being beaten, yet I kept on screaming.

Ula told me three weeks after the loss of her home that she was in a great deal of pain and had no will left to face her new reality – but nevertheless had to drag herself to move to live with her brother's family, to transfer the children to a new school, to acclimatize to a new place that was not hers, to lose her privacy, her freedom to talk to her children without her brother's family hearing, her freedom to sleep or dress the way she wished, her freedom to cook the dishes she and her family liked; but most of all she lost the possibility of continuing her education. She said:

> With the loss of my house, I lost my closeness to my husband and even my children, he sleeps at his parents and I sleep here with my children. We lost our ability to control our lives, we all sleep on the floor ... we lost it all, even our ability to cover the expenses for my college. I had only six months until graduation, to become a math teacher, to earn my own money, and have some freedom. Then, as a woman, I am expected to function, do everything for everybody, my husband, my brother, my children, my in-laws, bring new documents to the children's school, find new books, clothes, bags, and medicine for the family ... I know they are all suffering, they are all in pain ... but we women suffer the most ... the most.

Ula shared with me the effect of her immense loss, but added that her being a woman, a young mother, and a female student tripled her victimization. She concluded:

> Palestinian women must carry a heavy burden, I am doing it day and night ... non-stop ... not knowing what will happen to us in the future. Did you hear the story of the mother who lost her child, giving birth while held up at the checkpoint? *Nakabuna* [they caused *nakba*, i.e. they have caused us so much pain] and they have never stopped.

Thanato-power is the power that is the management of death, destruction, and violence. The use of thanato-power against women under military occupation is reflected in the following report in a *Ha'aretz* article entitled 'Twilight Zone: Birth and Death at the Checkpoint'. Gideon Levy states:

> Rula was in the last stages of labour. Daoud says the soldiers at the checkpoint wouldn't let them through, so his wife hid behind a concrete block and gave birth on the ground. A few minutes later, the baby girl died.
>
> They wanted to call her Mira. All their children have names that begin with M, from Mohammed to Meida, their youngest daughter. They borrowed baby clothes from Rula's sister – their financial situation after

three years of unemployment made buying new clothes out of the question – and they packed a bag to be ready for the birth. Now they are beside themselves with grief. Rula doesn't say a word and Daoud can't keep the words from pouring out.

(2003)

Ula's narrative, a narrative of woman's power and victimization combined with the thanato-power of the just-born dead body – the newborn who died during its mother's labour at the checkpoint – clearly reflects hegemonic conceptions of those made Other. The violent acts perpetrated against women raised by Ula include not only the visible losses of loved one's homes and land but also the harmful childbirth (as an example of bio-power) and death (of thanato-power) of newborn babies due to the refusal of the military to allow the expectant mother to pass the military checkpoint and proceed to a hospital. Her narrative of life and death merging with her history of continual loss challenges the hegemony through her power to continue walking the walk despite the severe loss while opening into a renewed way of conceiving what happens to women's life and death in the context of constant military occupation.

Levy's illustration of the hardships faced by Palestinian women like Rula must be taken in conjunction with a recent study released by the Human Rights Council:

> According to the Information Health Centre of the Palestinian Ministry of Health, from 2000 to 2006, 69 cases of Palestinian pregnant women giving birth at Israeli checkpoints had been recorded with peaks reached in 2001 (18 cases), in 2002 (24 cases), in 2003 (8 cases) and in 2004 (9 cases). Of these, 45 took place in the West Bank (out of which 11 cases occurred in Nablus and 9 cases in Ramallah), while 14 cases were registered in Gaza. In 2005, only three cases were reported in the West Bank and Gaza, while two cases occurred in the West Bank and none in Gaza in 2006.
>
> As a result of the checkpoints, 10 per cent of pregnant women who wished to give birth in a hospital had been delayed on the road between two to four hours before reaching health facilities, while 6 per cent of them had spent more than four hours for the same journey. Before the intifada, the average time to reach health facilities was 15 to 30 minutes. These hazardous conditions were mainly attributed to impediments faced by ambulances and medical teams when trying to transport women in labour through checkpoints, and to inspections or attacks perpetrated by Israeli forces against ambulances and their patients.

(2007)

Ula's voice and the many unheard voices of Palestinian women that are discussed in this chapter painfully illustrate the explicit effect of violence against women through militarization and occupation.

THE QUESTIONS, BACKGROUND, AND THEORY

Historicizing the context of violence against women by taking into account the political and economic realities and dynamics of the region enables a more complete analysis of contemporary power relations, hierarchies, and positions in relation to Palestinian women. I focus on violence against women in conflict areas both because of my own subject location as a Palestinian feminist and to offer an oppositional perspective against the 'new imperialism', the colonial and neo-colonial powers that are on the rise as evidenced in the continued Israeli occupation of Palestinian land, the US and allied powers occupations of Iraq and Afghanistan (and, we must remember, Haiti), the 'soft' occupation of much of the globe, and the rather harder occupation via the presence of 737 US military bases in sixty-three countries (Dufour 2007), and the world's denial of women's suffering in the various conflict zones. I also firmly believe that the interconnections between the local and the global are crucial to our discussion. That same global dynamic which denies the realities faced by the Palestinian people also refuses them the right to justice, safety, and protection, allows military personnel to threaten women's health, contributes to and conducts infanticide, and more. Those powers are the ones that have permitted local colonizers, by omission and commission, to demolish Ula's house and violate her family, home, education, economic stability, and spatial security. Ella Shohat theorizes the complexity of the situation for women like Ula: 'In a world of transnational communication the central problem becomes one of tension between cultural homogenization and cultural heterogenization, in which hegemonic tendencies are simultaneously "indigenized" within a complex disjunctive global cultural economy' (cited in Alexander and Mohanty 1997: xxi). Thus, the need to uncover the ongoing interplay between the cultural, the political, and the economic in the context of the interaction between the local and global is central. The theoretical anchor of my analysis is thus based on the legacy and continuity of, and also the fractures between, historical colonization and its continuation within the new image politics of imperialism and occupation and the veiled politics of 'freedom' and 'homeland security'. This chapter will specifically examine violence against women in the

Occupied Palestinian Territories (OPT) while keeping in sight the global geo-political-economic context in which that violence occurs, and will consider the effects and intersections of that violence with the struggle for women's agency in conflict areas around the world.

Allowing the voices of women to emerge and talk – not just to those within the conflict zone, but more importantly to those outside – and acknowledge for themselves the horrifying impact of violence perpe-trated against them in the context of war is, in my belief, nothing short of a political necessity, not simply as an act of personal therapy but also as a way of assigning 'meaning' and in order to continue to create feasible narratives from shattered lives. The importance of initiating a dialogue that can be used to implement a discourse on violence against women in conflict areas for critical political–feminist theory became evident to me when I worked with Palestinian women in the context of constant uncertainty, political unrest, and trauma.

The many discussions that I have been privy to with various Palestinian authorities as an academic and an activist regarding the politics and the poetics of an emerging Palestine, both as state and identity, revealed for me that often those with authority both in the West and in this region seem to want to dismiss violence against women as a political issue. The often-used refrain is that 'we have many more important issues to worry about' or that if we 'show our dirty laundry those in the West will attack us and vilify Arabs and Islam'. Invariably, when I have shared the voices of Palestinian women with international organizations in conferences and other forums, one of the first questions asked is: 'Please talk about "honour killing", discuss the hardships that the rape crises centre faces, share with us the Palestinian criminal justice system's failure to combat violence against women.' Thus, while I under-stand the patriarchal implications of the dismissal of violence against women by the power holders in Palestine, I am fully cognizant that the power/knowledge dynamics in play both in terms of external dominant powers as well as the internal ones means navigating issues with extra caution so as to not create the perception of *dramatizing* the already dramatic and *culturalizing* or even *Orientalizing* the analytical context. I believe that raising the issue of the ways in which the dynamics of violence against women plays out in conflict areas – as Ula's case and the various other voices heard in this book clearly illustrate – has the revolutionary potential to re-conceptualize the nature of such violence, uncover its relationship with the emergence of women's agency, and show the way occupation and colonization operate through the bodies

45

and lives of women: Rula and Daoud suffered under the Israeli 'security measures'; Ula suffered from the violence of military occupation. Such violence against them, as examples of violence so often unacknowledged, violated their rights to safety, security, and housing and also increased their vulnerability to health problems and economic, social, spatial, and internal patriarchal violence and abuse.

A well-known and oft-repeated theme in Foucault's work is his conceptualization of the 'individual' as a construct of discursive modes at play in culture and the critical interactions of knowledge and/as power. In *Discipline and Punish* Foucault acutely describes the effects of the panoptic gaze whereby the individual is under constant social surveillance, and more importantly created and articulated by that observation (1975). Palestinian women and men are under constant surveillance and control to such an extent that even childbirth can be considered a tool in the hands of power holders to further control and dominate. Not surprisingly, the most salient criticisms of Foucault resist what is perceived as his conception of the totalizing effects of knowledge and power on the formation of a subject, a systematic encoding by cultural forces that Foucault's critics believe has left the subject without any agency to resist the ostensibly totalizing forces that shape her. In his later writings, Foucault elaborated his conception of the subject as incoherently defined by the power/knowledge nexus and argued that the very nature of an articulated subject allows for discursive interventions (1980). As is well known, Edward Said would take this very possibility as the theoretical premise of his *Orientalism* in order to illustrate the ways in which the epistemic practices of hegemonic power can also be its own undoing, since the discursive network that is posited as 'reality' is, according to Said, both decidedly 'unreal' and flimsy (1979).

If we begin with Foucault's premise and conceptualize the subject as potentially articulated through discursive constructs and also consider the possible interventions into that construct as outlined by Said primarily in colonized contexts, we can examine the false dichotomy that is also discursively created in hegemonic culture between concepts of women's 'victimization' and women's 'agency'. This (ostensible) dichotomy continues to play out polemically within feminist studies itself, particularly when feminist theories attempt to posit and negotiate the social effects of violence against women. Books such as Naomi Wolf's *Fire with Fire* (1994) and Katie Roiphe's *The Morning After* (1994) criticize and characterize some feminist work as 'victim feminism' and offer instead what has been termed 'power feminism'. As the titular reference itself might suggest, 'power feminism' wants to stress women's individual agency and responsibility against hegemonic forces while arguing that a relentless emphasis on women's victimization in fact reinforces sex and gender stereotypes of women as weak, vulnerable, and fragile – perpetually at the mercy of powers that be. In contrast, advocates of power feminism believe that they are arguing for women's individual agency as the basis for women's ability to exercise choice and responsibility. Thus, they contend that 'power feminism' will empower women, and within its theoretical parameters rename the hitherto powerless women not as 'victims' but as 'survivors' (for a more expanded discussion of this debate, see Schneider 2000, especially the chapter entitled 'Beyond Victimization and Agency').

As productive as this debate has been on some fronts, from my perspective such a binary discourse – as it is inevitably locked in to an either/or proposition – fails to acknowledge the complex nature of colonization and the way it operates through the systemic oppression of women and fails as well to understand the uniqueness of women's active and proactive efforts to resist such oppression. The risk of such binary thinking in terms of 'powerful'/'powerless' or of 'victim'/'survivor' is further exacerbated when we attempt to analyse violence against women in conflict zones, as seen for example in Ula's case, for in such spaces these seemingly oppositional labels become at once both feasible in application while creating yet another source of oppression through the very applications themselves. The fundamental inadequacy of these binary acts of naming necessarily overlooks the complexity of the daily struggles women undertake in conflict zones. The sometimes-facile use of 'victim' or 'victimization' in the prevalent discourse becomes a two-edged sword in that such naming both creates and identifies a political and feminist problem. In general, when violence against women occurs, victim claims are often the *only* way that these women can be heard. Of course, a discourse on violence against women that only stresses the status of 'victim' or the process of victimization can also be counter-productive in that it can and too often does further encourage stereo-typical beliefs about women as passive, vulnerable, and weak, or about women's society as pre-modern and/or backward. More importantly, as my own research in the region has shown, the specific dynamics in play can also trigger very pernicious attempts to 'protect' and safeguard women which often lead to further oppression and social control (see Merry 2006; Shalhoub-Kevorkian 2003b, 2005a, 2005c, 2006). Martha Minow has also noted the double-edged nature of claims to victim status, observing that the use of victimization claims make powerful appeals for sympathy, compassion, and solidarity, and finally also raise social consciousness around the issue at hand (1993). That said, such claims also suppress and override the societal and structural dimensions of gender discrimination while undermining the value and power of women's personal strength, capacity, and agency.

In addition, Razack's analyses regarding the portrayal of the 'Other' woman by Western feminists – and I would add by the colonial settler projects and occupation forces – as burdened by culture and hindered by their community from entering modernity keeps the otherized woman 'squarely within the framework of patriarchy understood as abstracted from all other systems' (Razack 2007: 3). Razack's insightful writings and theorization points to the way women's bodies are present to mark the society's backwardness. Palestinians are constructed by the West and by the Jewish state as terrorist pre-modern Others, as 'bare lives' against whom violence is authorized as necessary. Ula showed us how violent events happening in violent spaces and conflict areas are open spaces to further violence, and that political oppression and spatial occupation are anchored through race, class, and gender. The raced and gendered dimensions of the Israeli colonial project are well articulated by David Remnick:

> 'The situation between us', [Moshe] Dayan creepily informed the Palestinian poet Fadwa Tuqan, 'is like the complex relationship between a Bedouin man and the young girl he has taken against her wishes. But when their children are born, they will see the man as their father and the woman as their mother. The initial act will mean nothing to them. You, the Palestinians, as a nation, do not want us today, but we will change your attitude by imposing our presence upon you.'
>
> (2007)

Dayan's statement is only one example illustrating the manner in which colonial violence is well-calculated and planned – and thoroughly gendered. Colonial settler violence creates exceedingly violent contexts wherein instances of violence are not only endorsed but also advanced 'silently' with Empire's support. What I am saying here is that theorizing violence against women in conflict zones should not be incarcerated in the analyses of internal patriarchy and victimization of women, rather, that one must look at abuse and victimization as a product of the interlock between the various colonial hegemonic systems of Empire that are raced, classed, sexed, and gendered. An analysis of such interlock should never deny women's agency a theoretical apparatus, as I will be showing in the following section.

ARTICULATING WOMEN'S AGENCY AGAINST TOTALIZING THEORIES

The drawing reproduced here was created by Salam, an eight-year-old girl who suffered from the demolition of her East Jerusalem-area home in the winter of 2007 (see Figure 1). Salam wanted to show, despite the demolition of her house, that she still held onto its memory and beauty in her mind, as reflected in the colourful curtains, the warm windows, and the pet pigeons singing inside the cage in her drawing. The colours she used express hope. In an accompanying text, she wrote: 'When the house was demolished I started crying.' With a sense of empathy on her part, Salam recounts her failed efforts to release her pigeons from their cage; their steadfast refusal to flee and live a life in exile overpowered her pleas for their flight. She stated:

> We all tried to let them free ... but the birds did not fear the demolition, and when the bulldozers demolished the house, they were still inside, in

Figure 1 Salam's drawing.

their cage and then within the house's ruins. I was so upset. I was very afraid and crying. But then when I saw them managing to get out of the ruins of the house, I was very happy. They wanted to stay with us; they got out of the ruins and flew towards me. My father rebuilt their cage, and they are still with us.

Salam's story is the story of a young frontline girl who needed to confront the violence of the Israeli occupation unleashed against her home, her family, and her precious pigeons. Her voice of victimization and agency demonstrates to us the way she gathered power in her moment of despair from the uncontrollable birds that symbolized the power of hope, love, belonging, and survival. Her pigeons' steadfastness becomes a language by which Salam asserts her own conclusions arising out of the demolition. In artistically using her pigeons, she personifies how the belittling feeling of anxiety that overcame her when the house was demolished was tempered by her refusal 'to be displaced'. With Salam, it was hard not to feel her victimization without seeing her agency, her pain without her steadfastness. Her innovative agency is reflected in her ability to use the pigeons as a catalyst to confront victimization. As a representative of the destruction and violence in violated spaces endured by many other girls and women, Salam's experience and response calls for an analysis of the innovative agency of women when dealing with violence. As such, this necessitates the incorporation of a theoretical understanding of women's agency alongside any analytical framework addressing violence against women in conflict zones.

I understand and define women's agency as the power, motivation, and energy that are created and/or exist in space and time, that are held by individual women or a group of women in life situations, and which are used to bring about social change. I am primarily conceptualizing women's agency as a geo-political, bio-political, thanato-political, and social location that allows women to act, move onwards, and bring about transformations. Agency is inherently situational. As such, I have come to understand agency not in the abstract but in the actual examination and identification of hierarchies of power and, more specifically, in how women's agency, as a concept, is allowed to circulate within those power hierarchies. It will come as no surprise that some women are circulated as icons of 'modern' or 'liberal' citizens within liberal democracies while others who may be struggling for freedom, or fighting national struggles, or simply trying to survive, or to preserve a certain measure of cultural authenticity, are often depicted as backward or hapless victims in the binary discourses of populist conceptions of agency.

This has led to a false bifurcation between those who are seemingly 'cultureless' and those who are discursively formulated as the Cultural Other. On the one hand we have the modernized, 'civilized', citizens of the Western empires and on the other hand there are simply those who are elsewhere, the 'cultural primitives' outside the Western sphere who deny the many Salams a voice within the process of theorization. This discursive divide becomes even more apparent when the issue being discussed is violence against women living in conflict zones. Such a dichotomous method of analysing the 'Other' woman ignores the power of Empire and the fact that she does not have equal access to the processes of deliberation, nor does she have the ability to have her discourses of liberation circulate freely. The inherent dichotomy of the dominant discourse ignores how power shapes both the process of liberatory struggle as well as the circuits of power which inscribe, describe, and circulate the notions of how 'we' (read the dominant culture) are to view such struggles.

The problem becomes even more acute when we are specifically discussing violence against women in the occupied territories of Palestine, for there is a tendency to culturalize the violence as a way of dismissing it. Somehow, violence against women in Palestine is always a matter of culture ('it's their culture'), while acts of violence in the West are always outside of ideology and open to legal action, Western psychology, or individualizing narratives. The rape of a Western woman is symptomatic of an individual, criminal aberration on the part of a male, while the rape of a Palestinian woman is endemic to her cultural heritage. When celebrated cases such as that of Scott Peterson, who killed his wife and unborn child, are circulated in the media, the event is usually not diagnosed as a product of the culture of the United States, a culture that practices violence against women, but rather the deviant act of an individual criminal. Such popular and ironically culturally sanctioned analysis reflects the hidden racism that allows these interpretations to circulate unchallenged. Veens Talwar Oldenburg put it well in writing in opposition to those 'who continue stubbornly to find cultural fingerprints at the scene of crimes against women of "inferior" culture' (2002: 227).

This absolute binary of the cultureless versus the cultural 'Other' disavows the politics and power inherent to all violence against women and invokes culture as a way to dismiss the abuse (see Volpp 2000, 2001). Moreover, culturalizing gender subordination to apply only to certain racialized bodies and analysing gendered violence as a product of cultures when such violence committed upon the Other is a method of stigmatizing and thus of excluding the Other from holding a status as a legitimate citizen with inalienable human rights. Simplifying an analysis and narrowing it to 'culturalized' explanations that assert cultural bases for the oppression of women constitutes an implicit need to uphold the hegemonic 'Self' as superior.

As an academic, I necessarily participate in the discursive networks which disseminate 'knowledge' and thus must take account of the power relations, the systems of belonging and exclusion, and the categories of analysis that obtain in such networks. I hope that I bring this awareness to a feminist analysis of women's strategies for survival, their understanding of agency and victimization, as I unlearn my own means of participation within networks of discursive power. When investigating the subjectivities of those who have been denied basic human rights and a voice, particularly women in war zones and conflict areas, I have to examine how these women are daily constructed for our consumption. In an attempt to reconfigure agency, we have to take note of which constructions are encouraged, and why. In fact, the most intriguing aspect of studying and attempting to conceptualize 'agency' in a conflict zone is to be attentive to and acknowledge the hidden struggles for change, the invention, mobilizations, and productions that characterize counter-hegemonic discourses. Questions remain, however: what possibilities for mobilization are produced by the process of colonizing and by the occupying projects? Moreover, what is the mobilizing power in Salam and other women whom I have met, talked to, worked with, and learned from in the occupied territories, the power that coalesces their agency so they can construct and execute their strategies for survival, whether through language, actions, narratives, love, or even silence? What fuels the construction of new political spaces of resistance? Conversely, how do we negotiate the position of those who situate themselves within, rather than in opposition to, hegemonic powers and uphold the dominant discourse simply by their location within culture? Is this agency or a parody of the privilege of location? In the contemplation of agency throughout the book, I also explore the aligned processes of invention and imagination.

Additionally, a central issue that remains in conceptualizing agency is the exploration of the limits that (re-)appropriation, parody, or other mimetic strategies might play in the formation of agency. As Mary Louis Roberts reminds us, parody's ruling irony is that 'in situating themselves within, rather than in opposition to, hegemonic forms, mimics reproduce and uphold those forms as much as they undermine them' (2002: 106). Thus, are all acts of personal deployment within a situational framework in the end agency, or are discursive re-appropriations a critical part of the apparatus of understanding agency?

Salam, Ula, Maha, and other women's resistance to various kinds of domination take an active stance against the fabrications of the dominant discourse. But – and in order for us to understand the ways in which women fight back, tolerate, reject, react, become proactive, or postpone any reaction to violence against them – one needs to not only look at the macro-political power-plays but also at women's micro-political refusals to subjugation. Observing Palestinian women's agency and modes of dealing with victimization requires close examination of the structural determinants of knowledge. By taking into account the ways women in war zones and politically conflicted areas are differently situated within given social locations, one is able to examine the way they are differently affected by the dynamics of knowledge and power. By being attentive to the various strategies they use to overcome oppression, we can begin to answer a series of questions: how do women survive in militarized spaces? Who might these women become? My refusal to accept the de-politicization of women's experiences in the name of 'culture', including violence against women, goes hand in hand with my assertion that it is misleading to understand violence against women in terms of internal cultural, religious, or localized oppression.

I believe that we cannot begin to understand women's ordeals in politically conflicted areas and in war zones without attempting to understand the *interrelatedness* of victimization and agency within the context of Empire. When women act on their own behalf under conditions of oppression and political occupation, it does not mean that they have overcome such oppression, or that they have ended their abuse. Once again, victimization and agency are not an either/or phenomenon, nor are they something static, isolated from the constant transformations and shifts in systems of power. The complexity in understanding violence against women (VAW) in general and in conflict areas and war zones in particular requires an analysis of the rhetoric of 'victim'/'agent' as politically constructed, serving the political purposes of those who have the power to circulate the constructs in the first place. The social and political construction of women's agency and victimization, their actions and responses to violence, their resistance to abuse, should be analysed within the specific context of political and social forces that not only incur the violence but also discursively create the concepts of agent or victim. We should be cautious in our attempts to conceptualize and then discursively analyse the 'victim' or the 'agent'. Victimization is not total failure and annihilation, nor is agency total victory over abuse; neither should be dramatized or romanticized. In this project, I am arguing for a rejection of simple dichotomies, and want to examine the complexities and contradictions facing women and affecting women's lives, particularly in conflict zones. The question remains as to how our conceptualizations of 'victimization' and 'agency' affect the acts of survival and resistance to abuse, and how does the specific context of the abuse – historical, economic, gender-based, social and political – either further burden or enable abused women to resist their oppressors?

THE DYNAMICS OF SILENCING: INVISIBILITY AND HYPERVISIBILITY

The voice of Ula at the beginning of this chapter, the unheard voice of Rula as she gave birth at the checkpoint, and Salam's voice found in her drawing of hope, are all the frontline voices of women who have experienced both victimization and survival. They are voices which bring with them the realities lived by women who fight with 'nothing left' so as to resuscitate life and to attempt the creation of new options for themselves or their children from out of the rubble. Listening to them, voices coming from such great power, a question within me begged for an answer: who has the right to produce what we think of as 'knowledge' about conflict zones? About the violence that is war? Who is best qualified to talk of life under militarization in conflict areas, and about the specific silences that are perpetrated against women during times of political occupation? Perhaps the obvious answer is that those who are blinded by tears but motivated by their losses have the most right – but do they have the 'appropriate language' to speak their truths within existing systems of power?

The voices of the (materially, psychically, or psychologically) occupied, particularly of women, are never secure from those who hold the power of discourse, for those in power have always had the sole right to decide what 'truths' shall circulate within a given regime; they have decided what constitutes victimization, and most importantly, they often (pre-)determine the limits of which survival strategies can be put into play by the victims themselves. Palestinian women I spoke with have repeatedly told me of the kind of 'gagging' they experience daily, as if a hand were clamped over their mouths, and more importantly, that almost no one has even *acknowledged* their suffering, let alone attempted to try and end it. So I ask: why can we not hear or acknowledge Ula's voice, her cries of lamentation rising from the ruins of the conflict in Palestine? Why can we not acknowledge the voice of Salam who used her depiction of her birds to reveal violence against her? Why can we not hear Rula's voice calling for a safe delivery of her baby? As arguably the most overlooked aspect of the dynamics of silencing, where does the unflagging power and agency Ula, Rula, and Salam come from in the face of continual violence? To a certain extent, the answers to some of the questions are obvious, but I want to elaborate on the process and concept of agency within the realities of a power dynamic in which one would think agency could not obtain as a viable option. Hopefully, the women's voices that I want us to listen to in this project will detail the complex nature of the oppression as well as of the strategies of resistance. But I hope that through these voices we also recognize the discursive constraints that are endemic to the power/knowledge nexus and the ensuing power structure. Understanding the dynamics of silence and silencing enables us to understand the intricacies of abuse that is violence against women. By analysing the dynamics of the silencing and agency of women's victimization, while we begin the process of hearing their voices, we can perhaps create new sites for a different kind of knowledge that is not complicit with hegemonic circuits of power where what is available for consumption (within the seemingly unavoidable nexus of a colonial capitalist and consumerist global structure) only reinvigorates the power structures that allowed for its consumption in the first place.

Endemic to violence against women is a corresponding move to silence them; for like the proverbial three monkeys, colonial racialized culture does not want to see, hear, or speak of the violence enacted on the psyche and bodies of women. This perpetual attempt to negate the voices and narratives of women who have suffered violence is further aggravated in conflict areas wherein material strife, political unrest, or war foregrounds the existing tensions of a gender-biased world. In a militarized zone, these acts of silencing become acute, and as illustrated by Cynthia Enloe, everything comes to be 'controlled by, dependent on, while deriving its value from, the militaristic structure and its institution' (2000). In occupied Palestine the attempts to render women's agency and victimization as silent has been conceptualized as a matter of 'national security' mainly by those constructing Orientalist and Orientalizing discourses. To gain at least a working understanding of how the elision of violence against women comes to be subsumed under the rubric of protecting/serving the powerful, we must go back to the beginnings of the political conflict in Palestine and do some genealogical analyses of the context.

In a presentation I gave at the Yale University School of Law in April 2003, one of the doctoral students refused to hear a narrative on the sufferings of Palestinian women. He argued with me, shouting that Israeli soldiers have never abused or sexually harassed Palestinian women. He stated: 'A Jewish soldier sexually abuse a Palestinian woman?! It never happened. We never come close to Arab women!' The vehemence of his refusal to hear was almost palpable: a volatile mixture of denial and anger – a material abjection of Palestinians that one could almost touch. Was he in denial of the effect of Zionist colonization on Palestinian women? Was he afraid to acknowledge the historical and current abuses and traumas? Did he mean that it is dishonourable for someone in a position of authority to abuse women, or that the class of the Israeli soldier in his expression of desire – even if violence is the expression of that desire – towards a Palestinian woman is somehow abridged? Did he mean that we, as Palestinians, have no right to invoke our rights? The abhorrent masculinization of the discussion and his explosive anger made me wonder: why this denial? Indeed, why the fear? While the anger of the student is multilayered and complex, the reasons for this anger on some levels are easily understood: he firmly positioned himself on one side of the (ostensible) Arab/Israeli conceptual binary or cultural divide.

Political unrest in Palestine started before 1948, increased during the 1960s, 1970s, and the First Intifada (beginning December 1987), and has steadily increased during the last sixteen years – including the advent of the Second Intifada and the violent continuation of the settler-colonial project of the Jewish state. Following the Oslo Agreement, the occupier has continued to violate the rights to freedom of Palestinian men and women. The Palestinian resistance movement continued, in different forms, to fight against oppression, while many national and international efforts were trying through *peace*-keeping efforts to ensure socio-political stability. The militarized social space – coming at the critical moment of 'emerging statehood' – created an atmosphere wherein the political and ontological choices of Palestinian men became inherently liminal: conflations between the family and state, land and honour, protection and oppression, and purity and danger happened almost simultaneously.

Silencing, by those in power, of women's victimization and their freedom fighting when so required and highlighting these when 'politically appropriate' should therefore be part of the matrix of our analyses. Looking at the processes of silencing primarily as a political issue reveals the tendency of the dominant discourses to culturalize violence against women when it is perpetrated by Palestinian patriarchal powers, and even justify it if it serves the 'security' of Empire. Conflating issues of violence against women with liberatory efforts to 'save' Palestinian women from the 'primitive' or 'terrorist' Arab male has been a common move of the Western press and Western interventions. Such a discursive move, if it is unchallenged, endangers available spaces of invention, transformation, and agency. In a space as highly politicized and militarized as the OPT, power relations are a crucial unit of analysis and sexual politics becomes central to the process and practices of colonized control.

As we listen to the voices of Palestinian women, it is critical to understand how concepts of 'silence' and 'silencing' also define both the victim and the agent – at once making her invisible in part through refusal to acknowledge the violation of her rights as a Palestinian woman under military occupation, or hypervisible when her victimization serves power holders. In studying contemporary relations of power and social hierarchies, including the archaeology of state practices during political conflicts, I want to examine the ways in which specific voices and images of women are advanced for consumption while others are muted. In 1996 the Taliban took power in Afghanistan (with considerable covert aid from the United States), yet only in the wake of 9/11 did the victimization of Afghani women by the Taliban regime and the imposition of the *burqa* become of ostensible concern for the United States. Suddenly, the oppressive gender-biased culture of the Taliban became a rallying point for US military action and other aggressive strategies. Similarly, the voices and faces of Iraqi women became heard and seen in the world's most powerful media as these supposedly became a source of US moral outrage and a symbol of Saddam Hussein's tyranny. But instead of re-circulating these well-known and well-rehearsed conceptual imaginings, it is absolutely more productive for us to think of ways in which women can create their own meanings, circulate their own signifiers.

To make my point clearer, I present the following, an excerpt from a BBC article published in June 2003:

UN officials in Baghdad say they are very concerned that religious extremists are intimidating women and girls into wearing the veil. In particular, some radical clerics have demanded that women – even Christians – wear the veil. The UN officials have also expressed alarm at a reported rise in rape. Since the end of the conflict in Iraq, radical factions in Iraq's Sunni and Shi'a Muslim communities have been asserting themselves in the ensuing period of instability. One Iraqi UN staff member recently received a handwritten letter at home saying she would be killed unless she started covering her hair. The spokesman for the UN Children's Fund, Geoffrey Keele, said that in some areas there had also been pressure on schoolgirls to start putting on the veil. 'It's an issue of people's rights – it's an issue not only of women's rights, but human rights – and people have a right to choose whether or not they wear the veil, what religion they practice, how they practice that religion', he told the BBC. UN officials have raised the issue with American and British forces. They also say Iraqi women can no longer drive or walk in the streets at night as freely as they did in pre-war Iraq. And women have been victims not only of intimidation, but also of the lawlessness of the last few weeks, says the BBC's Caroline Hawley. No statistics are available, but Iraqis say there has been a significant increase in rape.

(BBC 2003)

As the excerpt reveals, it is absolutely remarkable how discrete issues are conflated with a sleight-of-hand ease to once again stage the place of the Other – an 'elsewhere' that always already obtains as 'not of the West' – and not wholly surprisingly, the iconic signifier of this elsewhere is the veil. In this instance the liminality to which the veil has been subjected is almost laughable in its obviousness: we shift from the veil being a signifier of bondage and backwardness, to the aggressive and brutal intimidation of the Arab male over Arab women, to a further (if somewhat unexplained) conflation of forced veiling with rape, with individual and religious freedom, and the general state of lawlessness in a space that has been recently occupied by invading forces! Perhaps more astonishing is the fact that since this collage of separate issues presented as 'news' under the rubric of the 'veil' went unchallenged, it reveals to what extent the veil fits the macabre outline of the Western cultural imaginary. As we all know, in a capitalist culture the first and foremost impulse is to produce what the consumer wants. I believe it is our responsibility as feminists to create the need and desire for alternative discourses in which things cannot be swept unexamined and unchallenged not under the proverbial rug but, in this case, the proverbial veil.

Palestinian women were well aware of the ways in which Israeli troops were trying to infiltrate their homes and tear apart the fabric of their culture. So the veil for some of them – far from being the oppressive mechanism of an evil Arab empire – became a place of refuge, a way of coping. This is not beyond comprehension when we think of the atrocities of war, the terrible exposure to which women are daily subjected. In the occupied territories, Palestinian women are daily stripped down to their flesh; some of their narratives speak as if they were probed to the bone: 'Every time I visit my son in jail they undress me, they touch my body, open up my legs and look inside, they ask all of us to stand naked in front of each other ... I decided that I am not going to visit him in jail anymore, I can't take the humiliation' (for more detail, see Shalhoub-Kevorkian 2005a). In the context of such violations, we should remember that the veil, after all, is a covering, a shelter.

Militarization is never gender-neutral; as Enloe argues, it is a personal and political transformation that relies on hetero-normative ideas about femininity and masculinity. In her book *Maneuvers*, Enloe provides an international overview of the politics of masculinity, nationalism, and globalization that includes many different areas of the globe, including Japan, Korea, Serbia, Kosovo, Rwanda, the Philippines, Britain, Israel, and the United States. Enloe outlines the dilemmas feminists around the globe face in trying to craft theories and strategies that support militarized women, locally and internationally, without succumbing to the prison of militarization themselves. She explores the complicated militarized experiences of women as prostitutes, as rape victims, as mothers, as wives, as nurses, and as feminist activists, and she uncovers the 'maneuvers' that military officials and their civilian supporters have made in order to ensure that each of these groups of women feel special and separate (Enloe 2000). This militarized milieu is exacerbated when a politically conflicted area faces material violence and bloodshed for almost sixty years – as is clearly the case with the Israeli–Palestinian conflict.

The conditions of women's lives in the Middle East are closely linked to the history and dynamics of inequality, colonialism, and imperialism in Europe, Africa, and elsewhere. When we trace imperialism back to its roots in European history, we better understand the violent patriarchal history of the persecuted Jews and the Holocaust. We also comprehend the emergence of what Said calls 'Orientalism', in addition to the stigma against the Arab male and female 'Other', as well the denial of the Palestinians' rights. The history of gender violence in Europe, as

59

dramatically reflected in the witch-hunts and inquisitions of the Middle Ages when several million women were systematically tortured, disfigured, and burned alive, is now common knowledge (Chesler 1972; Mies 1986).

In *Imperial Leather: Race, Gender and Sexuality in the Colonial Contest*, McClintock argues:

> Imperialism is not something that happened elsewhere – a disagreeable fact of history external to Western identity. Rather, imperialism and the invention of race were fundamental aspects of industrial, Western modernity. The invention of race became central not only to self-definition of the middle class but also to the policing of the 'dangerous classes': the working class, the Irish, Jews, prostitutes, feminists.
>
> (1995: 5)

The European imperialist regime from its outset created a violent encounter with pre-existing hierarchies of power and affected the gendered dynamics of the colonized cultures. Colonized women, before the intrusions of imperial rule, were usually disadvantaged within their own societies. Imperialism and colonization imposed on women the necessity of negotiating the gender power imbalances not only within their own societies and their personal relationships, with their own men, but also with the violent hierarchical and militaristic structure of men and women of the imperium. This colonial situation positioned women as icons; women were to uphold social 'boundaries' and 'rules', bear sons and daughters, carry out particular economic responsibilities, and protect the unity of their families, including its sexual purity. This history, later established in law and bounded by gender patterns of disadvantage, deeply affected political conflicts and wars.

POLITICAL CONFLICTS AND VIOLENCE AGAINST WOMEN

The general increase of violence against women in conflict areas or war zones was translated into changes in the physical, social, spatial, and psychological settings and had a particularly pernicious expression in sexual abuse and sexual politics which are also exponentially higher in these areas. For example, history is replete with examples that show the connection between colonization, political conflicts and wars, and sexual abuse. Philippa Levine, in an article on the First World War, discusses the discourse of the imperial powers and its association with the sexual anxiety of the British colonizing powers. She shows how race was a crucial ruling strategy and how racial subordination was a very critical means of imperialism. Such racism, she explains, brought about an increasing link between racial mistrust and a vision of the sexual disorder of the 'untruly' women (1998). Beverly Allen, for another example, in discussing what she has called 'rape warfare' in Bosnia-Herzegovina, reveals how genocidal rape becomes part of the macabre methodology of an 'official' Belgrade policy. Such rapes caused the Hague International War Crime Tribunal for Yugoslavia (ICTY) in February of 2001 to conclude for the first time that rape and sexual enslavement were violations of sufficient gravity to be considered as 'crimes against humanity' under international law. Sexual abuse in times of war varied in its visibility, invisibility, or hypervisibility depending on the conflict in question, but for the most part women survivors are faceless. The rape of the Nanking, both the rape of German women by Soviet troops in 1945 and 1946 and the rape of Soviet Ukrainian women by German troops after 1942, or the rape of Indian and Bangladeshi women are too often analysed in a manner that further militarizes raped women. In Guatemala, an ethnographic research project discussed rape by soldiers during the civil war. It challenges the claim that local cultures silence survivors of state-sponsored rape while emphasizing the role of national and international forces in conspiring towards a position de-politicizing rape and silencing rape survivors (Hastings 2002). Thus, militarized rape has gained visibility in international politics due to the mass rapes that occurred during both the genocide in Rwanda in 1994 and Bosnia during 1992–5, yet it remains uncovered and even de-politicized in areas such as Haiti and Indonesia where only through the work of women's organizations have the rapes became re-politicized and made visible (Enloe 2000).

Rubina Saigol presents women's bodies as arenas of violent struggle when she argues that in South Africa an important part of nationalism has been the way women and their sexuality are treated as the symbols of culture, tradition, and home (2000). In a situation of national conflict, this leads to the women of the enemy being forced into a similar symbolic role. This is why, although violence during communal, ethnic, and international conflicts is directed against everyone, women are violated in a specific sexual manner, namely, through rape. Yet 'not only are they raped, their bodies are marked in particular ways that are meant as reminders of their being women, the honour of the community/ nation' (2000: 116).

Sexual politics and sexuality during war has also been discussed by various Middle Eastern and Third World scholars such as Accad who argues that women's sexuality should be conceptualized as the central problem in the Middle East. She goes so far as to boldly state that where 'an analysis of sexuality and sexual politics [to] be truly incorporated into the revolutionary struggle in Lebanon, nationalism [there] could be transformed into a more viable revolutionary strategy' (Saigol 2000: 38). Once more, war crimes and the state merge over the body of the brutalized woman.

VAW does not only affect women in war zones and politically conflicted areas but also affects countries that colonized, invaded, and occupied other countries. One very clear example is reflected in the Abu Ghraib case, where soldiers physically and sexually abused both men and women; the response of the US administration was a de-politicization of the abuse and a shifting of the blame onto individuals. Violence in general and as afflicted against women in particular is a tool in the hands of the colonizers and a politicized and highly charged space in conflict areas.

THE MORPHOLOGY OF MILITARY OCCUPATION

My aim in the following is to describe the morphology of the colonial Israeli model that uses women's bodies and lives and violence against them as markers to serve their political occupation. Moreover, I would also like to emphasize the complexities violence against women raises when it is challenged internally by local feminist activists. VAW – as we learned from the way Rula was violated through her birth at the checkpoint, and as depicted throughout the book – calls attention to the way Palestinians in general and Palestinian women in particular are transformed into 'exceptions' and 'bare lives' that can be violated through 'legal' racialized security measures based on political 'exception' as the main arbiter of ruling reality. Such 'exception', as portrayed by Agamben (2005) and as reflected for example in the American 'Patriot Act' or the Israeli 'security theology', turned people's lives from lives worthy of living to 'bare lives'. The apparatus that is illustrated in the following chapters not only increases gender violence but also actually employs it to promote the colonial project.

The effect of political conflicts and the colonizing policies and context are transformed and translated in varied and violent ways relative to spatial and racial contexts – as in the case of Palestine. In 'Occupation:

Violence and Women in Israeli Society', Erella Shadmi exposes the deeply embedded roots of violence in Israeli society. The fact that Israel was founded and continues to exist by virtue of its armed forces creates a society wherein power and militarism become the salient expression of its culture as well as paradigms for its societal imaginary wherein the history of the occupation is concealed under the mythography of security (1993). Galia Golan, in her analysis of gender and militarization in Israel, indicates that the major effect of militarization on the status of women there derives from the centrality of the army. She shows how the patriarchal values of the army have reinforced inequality and how the male-dominance of the army in general affects the social and political relation of the colonizing system to women (1997). In addition, research has shown the way in which highly militarized spaces in Israel have correspondingly militarized the criminal justice system and its response to violence against women (Adelman 2003; Shalhoub-Kevorkian 2004c). Adelman concluded her discussion by stating: 'The Israeli case ... may constitute a rather extreme example of the militarization of society and domestic violence. It is nearly impossible to analyse any aspect of Israeli life without noticing the effects of militarism' (2003: 1145).

As a result of the occupation, a similar mythography is engendered in Palestine and comes to obtain there as well, translated through the material realities of the oppressed (as opposed to the brute presence of the oppressor). In studying crimes against women in Palestine, I found that the continuous occupation and the resulting political violence and economic hardship has increased the power of the existing patriarchal system and has considerably weakened the rule of law – for military occupation is done 'legally' (Shalhoub-Kevorkian 2002, 2003a). Additionally, the daily casualties and indignities of life combined with the demolition of houses, the closure of large areas, and the closure of educational institutions has to say the least made violence the primary language of communication. The daily struggles just to survive, coupled with a political ideology that believes in the crucial need to stop the constant displacements and to liberate the land, and the prevailing despair, has led some to believe in death and martyrdom as the best way of living (Al Sarraj n.d.; Shalhoub-Kevorkian 2007a), or if you will, the only feasible expression of life under occupation.

Thus, it is not surprising that, given such a political climate, local feminist and human rights activists sometimes refrain themselves from protesting against the disclosure of internal patriarchal violence against women in such forms as early marriage, deprivation of education, and even 'honour crimes'; raising the issue of violence against Palestinian women by Palestinians is dangerous as it has the potential to empower the Western imperialist discourse and further *culturalize* it – let alone Israeli ones. However, such a protest against disclosure again erases women and their voices to the benefit of hegemonic Empire. Yet the conflict zone is a spatial and political concept that in my opinion is open to more optimistic revisionist possibilities. Kaplan *et al.* locate the dynamics of such re-conceptualizations succinctly when they write in the introduction to their volume *Between Woman and Nation*: 'We have the never ending experience of nation making, through which the vulnerability of certain citizens, some of whom are often in question, can be mapped. Often these subjects stand on the edge of contradictory boundaries – equality and liberty, property and individual self-possession, and citizenship itself – that the modern nation-state cannot resolve' (1999: 6). It is both my goal and hope that through 'voicing', the morphological analyses and the kind of mapping to which the passage refers will commence. One of the foundational premises of modern feminism has been that the personal is political, and the Palestinian case necessarily takes such a dictum to both its logical and material extreme when emphasizing ways in which the political – and indeed the international – are personal. It is our challenge as critical Palestinian feminists, through the personal narratives of Palestinian women, to enable a more optimistic re-conceptualization of women's ordeals, victimization, and agency.

My scholastic and activist aims remain harmoniously connected, and these are expressed through a personal commitment to providing the women of Palestine with a forum for their discourse as well as enabling them to set up a praxis network wherein such discourse can continue into the future and can function independent of any external presence. My efforts are but only a beginning; there are so many cases that are unvoiced, unheard, and nullified. People are dying daily, houses are being demolished, and children are traumatized. I live there, mother my children, and work with women frontliners, girls who struggle daily to reach their schools while facing sexual and psychological harassment and torture, mothers who have lost their children. I have my team working in Jenin, Nablus, Jerusalem, and Bethlehem. The potential loss of friends and family members is something I have to negotiate daily in this militarized social and political space.

It is ironic that within the militarized space of the Palestinian–Israeli conflict, violence against women and the endemic violence of the war itself is presented as an either/or situation – any discussion of the former must be silenced, while the latter is sanctioned as a part of legitimate politics and other liberatory agendas. However, as a Palestinian feminist and activist I do not hesitate to point out that the two kinds of violence are hardly discrete phenomena but rather are integrally linked as the violence of war proliferates violence against women. Violence against women cannot be examined, discussed, or raised as a social issue distinct from the concerns of the 'state' under siege, for the women of Palestine are besieged as well, not just as Palestinians (as *homo sacer*, bare life) but also as women (*femina sacra*).

Gender analyses of violence, as we have seen, cannot be conceptualized without understanding the process of knowledge production as such epistemic practices intersect with the specific prevailing cultural and political conditions. The story of the seven and half million Palestinians who are stateless refugees all over the world, the international community's denial of and refusal to blame Israel for their tragedy, and the continual displacement, occupation, and victimization of the Palestinian people cannot be divorced from our analyses of violence against Palestinian women. As displaced people robbed of control over their own resources, deprived of national territory, identity, and freedom, and forced to be a minority in their own land, Palestinians have consistently required their right to *right*.

Theorizing from the viewpoint of Palestinian women's struggles, and based on the scholarship of Rosemary Sayigh (1983), one learns that to understand gender violence one should not focus on the social dimensions of women's oppression (mainly the effect of tradition) but rather one should link the analysis to the role of Israeli occupation and the interlock of race, class, gender, and sexual politics with local and global factors affecting the political economy of violence against women. Such linkages play a crucial role in re-producing women's social oppression and affect gender violence.

Moreover, to understand such violence, it is imperative also to historicize and understand the role that women played in the Palestinian resistance movement, as well as the continuous political crisis that has shaped and re-shaped Palestinian identity, including the role women have played in building alliances and solidarity groups in society. Julie Peteet, in her book *Gender and Crisis*, discussed the issue of women's participation in the Palestinian political struggle, stating that while the first record of women's participation in these struggles begins in Haifa, Yaffa, and Jerusalem in 1947, the emergence of an identifiable women's movement began even earlier in the 1920s following upon the growing Zionist political policy and during the British Mandate (1991). In *The Nation and Its 'New' Women: The Palestinian Women's Movement 1920–1948*, Ellen Fleischmann showed that the Palestinian women's movement during the early and late 1920s aimed at establishing new spaces for women to engage in the struggle for national liberation (2003). The fact that Palestinian women are considered 'preservers of the culture', as biological reproducers, the icons of their nation who signify the national/ethnic uniqueness of their people, and yet are also political actors in the liberation struggles – including participating in social, economic, and national resistance activities – actually increases their vulnerability to gender violence.

Not surprisingly, the historical role of the patriarchal tribal system has continued to evolve within the ongoing context of occupations by the Ottomans, British, Jordanians, Egyptians, and Israelis. These colonizations and occupations and the attendant political uncertainties have necessarily come to privilege tribal laws and tribal justice. More importantly, the colonial regimes and their support for the emerging primacy of the tribal powers has specifically served to agitate issues of gender, sexual abuse, and, as I stated earlier, concepts of boundaries between the woman's body and the state. The conflation of the two is also a critical moment in the development of the tribal, as this tribal matrix is articulated outside formal juridical doctrine and is open to improvisation. Thus the tribal has gained a tremendous amount of power, since it is executed within a kind of 'applied juridical' forum. One good example is related to the way the tribal heads authorized by the Israeli occupation are left to deal with crimes against women, and Israel even allows them to issue death certificates using Jordanian health law to justify the practice. This juridical power opened up a large space for masculine manipulation and, as I have shown in my study on femicide, this has assisted patriarchal authorities in hiding cases of women killing. While collecting data on cases of femicide or the so-called honour crimes, I discovered a death certificate of a woman aged twenty-eight of whom the *Muktar* (tribal head) claimed on the form had died from 'old age' (Shalhoub-Kevorkian 2001). The liminality of these boundaries – between body and state, civil and tribal law – has deeply affected women's socio-political and cultural roles, creating inflexible and binding rules to control female sexuality and mobility.

In addition, and as I have found through the group therapy sessions that I have facilitated during my clinical work as a therapist, the issue of mobility is a critically important one and mimics in ironic and dissonant ways the alignment of body and state that I have been speaking of; for the private restrictions faced by women are mirrored in the material restrictions of living in an occupied, militarized space. The presence of the Israeli army and its military operations cut off roads on a regular, almost daily, basis. Thus, women face the restrictions of patriarchy and the restrictions inherent to a 'state' under siege. They become literally isolated – cut off from family and friends. In my other published work I have presented extended excerpts from women's narratives (Shalhoub-Kevorkian 2005a), and one of the repeated themes has been the sense of elation, emancipation, indeed joy, that has come from having been able to build a community through voice therapy and the physical gathering of the group itself. This was a community created out of the imposed immobility – a space of freedom created not outside, but *within* the prison itself.

Palestinian women in the First Intifada believed that victory in the political sphere had the potential to be aligned with corresponding changes in society. Initially, political mobilization was well connected to social mobilization as part of a transformative vision of society as a whole. However, as the years of occupation have continued, Palestinian women have come to understand the strategies of the colonial Israeli oppressor and the ways in which – instead of being considered agents of social change – they have become pawns in a process that is actively engaged in disrupting any alliance between the political and the social. While I doubt that feminists would argue with the latter contention, the question of methodology remains problematic and divisive: how do we articulate a transformative analysis that is able to take into account the contextual specificities – the space and place, if you will – of the site of our investigation. Chandra Mohanty (among many other feminists) has urged scholars to contextualize our analysis locally, and to concretize the effects of such analysis on women (2003). Thus, in attempting to voice the violence against women, to bring their narratives to the surface, we must necessarily be attentive to the micro-politics of the cultural space that obtains in Palestine, as well as the macro-politics of the conflict, as these are inseparable from any conceptualization of 'Palestine' and the global economic and political systems which created it. Thus, though the voices of the women are necessarily pluri-vocal and multiple, they are nevertheless embedded in and born out of the singular political matrix of 'Palestine'.

In the Middle East, the connection between nationalism and feminism has been deemed paramount by various researchers (Kandiyoti
1991; Abdo and Lentin 2002; in this regard also see Chapter 3 in this
book). Women have been used in national liberation struggles, such as
in Algeria and Iran, to name a few, and upon achieving 'independence'
have been sent back to the kitchen. Sondra Hale raised a key question in
her discussion of Eritrean women who joined combat forces in resistance
struggle: what happens after a revolution has been successful? As a
Palestinian woman, I necessarily wonder about a post-independence
Palestine. However, I want to engage my current energies in building
what I call *Palestinian-sensitive strategies* that I believe will be essential
tools for survival when we have been liberated from occupation. Arab,
Palestinian, and other women from the Middle East are faced with such
obstacles when taking liberatory steps.

When discussing violence against women in the Middle East and in
Muslim societies, Western Empire propaganda claims that oppression of
women is part of the culture and is supported by the women themselves.
I have often heard the accusation that the reason for violence against
women is religious fundamentalism and Islam. But the logical, corresponding question as to why there has been such a rapid growth of
fundamentalist movements is only rarely asked. Nor do we usually ask
why in most theoretical and media analyses of the Middle East, including the specific topic of violence against women in the region, Islamic
fundamentalism occupies centre-stage and is posited as a simple answer
to complex and multilayered problems. The contradictory effect of the
growth of nationalism and fundamentalism raises additional feminist
challenges, but as Gita Sahgal and Nira Yuval Davis have shown, one
should not forget that the failure of capitalism and communism to
provide material, spiritual, emotional, and social safety for people
encouraged the global rise of religious fundamentalism (1992). We
end up with a situation wherein women in the Middle East and Islamic
countries need not only fight for equality, anti-discrimination, and
social justice, but must also fight another tool of colonization: the
Western propaganda machine.

Shahrzad Mojab, in analysing women and the Gulf War and discussing the effects of 'gender determinism' and the fragmentation of the
feminist movement, particularly in the West, has argued:

> The absence of a conscious feminist internationalism is closely related to
> the tendency of feminist movements in each country to draw an iron

curtain around themselves, and to segregate the struggle for justice and equality along gender lines ... [This] tendency is rooted in a worldview, ideology, or theory that assigns gender an over-determining power ... Gender determinism is theoretically untenable and politically destructive. The oppression of women, inequality and other ills related to male domination may end, if ever, only when the entire system of power relations change; men are part of this system and it is impossible to eliminate oppression without changing men.

(1997: 75–6)

I would like to stress that global political colonialism, capitalism, and patriarchy are closely intertwined. Moreover, as Chomsky explains, the role of the media is very important to our perceptions of feminist movements around the globe because the media is controlled by the organized power of the state and the market. Feminists should abandon a policy of isolationism and, as per Mojab's argument about feminist internationalism, work to build a combined force of people who demand a just political, social, and economic system that challenges ideological, political, and structural gender oppression. In my attempt to conceptualize the situation of women in war and conflict areas, I hope to de-marginalize women and place them at the centre of a multidisciplinary analysis that focuses on both theory and praxis. In exploring the lives of women facing multiple discriminations on the basis of their nationality, ethnicity, gender, class, and other identities, we will reveal how such factors interact within the conditions of patriarchy, sexism, and racism.

Using critical race theory in an analysis of violence against women in South Africa and Palestine, Wing applies two main concepts: the outside/inside dichotomy and what she calls 'spirit injury'. She argues that during conditions of occupation and political oppression, men within an oppressed group feel emasculated and cannot be men in culturally acceptable ways; as such, they have a sense of having lost control over the public sphere and so resort to expressing their *maleness* by exerting their frustration through women in their private sphere (2000). Thus, external political violence and oppression is inevitably reflected in the social and even more so in the personal spheres. Customs, cultures, and religious beliefs become a psychological refuge against the tyrannies of the occupier. At times, people might turn to a glorification of the most repressive patriarchal traditions in order to restore and preserve some sense of self (see Wing 1994). Violence affects women from outside and inside, constituting 'spirit injury' (2000); Wing points out that it is not just women but the entire society at large that suffers from such violence. Wing speaks of Patricia Williams' concept of 'spirit murdering', explaining: 'a fundamental part of ourselves and our dignity is dependent upon the uncontrollable, powerful external observers who constitute society' (2000: 333). Wing further argues that due to the violence and devaluation both outside and inside their world, 'women cannot help but be profoundly silenced and experience a loss of self-actualization' (2000: 333). The spirit injury becomes 'as devastating, as costly and as psychologically obliterating ... as robbery or assault' (Williams cited in Wing 2000: 129). I agree with Wing's contentions here to a certain extent, but would like to take it one step further and claim – based on my clinical experience – that oppression can also have the opposite effect; it can empower and turn women into creators of survival strategies and of methods of resistance; as such women become more than passive recipients of oppression. All of my hope is vested in this belief.

In attempting to bring forward the muted voices of women, I want to pay particular attention to the narratives of young women. In my previous research, what 'listening' has unearthed are the ways in which Palestinian women are continually shaping strategies for coping, for creating optimistic possibilities, and for community building. My specific focus on young women is important for the obvious reason that these women are the future of Palestine, but also for the less obvious reason of examining the ways in which the quotidian and colonial conflation of state/family/woman/property is being disrupted by the younger generation, for such disruptions are occurring. These young women are fighting with determination to survive and are valiantly attempting to change the norms. They are entering the public sphere while demanding justice in both private and public spheres (see Shalhoub-Kevorkian 2007a). Their feminism is based on fighting both internal and external violence. As I mentioned earlier, the lack of mobility is a very real issue in Palestine for women. Young women are refusing to accept roadblocks that prevent them from reaching schools; refusing home imprisonment; refusing early marriage as a mean of surviving economic hardship or social insecurity. They are creating new ways to play, cope, share, walk, and live.

Young women are demanding that we revise and review our perceptions towards militarized societies. They demand a re-visiting of the meanings attached to our analyses of militarized areas and understanding of violence against women in conflict areas as a political crime engendered by colonialism. They ask for an acknowledgement of violence against women and of women's presence in what was considered to be a *no-woman's land* (Higonnet 1993). They are transforming the historical and political debates around the meanings and causes of violence against women. Political conflicts are not divorced from their representations, and the reality of violence against women is not divorced from the militarized and masculine space. Re-thinking the representational strategies through which we articulate violence against women is crucial to our understanding of justice and injustice, to beginnings and endings, and it is integral to building peace as opposed to war.

Political conflict and war crystallize the connection between the public and the private; it stresses how the personal is political and does not disengage the 'home' and the 'front' as discreet or discontinuous spaces, for they are one and the same.

THE POLITICS AND POETICS OF WITNESSING: JENIN

In this section of the chapter, it is not my intent so much to 'represent' the ordeal of women living in war zones and conflict areas, for as Gayatri Spivak has suggested in her body of work, representation can refer to a range of relationships: a vexed dynamic that includes having authority over, standing in for, or appropriating the voice and ontology of another (Spivak 1985). I will use the metaphor of 'translation' (Waller and Rycenga 2001: xxii) that manifests itself as the process of moving between incommensurate languages – and, in my analysis – cultures, borders, and boundaries, revealing the limits and possibilities of each as I try to disseminate my own experiences in the region and attempt to build a community through the voices and narratives of women, and in so doing hopefully create a link across heterogeneous times and spaces.

As a Palestinian mental health worker and criminologist who has worked in the field since 1983 and who established the first hotline for abused girls and women in Palestine in 1994, I could neither comprehend nor absorb the horror stories regarding the Israeli atrocities against and the incursions into various cities in the West Bank and Gaza. I could only try and comply with my internal urge to offer personal and professional help in Jenin, although I knew that as a Palestinian citizen of Israel that I was not allowed to be there. Another reason for the persistent tug within me to do something came no doubt from the fact that most of the Jenin camp inhabitants come originally from my hometown of Haifa. It was a group of mental-health workers led by Bill Thomson, activists and therapists from all over the world (we were twenty-eight altogether), who were ultimately able to smuggle into the camp myself and my friend Sama Aweidah, a fellow Palestinian feminist. Getting to the camp was a harrowing experience in itself: Israeli soldiers were shooting at all trespassers, including us.

The level of destruction we saw was completely and utterly disturbing – in short, 'life' in the Jenin camp was a scene of death. One walked about feeling in turn sad, hopeless, enraged, and more. Conversation with people was difficult, for most of them were at a loss for words. The only ones who were able to communicate with me were the medical teams and the youth groups composed of men and women who had managed to self-organize in order to offer help and support, to find food, call a doctor, and search for lost relatives or friends. While I walked among the ruins hardly believing my eyes – destruction, loss, death, fear, despair – I was aware at the same time of an indestructible hope within me, a hope that one day the situation will change.

The narratives I share with the readers in this chapter are based on those I personally collected – experiences and stories shared with me by the Jenin camp inhabitants. I was later able to bring my experiences and the testimonies gathered to the organizations I work with. What I hope to reveal through these narratives is the nexus of relationships between 'witnessing', that which is coerced into silence or has been hitherto unspeakable. I have chosen to privilege the intersections of these factors in my mind, perhaps as a way to explain – if to no one but myself – my persistent hope for the future in the face of such despair.

The voices in this section of the chapter are of Palestinian women who suffered from the atrocities of the Israeli occupation. Their testimony demonstrates how written history is not necessarily 'her-story'. This discrepancy too often affects the way we theorize and do research, but affects in particular the effect of war and political conflict on women. Thus, raising global consciousness and mobilizing the international community's conscience – particularly in the case of anti-colonial struggle – is of focal concern for all feminist, humanist, and Palestinian activists. I believe that our failure to notice the discrepancy between women's participation and their marginalization in national and international politics and histories has denied women a voice. The Western media has completed this cycle of silencing (see also Sayigh 1996). Attempting to understand the complex socio-political, historical, and cultural dynamic of women's silencing and learning how to listen to the voices of those in pain, without stigmatizing and appropriating those voices, will allow us to break the long history of that silencing and shed light on the invisible victims of war – namely, women.

The voices from Jenin camp reflect the specific nature, structure, and process of survival that confronts the hidden survivors of war in the context of life in Palestinian society. I illustrate the multiple epistemologies of power and politics in play, and pay particular attention to locating these voices within a specific neo-colonial militarized context. By bringing myself, a Palestinian woman, into this narrative, I want to challenge the hegemonic patterns of Western scholarship – the production, publication, distribution, and consumption of 'knowledge' by and for the West. I believe in the power of oppressed women's discourses, hoping that women's narratives of contestation can create alternative spaces. Moreover, bringing women's voices to the foreground enables us to acknowledge the variety of roles women assume in conflict zones, a space that is generally understood as the *domain of men*. Women have used their roles to enter the public space in newer ways, shaping it to their own purposes, demanding that their voices about war, pain, and justice be heard. These voices that speak out against oppression demand that our previous perceptions about war and conflict zones be reviewed and if necessary revised.

Umm Shahed, a mother of a martyr, told me that she learned three days before my arrival at Jenin camp that she had lost her son. She had wanted to believe that he was in prison:

> I hoped and prayed that they have imprisoned him, for at least in prison they could be with each other, all the *Shabab* [young men] with each other ... but today I know I lost him ... he was too young to die. I know he died as a *Shadeed* [martyr] fighting for and defending his country, but he had yet to enjoy life, his young eyes hadn't seen anything beyond Jenin ... He always wanted to visit Haifa. We came from Haifa, and he wanted to see the sea, the beauty of Haifa ... Maybe up there [i.e., in heaven] he can see Haifa and maybe see the world. In here, in this world, there is no life except this life – what you see today – nothing but destruction. And no hope despite all the hope in our hearts. Death is hard, and the death of a child is the hardest. You feel guilty that you are living. I really wished I had died in his place ... but maybe this is the only thing that could bring hope and plant strength in his brothers' and sisters' hearts.

I saw a group of children screaming, and calling for help; they told me that they had seen the hand of a baby. 'Maybe it is Samer's sister's hand; she died as a *Sheheedeh* [female martyr] during the *Kasf* [the shelling and bombing].' I was afraid to look, but hid my fear and was searching for the hand when one of the members of a medical team asked us to move so that they could get the body out. We moved aside and started talking amongst ourselves. It was the first time in my life that I hated my profession; I hated the fact that I was a mental-health worker. What I wished for most of all was to run away from the painful scenes and experiences and the inevitable traumas that the victims would have to endure. I felt them crying without tears when they discovered the baby's hand.

One day when they discovered a large blue pot, Samer told his friend that it belonged to his uncle, and that it was the one they used to wash their baby. He actually carried it with him all the way while we were walking; he was planning on giving it to his uncle: 'I am sure the baby will be happy', he claimed. I said that it must be hard to witness this destruction everyday, the bodies, the loss, and the camp. Young Shaima was the only one who responded to me, saying: '*Ya Elahi ... Ee'sh Kaman Bedu Ysir Fina* [Oh God ... what more will happen to us].' Then they all started telling me how much they loved the camp, and that they will do whatever it takes to rebuild it 'exactly as it used to be'. Then one of them asked me who I was, and I told him that I am a Palestinian from Haifa who came to be with my people and the families in Jenin.

While walking, I saw a house cut literally in half, one part totally destroyed and the other half standing there as a macabre marker of the life that had once taken place there. 'How many people used to live in this house, *Khalti* [aunty]?' I asked and Umm Riad answered: 'I am not sure exactly, but it was my husband, my four sons and their wives, my three daughters and nine grandsons; three of them were less than two years old, one was one month – but he died.' 'How did he die?' I asked. She replied: '*Alla Yekhalliki ... Ma Tiftahi J'rouhi* [God protect you, do not open my wounds].' When I asked her what happened during the incursion of Jenin, she replied:

> I did not know how to handle so much pain. Every hour we heard a new story, a new rumour. Despite the home imprisonment and due to the fact that our houses are connected to each other, we were able sometimes to talk to the neighbours and learn about the outside situation. We learned that our neighbour Abu Mahmood was killed in front of his kid's eyes. We learned that two Israeli soldiers electrocuted our other neighbour, a young newly married woman, while they were arresting her husband. Now her husband is in prison, and he thinks that she is about to have his son, no one was able to inform him about her *Istishhad* [martyrdom]. I was

trying to calm down my daughters-in-law and my own family. It was terrible ... we were 36 people in one room that barely could hold six or seven people. We were unable to breathe or move, unable to talk most of the time, unable to cry, unable to look outside. All we heard was the voices of the soldiers while they were invading the house. They went into the house, broke all the furniture, the machines, the doors, the windows, even my [eleven-year-old] son's schoolbooks were shot. Madness isn't it?

Um Riad explained to me how home imprisonment caused so much pain and inconvenience, particularly for the women. She explained:

It was three weeks after my daughter-in-law delivered her first baby; she still had heavy bleeding because we never managed to take her to the hospital – the political situation prevented them from leaving the camp, and her health was in bad shape. She was with us in this small room, with three other women who started menstruating and four children with diapers. In the room, the smell was very bad. We were unable to open a window or a door, and going to the bathroom was a very risky task. The smell of the blood filled the room, and the old man [referring to her husband] got very upset, and decided to ask all the menstruating women and children who urinated on themselves to sit in the corner. On day eight I also started menstruating, and sat with the filthy woman. I personally knew that being a woman is a curse, but never imagined how much of a curse it is. You know, my twelve-year-old granddaughter promised that when she is free from home imprisonment, she will kill herself and many other Israelis. She wanted to die with dignity like a martyr.

At night, I noticed that this granddaughter was trying to hang herself with a rope she had found. Women's destinies and hardships seemed in the beginning similar to those of their fellow men, but when you listen to their voices, you understood the very specific ways in which the hardships are so much greater on them. In this imprisoned house, they were literally isolated, objectified into 'bleeding objects'.

From being in the presence of these women, one learns the way military spaces *create* violence against women. In fact, the strength these women demonstrated clearly revealed their indispensability to the causes of national liberation, not only as actors in the material revolution but as producers of an ideology that carries the potential for radical social change. Through their experience of oppression, they have learned most effectively the dynamics of oppression and how to negate it. They may see aggression to be necessary, but they propose new ways, strategies, and targets in order to cope. Their unique activism in the 'battlefields' and their courage in the face of daily adversity contrasts with social expectations that they should be passive and absent.

In a space where the powerful wage perpetual war against the powerless, and when violence and destruction is daily used in the name of liberation and the protection of human rights, to 'put our siege under siege', as the Palestinian poet Mahmood Darwish (2002: 57) has put it, is a must. It is the women who are the frontliners in that cause. By naming the nameless and shedding some light on the hidden casualties of war, I hope to take the reader along with me on the journey as a Palestinian woman/feminist/activist and so help others see through my eyes what I witnessed, what I lived.

The complex relational dynamics between what is 'witnessed', what is spoken, and what is 'heard' in the unspoken or the unspeakable – the 'truths' of war and political violence – is understood within the lines of the women's stories. By moving from the historical to the personal, the visual, the cultural, the psychological, the gendered, and then moving back to the political Empire, I hope to shift the global vision from material questions and concerns of war into larger, perhaps more abstract, questions concerning the mutual interaction between the personal and the political, between men and women, trauma and memory, witnessing and testifying, between theory and history.

Women's stories revealed militaristic atrocities often and many times over, yet there is still so much that is silenced and muted by the survivors, victims, and criminals. The most frightful lesson I learned through my 'witnessing' is indeed the understanding of how conflict zones are complicit with silence as opposed to the latter being a result of the former. Perhaps these voices will enable us to resist what seems to be an amnesia of our own choosing.

CHAPTER 3

VEILED POWERS: CONCEPTUALIZING WOMAN AND/AS THE 'NATION'

It is difficult to start a revolution, more difficult to sustain it. But it's later, when we've won, that the real difficulties will begin. (Giles Pontecorvo, 'The Battle of Algiers', in Jacqueline Siapno 2001)

On her way to school, fourteen-year-old Tamam stopped to speak to me. Pointing to her battered backpack, she asked me what I thought she carried on her back. I was somewhat bewildered by her question, so she answered me herself: 'Do you think I carry only books in my pack? I carry the burdens of the Palestinian people.' I relate this brief and multilayered exchange with a young girl because, it seems to me, it epitomizes where we must begin any discussion of 'women and nation' in Palestine. It is also critical to remember that in this instance the 'nation' is, as of yet, a concept only; it does not materially exist as such. Additionally, what Tamam's comment reveals is that in the case of Palestine we need to reprogramme our thinking on what it means to 'build a nation' and of what such a 'nation' might consist.

The history of the region is perhaps an all too familiar and almost tedious case study of marking, as on an imaginary map, a 'nation' and then an attempt to articulate a corresponding 'nationhood' through actual geographic borders and boundaries. What strikes me about Tamam's words is that in the broken enclaves that constitute Palestine, navigating the soldiers and tanks at checkpoints to get to school is an act of nation-building. Surviving another day and arriving back home safely is an act of nationhood and citizenship – an act of belonging. While her words may certainly seem atypical of a fourteen-year-old girl, perhaps even somewhat dramatic or hyperbolic to Western ears, nevertheless they ring true for the experiences that grow out of the region. In truth, Tamam – in addition to her schoolbooks and supplies – does carry the burdens of her people on her back.

As I emphasize again, violence against Palestinian women must be central to any critical analysis of the region; it must be the aim of the discussion awareness of the social, the political, or even the psychological dynamics of the area. In this chapter, I argue that the concept of 'nation' and 'nationhood' in conflict areas does not exist outside of an analysis of violence against women.

Within dominant discourses of violence against women in conflict zones, the failure of women to fight back against Palestinian patriarchal violence remains as one of the most frequent problems discussed – if not the most common accusation made against women who in actuality are fighting and resisting the oppressions inherent to conflict zones. Such deeply embedded, gender-biased assumptions about Palestinian women within the dominant discourse (even on the part of those who are ostensibly feminist) are among the most difficult and challenging aspects of thinking about violence against women. In attempting to challenge the popular representations of Palestinian women, it is critical for our understanding that we re-examine the myth that 'cultural' or 'religious' factors hinder these women in their struggle when it comes to violence against women. The tendency of the dominant discourses to blame women contrasts with the overwhelming evidence of the ways in which Palestinian women are actively fighting and resisting the occupation as well as the manifestations of violence endemic to the situation.

There is a paucity of research discussing the specificity of Palestinian women's experiences. Focusing on the experiences of Western women in non-conflict zones and using those examples as proxies for all women everywhere further marginalizes and excludes women in conflict zones. I am not suggesting that there are no common threads uniting the dynamics of violence against women, or that there are no similarities between abused women; however, the very different living conditions of women living in conflict zones resulting from national struggles and conflicts needs to be accounted for because of the way in which they operate to shape women's experiences. Significantly, national struggles and the effects of political oppression should not only influence our orientation towards abused Palestinian women but should also become the foundation for an understanding of how the specificities of the Occupation profoundly frame the way Palestinian women perceive their choices in resisting the abuses inflicted upon them.

In speaking about violence against Palestinian women, I am particularly thinking here of the way colonization and the military occupation's violence interact with and affect internal patriarchal violence
both within the Palestinian family and the society at large. The fact
that Palestinian women are active resisters and fighters with significant
personal agency garnered at tremendous personal cost is often overlooked and actually contradicted by the popular narrative (particularly
in the West) which presents the notion that they accept and tolerate the
abuses inflicted upon them by patriarchal Palestinian power holders.
Therefore, an important starting point must be an attempt to understand
the conflicted role of Palestinian women during this period of nation-
building and national struggle.

In discussing the devastating impact of the occupation and the resulting violence experienced on a daily level, Palestinian women facing
abuse emphasized to me their need to continually try to balance their
own personal needs and desires with those social needs of a people
trapped in a zone of conflict. The range of conflicting loyalties they
experience – their perceived responsibility to be loyal to their men,
to the 'nation', in addition to their need to protect themselves –
compounded with the lack of alternatives immobilizes some women
from being able to adequately address their own right to live safely and
free of abuse. Palestinian women who experience violence inflicted on
them from inside the family or society expressed the feeling that they
had reached a crisis point in terms of their balancing act of their divided
loyalties whereby they are burdened with the additional dilemmas of
trying to understand and contextualize the violence that originates from
within their own society. Some of the women spoke of the confusion
and suffering that ensues: their disbelief around the behaviour of family
members and the corresponding shame, guilt, sorrow, anger, and even
madness that all too often results from this dilemma. Some fear the
stigma of 'family dishonour' and blame themselves. Some displace their
anger upon themselves and accept compromises that jeopardize their
future – such as early marriage, deprivation of education, or loss of
work – in order to maintain the internal dynamics of their families.

Given such conditions, what is clearly at stake is not only women's
self-perception but also the critical relationships and support networks
that their survival is dependent upon. Women in the region often
expressed the acute conflict they feel between their individual needs
as victims and survivors of abuse and their social responsibilities as part
of an oppressed group, that is, that they should express their solidarity

against the daily attacks of the enemy. This conflicted loyalty creates a serious dilemma for Palestinian women. Author bell hooks (1995) has written about similar pressures on black women when their efforts to assert agency over their lives are perceived as attacks on black manhood; if they seek outside help they are seen as betrayers. This form of double-bind also afflicts Palestinian women. For Palestinian women, this issue of divided loyalties is exacerbated by the daily reality of violence. Their internal conflict around their own needs, their families' needs, and those of their society at large is particularly acute, as my work with Palestinian women who were mothers of martyrs and women acquainted with political prisoners has taught me. These women revealed how internalizing the conflicts created by divided loyalties by maintaining the notion of the 'strong' Palestinian woman, hinders the acknowledgment of one's own pain and vulnerabilities and significantly constrains women from seeking help or dealing with hurt, loss, and trauma.

The discussion of violence against Palestinian women must be located within the broader debates about violence endemic to struggles against oppression and nation-building. One of the major problems associated with obtaining an accurate assessment of violence against Palestinian women is that there is a great deal of fear and distrust of statutory agencies responsible for reporting such violence resulting from the fact that they are often perceived as powerful, male-dominated institutions. In addition, the constant violence wrought by the occupation hinders the ability of any formal or informal system of social welfare and security to function effectively to help abused women when needed.

Perhaps even more importantly, violence against women is not openly discussed by women who are victims of such violence for fear of exposing the Palestinian community to external criticism; as detailed in the previous chapter, such criticism generally narrates such violence in purely 'cultural' terms, for example, by concluding that Arab culture is inherently violent. Similarly, an approach in the dominant media has been to adopt an overly generalized religious view wherein it is assumed that Islam authorizes and allows violence against women. As a result, too often a disclosure of such abuse is a double-edged sword for these women as they are not only rendered unsafe within the society but also face Western racism from without, where reports of abuse are treated as confirmation of the inevitable stereotypes.

Palestinian women are particularly dependent on support from social and family networks, and this makes disclosure especially difficult. If the abuse originates from within the family, the situation becomes even harder. Many of these women fear that disclosure of abuse would be perceived as betraying the family or society, and such disclosure can generate fears of reprisal, further marginalization, and even exclusion. Moreover, my various studies in the region have shown that Palestinian women often come to feel alienated from local and international law enforcement agencies, although these ostensibly exist to protect their human rights (a topic I discuss in greater detail below).

Furthermore, the dynamic involving the ways in which Palestinian men come to be involved in issues concerning violence against women is a critical issue for consideration for scholars, activists, and social service agencies. The dominant discourse generally represents Palestinian men as 'terrorists' and 'violent'. Not surprisingly, Palestinian women are very conscious of these negative stereotypes, and the circulation of these stereotypes hinders many Palestinian women from utilizing available human rights discourses to combat abuse for fear of reinforcing the pervasive racism and further demonizing the demonized. Given this set of circumstances, it is not surprising that Palestinian women express reluctance to engage publicly with the issue of violence against women.

Thus, we can see the bisected way in which the effects of violence against women in the region has to be understood: as part of a global politics of denial; the importance of the dynamics of national struggles within a conflict zone as well as within the framework of the general socio-cultural mechanisms of the local society; and the centrality of the networks of the immediate and extended families. Family, society, culture, and nation – all can simultaneously be a source of affirmation for Palestinian women as well as a source of their oppression. In the case of Palestine, another additional issue is that of the conflict zone itself, as it is both highly militarized in addition to being significantly emasculating for Palestinian men who find themselves caught in a binary of oppositions as well. Palestinian women witness the constant humiliation of Palestinian men that results from the occupation, which further contributes to the climate of silence around the subject of violence against women.

Like so much else in the region, the silencing of which I speak is also split in its effects. On the one hand, the silencing of abuses can be seen as an act of solidarity with Palestinian society against the oppressive and racist narratives of the dominant Western discourse. However, by participating in such acts of silencing, Palestinian women are also materially denying their own needs for disclosure of their abuse and simultaneously contributing to their own further oppression. Here, silence plays the role of fuelling the problem, leaving women victims/ survivors feeling afraid, guilty, confused, and alone, while also turning silence into a weapon in the hands of men for use in 'protecting' the nation (including women, while also at their expense) from external hegemonic and racist attack.

This chapter, therefore, is an attempt to explore the construction of Palestinian women within discourses of violence against women in an environment of conflict and national struggle. Drawing upon the feminist insights of Palestinian women, I focus on an examination and problematization of the ways in which women and the violence committed against them are at once marginalized and centralized as contested sites of power. I contend that the role Palestinian women have played and continue to play as part of the legacy of nation-building practices is simultaneously liberating and confining. Data gathered in my studies highlight the different ways in which the reactions of Palestinian women to violence against them are compounded by the intersections of the nationalist struggle within the context of violent colonization, including race, class, and gender oppression.

In considering the case of violence against women in Palestine, one cannot evade the history that has led us to the present moment and, consequently, of how that history articulates the violence that women are subjected to. This in turn affects how women in the region are positioned both against and within any discourse conceptualizing a 'nation'. The history I refer to, of course, includes the British colonial state (Mandate Palestine), the Zionist settler violence of the former period, and the Israeli colonial state proper. Although my analysis here is not specifically concerned with the role colonialism and capitalism have played in the development of the nation-state, it will examine the effect of those two processes on gender violence insofar as I am arguing that consideration of such violence is fundamental to conceptualizing the 'nation' in Palestine and the Middle East more generally. Through the continued imposition of colonialist settler regimes in the region, existing economic and political conditions are aggravated, consequently exerting a negative effect on gender relations.

Within the liminal dynamics of what is conceptually and materially 'Palestine' the borders and boundaries of the nation-state become extremely confusing, to say the least. As I will demonstrate in Chapter 5, Israeli spatial policy and its Separation Wall have literally created isolated bantus that nonetheless still allow for the conceptualization of a 'nation' for the Palestinian people; however, such islands of survival and hope can hardly be classified as a 'nation' in the traditional sense of a bounded and contiguous space. Within this fluid dynamic, the Palestinian home (see again Chapter 5) is a particularly contested social and political space. Ongoing home demolitions, for example, strike at the core of the constant interplay of hope and despair that is part and parcel of both the survival strategies and survival psychology of Palestinians in the OPT. Additionally, the home space traditionally marks a woman's domain. I make that statement as a way to note a given reality, but what I show in this chapter are the ways in which 'traditional women's roles' in the region are continually and necessarily deconstructed. Because of the Western tendency to both fetishize and Orientalize Palestinian women, this crucial dynamic – the way in which Palestinian women are simultaneously working within the social, cultural, and political boundaries in which they find themselves while also deconstructing it – is often overlooked.

NATIONAL IDENTITY AND FEMALE BODIES

The examination of the intersections between national identity, nationalism, gender, and women's agency is multi-faceted. The historical patterns of colonialism and other forms of oppression would seem to suggest that there is an apparent affinity between nationalism, sexism, and gendered violence. This somewhat obvious observation, however, becomes complicated in vexing ways when we look specifically at Palestinian history. On the one hand, nationalism can open up radical possibilities for creating a sense of belonging, solidarity, and togetherness which may temporarily overcome pre-existing gender-biased barriers to such possibilities. As I state elsewhere in this book, Palestinian women have indeed taken up material positions as frontliners on the multiple borders that mark the conflict zones (see Chapter 4). However, as feminist research has repeatedly illustrated, 'nationalism' necessarily institutes new forms of power relations that give priority to men over women, thus further marginalizing women. Feminist researchers continue to engage in discussions that illustrate the contradictions between feminism and nationalism (see, for example, McClintock 1995; Jayawardena 1986; Enloe 1990; Yuval-Davis and Anthias 1989). McClintock, for example, has shown how not all nations in the world have given women and men the same access to basic human rights or allocated those resources made available by the nation-state in an equitable manner. Further, Enloe has argued that nationalism is affected by gender relations and a generalized, masculine control of existing power structures; thus, she has argued that women's status and rights will always be adversely affected during, throughout, and after the struggles of nation-building (1990).

While women's participation, or lack thereof, in nationalist movements often reflect the operant gender relations in society, it may be more useful, particularly in the case of Palestine, to explore those mechanisms, practices, and spaces outside the discourse of nationalism where women exercise power, control, and agency and are able to formulate their own notions of community. Abu-Lughod's argument is that one needs to look at women's discursive formulations and efforts to build communities in spaces outside of nationalism and nationalistic movements. By limiting our analysis to women's membership and active participation in national struggles – within the limited parameters of 'nationalism' only – we arrive at a skewed view. In this skewed view, women play a much-marginalized role within nation-building wherein they are seen only as caretakers and helpmates to men who inevitably become positioned at the forefront of nationalist struggles (Abu-Lughod 1998).

Having carried out several years of clinical intervention and research among women in Palestine, Israel, and Jordan, combined with my strong personal commitment to social and political justice in Palestine, I argue that women's agency and power should be analysed in its own right. Palestinian women have a long history of fierce independence and a genealogy of innovative female activism warranting a more elastic conceptualization of feminism, one that allows for a more complex relationship to emerge between feminist practices and the practices involved in conceptualizing a nation. We need to focus on ethnographies of culturally specific rituals and spaces, discovering within them women's agency and activism and contextualized within its indigenous and local form (see, for example, Shalhoub-Kevorkian 2003a and 2005a on mothers of martyrs and women acquainted with political prisoners in Palestine, where the role of mothers and families is structurally, culturally, and politically central). In my own clinical work and writings, I have pointed to the way in which women have participated actively in the Palestinian struggle for statehood, though their participation has not always been registered in a publicly visible manner. Palestinian women's 'absence', as Fleischmann (2003) shows, is only a function of a gender-blind historiography and politics that fails to notice the locations, spaces, and places where women have staked their claims and activism.

The nation – with its historical and cultural distinctions – is much more a territory of struggle between competing subject positions, narratives, and dynamic struggles for power than it is a bounded material space. For our purposes, we need to look on both a historical and theoretical level to address the questions raised by many postcolonial and feminist scholars with regard to the rise of nationalism in non-Western countries while also looking closely at the relationship between gender, violence, and nationalism in Palestine. Particular examination of the way nationalist discourses constitute the female body or privilege the struggle over the ownership of the female body *as a way to claim it for an imagined national body* would help us to build an understanding of the connections between conceptualizing the 'nation', nationalism, and women's bodies. The intellectual, historical, and material challenge of positioning women (particularly women's bodies) within the discourses of nationalism while looking at the Palestinian context opens up, as Julie Peteet (1991, 2005) and Rosemary Sayigh (1979, 1998) have discussed, an important avenue towards our understanding of the problematics of nationalism itself.

The constant material violence that Palestinian women and men experience has to be taken into account when we conceptualize both the psychology and the process of nation-building. We must question the male-centred process of nation-building in which women serve only iconic functions as mothers, wives, or daughters. What many theorists of postcolonial discourse have pointed out is that we must carefully interrogate what we mean by 'nationalist' within such a discourse. Historically, the relation between nationalist discourse and colonial domination affected the production of a complex nexus of discourses we now think of as belonging to a postcolonial analysis. For example, Partha Chatterjee's book *Nationalist Thought and the Colonial World* (1986) raises an important argument about how the dynamics of nationalism must be understood as a European discourse of domination that is then appropriated by so-called 'Third World' nations for self-empowerment in the struggle for independence. What Chatterjee points out is that, given the Third World's subjugation and lack of autonomy, this particular acceptance of 'nationalism' paradoxically speaks the language of the colonial powers despite its opposition to colonial domination. Furthermore, the salient aspects of colonialist/capitalist culture – such as its fundamental promotion of 'modernism', 'progress', and 'development' – and the investment in a corporate economy remain unchallenged. Thus, this conceptualization of nationalism replicates the

85

larger world order, destroys the creative potential of alternative discourses, and undermines, if not diminishes, the alternative imaginings of the 'nation' to the point of their being ineffective.

As Chatterjee and other postcolonial theorists have pointed out, 'nationalism' can and should be a pluri-vocal discourse, but unfortunately, such plurality is instead subsumed under Western models of nationalism and the concept of a 'nation'. Nationalism, therefore, is capable of producing a different discourse, one that is optimistically marked by political contest and struggle for a just distribution of power and resources. The problem with conceptualizing 'nationalism' only within the frame of its European, colonialist origins is that this downplays the power of indigenous intellectuals and individual agency (see Bhabha, particularly his 1994 work). Working from some of the paradigmatic premises of Benedict Anderson's *Imagined Communities* (1991), Bhabha conceptualizes the nation as an agency of ambivalent narrations that can be a force for subordination as much as an avenue for 'producing, creating, forcing, guiding' (1990: 3–4). Thus, rethinking the origins of nationalism raises the potential of refuting the cultural domination of the West in homogenizing and totalizing the unfolding possibilities of alternative narratives within the nation-space.

There is a great risk in believing what is implied, if not directly stated, in so much critical thought, that the hegemonic discourse of the West is an absolute power that cannot be challenged. As the French feminist critic Hélène Cixous has written (1986, 1980), if that discourse is an absolute alterity then it cannot be theorized – it is absolutely Other; but once we imagine that an alterity can be interrogated, we at once open it up to possibilities of recuperation. The idea that the meaning and power of Western epistemologies cannot be changed or transformed when brought into contact with local traditions and local struggles is dangerous, and therefore we must move beyond the East/West binary in order to understand its complexity (for more detail, see Liu 1994; Said 1983).

According to Derrida (1998), colonized, ethnic minority, and immigrant women occupy a place of 'cultural undecidability' and in this location may help to both establish the margins of the nation-space while simultaneously disrupting the concept of margin itself, thus allowing for an alternative way of reconceptualizing Otherness as an evershifting plurality of the people as one. Therefore, within such a dynamic of the nation where 'margins' are being continually reconfigured, the concept of the univocal national subject is undone, providing a narrative authority for marginal voices and so allowing for newer discourses by women, minorities, immigrants and those similarly oppressed. This splitting of the univocal subject of nationalist discourse enables us to recognize and reorganize the nationalist space as one that is contradictory and pluri-vocal. Again, we should be careful not to homogenize the categories of the oppressed into yet another totalized category of 'the marginalized'. We must, then, resist the tendency to explain specific modes of oppression by building totalizing theories, and instead look to each discursive system of discrimination as deserving a specific historical and political analysis.

Similarly, we must be careful not to project totalizing theories of a universal idea of women within conceptions of 'nation'. But what is extremely problematic, given the history of women and 'nation', is to totally reject a totalized view of women within nationalistic practices as well. For the historians of women's movements worldwide have shown that nationalist practices in the past have invented a totalized idea of women and have deployed that figure efficaciously in various local struggles. Laura Nader (1989) has shown that while women and nation – or women *as* nation – is a problematic and vexed construction, such a deployment in colonized areas has often led to emancipatory movements whereby women's struggle for emancipation has gone hand-in-hand with the national resistance movement. This is an instance of what I mentioned earlier, that in (re-)considering 'woman and nation', or even 'woman and/as nation', we need to operate out of a more elastic feminism that allows for contradictions to exist. I imagine a scenario such as what Gayatri Spivak references in her theorization when she calls for 'strategic essentialism' – a temporary 'essentialized' strategy used by women to present themselves and achieve certain goals.

In the Palestinian context, as we have discussed in the previous chapters, the relation between nationalism and women's struggles are integrally linked and the relationship between the two is complex and often problematic. The two Palestinian Intifadas of 1987 and 2000 epitomized the way in which nationalist discourse positioned gender issues. For example, in the cases of *Isqat* wherein Palestinian women were abused in order to extract political information that benefited the enemy, women's bodies served as a powerful weapon against themselves but also against Palestinian males who are always already positioned, by virtue of their struggles against occupation, to stand in for the nation. Thus, the use of Palestinian women to prevent the realization of a Palestinian 'nation' positions gender, particularly in the figure of the gendered citizen, within the struggle for nationhood. The way in which this particular instance has an acute gender valence is also revealed by the term that is used to inscribe it: *Isqat*, that is, the 'downfall'. Thus, the abuse of women is at once her downfall within the dynamics of the patriarchal culture, of which she is a (second-class) citizen, but on another level, the abuse also registers as a material downfall of the nation/state. Thus, women's victimization has been used by the masculine hegemony within Palestinian culture itself to crystallize the plight of the Palestinian people as a whole and to concretize the need for a separate independent state. However, in so doing the female body is denied its pain and agony through the focus, instead, on the large symbolic meaning that such abuse provides; violations of women's bodies become the violation of the very nation of Palestine itself. As intimated in Chapter 1, the proverb 'land before honour' has also been used to stress the need to preserve the national 'body' that is the land, but here land and honour actually conflate to enable the marginalization of women's experience. When the 'nation' is at stake, the significance of sexual abuse is as a crime against the 'nation state', the national 'body'.

The way nationalist discourse often seamlessly connects the national body with women's bodies was apparent in one of my encounters with a governor of Ramallah. The governor was appalled by the fact that my centre, the Women's Center for Legal Aid and Counseling, managed to help a young woman who had been raped escape from her village, as she feared being killed by a family member. When the governor called me, he stressed the fact that I had no right to hide women in such straits, stating: 'You can't hide them ... these are rape cases ... these are national security issues. By what mandate do you act? Who gave you the right?' Perhaps the conflations, semantic slippages and accusations in the governor's words are too innumerable (and some perhaps too obvious) to list, however, one cannot help but note the ease with which rape and national security become one in the same breath. Once again, the equation being presented is ostensibly thus: where issues of violence against women are perceived as a matter of women's honour (for it is clear that, to the powers that be, rape is viewed as a failure of 'honour'), such issues will be understood as a violation of the 'nation-state', thus becoming a matter of 'national security'. Furthermore, in this equation the discourse of nationalism is used to totalize women. The governor's concern is clearly not with the specific woman who was raped and had to flee to save her life. Indeed, his words would suggest that he is incapable of perceiving her specificity or humanity. His admonition that I have no mandate to hide victims of abuse places them into one homogenous category through which their individual experiences and traumas are elided as a matter of any concern, except for any violations of the 'nation'. However, as it has been my intent to point out throughout this book, the limitations and elisions imposed by this discourse are precisely what allow women to challenge its authority, thereby allowing women the possibility of creating alternative narrative spaces of their own, examples of which there are many in the history of Palestine.

Despite the many feminist critiques, my own included, that exist on the naturalization and essentialization of nation and women in conceptualizations of the nation-state, as well as feminist discontent with the often romanticized and eroticized narrative of women and nations that are pervasive in colonial and neo-colonial discourses (e.g. 'maternal love' and the figure of the pure and honourable 'virgin'), it is imperative to examine the relationship between women and nations in the narratives that have been created about women. Here, as elsewhere in this book, I repeat my call for a contextually specific critique of conceptualizations of the nation-state (the context being colonization and military occupation in the case of Palestine) because I think that such a critique is crucially important if we are to recuperate these existing narratives for more optimistic political ends. Even were it possible to achieve, I do not think the solution is to simply jettison concepts that hold within the region, but rather to examine them in order to take into account the very ways in which the cultural and socio-political space and Orientalist Empire make possible the 'nation as mother' or the nation as the place that houses the pure 'virgin', thus ostensibly protecting her womanhood.

The discursive constructions of the nation-state, with regard to women, are always already conflicted and striated. The constructions of women that normalize control over them by creating a seamless equation between women and/as nation also turns women's bodies into central sites of contested power. In this respect (as will be discussed extensively in Chapter 5), concepts such as 'home', 'land', and the dynamics of place/space come to be (re-)played repeatedly. Thus, 'woman' as concept – constructed, militarized, racialized, sexualized, and genderized – becomes a crucial site of inquiry. In the context of the nation-state, 'woman' endlessly rehearsed as repetition and recitation builds the political and cultural imaginary that constructs both the concept and the 'pedagogy of the nation', as Judith Butler explained, in order to produce the citizen-subject who mirrors its political desire (1993). But as Butler has pointed out in the general thrust of her work, it is in ceaseless repetition that semantic slippages occur. Thus, within such endless replication, the power of the 'authentic' or 'origin' is productively lost.

In their book *Between Women and Nation*, Kaplan *et al.* comment upon the essentialist nature of the modern nation-state:

> We propose that it is through racialization, sexualization, and gender-
> ization that the nation is able to transcend modernities and to become a
> timeless and homogenized entity. In this sense, women as a monolithic
> category – represented either in the particularistic discourses of nation-
> alism or in the universalizing discourse of 'global feminism' – is problem-
> atized and put in crisis not only because of their inability to bring into
> view the instability of a national or international order that transcends
> itself to the level of 'essence', but also because they guarantee agency to
> some while at the same time turning others into a spectacle.
>
> (1999: 7)

However, inscription of women, as described by Kaplan *et al.*, involves the problematization of the ways in which women are at once marginalized while also being centralized as the site of contested power. By implicating the local politics of gender in the production of knowl-edge, one comes to understand more clearly the role that violence against women plays in promoting and preserving both the nation-state and hegemonic systems of power. For nations include a political economy that not only affects the circulation of discourses and practices of the nation-state but one that is also related to the production and distri-bution of economic and political power which impose rules and laws that define the boundaries and spaces between the powerful and the powerless.

Questions remain how women's bodies and lives, how women and nation or as imagined nation, and how women's spaces are situated in between dominant power structures (including between the West and the non-West, the modern and traditional, public and private, reason and emotion) and thus how women are thereby transformed into con-tested sites that are subsequently used to mark contested borders in the wars waged by men. In the case of Palestine, the national desire and longing for liberation, for regaining the homeland, and the absence of a safe haven – even in one's own home – together territorialize women, linking and transforming them, their sexuality, bodies, and essence into tools in the hand of Empire. This in turn transforms the (home-)land into an ultimate gesture of national wish fulfilment. It seems that gender and sexuality become the narrative engine of this totalizing 'pedagogy of the nation' both as symbolic and material power during the process of national liberation and nation-building. This need to prevent any disruption in the nation's narratives once again has a bifurcated effect: on the one hand it instigates gender violence, but on the other hand the very mode and form of oppression encourages women's agency and creates opportunities for creative resistance.

However, what is unique about Palestine, and what we have to understand if we are to work with the queries at play in this chapter, is that agency and resistance are articulated within the discourses of 'nation' and 'nation-building' and are not necessarily always external to it. We should perhaps again recall Tamam's words quoted on several occasions in this chapter; she is in fact resisting her limitations by the simple act of going to school, but that act of resistance is being expressed within the discourse of the nation when she points out that what she carries in her backpack, in addition to her schoolbooks that emancipate her, are the burdens of her people.

In a recent study of mine on women, education, and occupation based on focus group interviews conducted in August 2005 in Qalqilia, Ramallah, and Hebron (Shalhoub-Kevorkian 2007c), young Palestinian women attending Al Quds University in Jerusalem expressed their position on their education through their national identity. Their discussion usually started with the words: 'Being a Palestinian woman ...' Thus, a motivating factor for obtaining an education, from their perspective, was their Palestinian identity. Fatmeh exemplifies this tendency, stating:

> Being a Palestinian girl, I feel that education strengthens my personality, it empowers my belief in myself, for when I argue with the Jew [she means the Israeli soldiers at the military checkpoints], I learn how to argue, how to face him, how to express the importance of reaching my university. One day, while I was arguing with one of them, he [the soldier] raised his weapon, directing it at my face ... he did that because he saw the books I had with me, since that time, while waiting at the checkpoint I had hidden my books, and if they [the military forces] stop the Ford [the taxi] I sit on them ... for if they see the books they take them from us and tear them up ... and then he wouldn't let me pass ... only because I am a student.

Like Fatmeh, many Palestinian women that participated in the study stressed the way in which the context of military occupation turned what might be considered a normal school experience – the daily trip to school – into an expression of the national need to cope with military occupation. The young women's racial background as Palestinians meant that every step they took was turned into a racialized, national-ized, and sexualized act. Young women told stories concerning the loss of their ability to reach their exams on time, of needing to line up for hours at checkpoints during the cold of winter or the heat of summer, of being searched and sexually harassed by soldiers, and of losing track of time and place after walking for long periods of time.

As with all aspects of life for Palestinians living under military occu-pation, the effort to obtain an education presents many challenges and hardships, including very specific gender abuses. As many young women explained, being a Palestinian or a veiled Muslim woman increases their vulnerability to gender abuse. Lana from the village of Sarra stated:

> It is hard to remember all the incidents … we need to walk on the by-pass roads just to reach school. Soldiers always hide behind the trees to scare us; they start shooting on us from all directions. Sometimes we used to climb the mountain and pass through Ein Il-Muzrab in the Il-Tal area, and the soldiers used to shoot at us from a house on top of the mountain. During the winter, we used to fall and suffer so much. I personally needed to cross two checkpoints, the ones at Sarra and Beit Ibba, to reach Nablus and when we reach Beit Ibba's checkpoint, the soldiers used to say that no one less that thirty years old could pass … but we are all under this age, we are all students … stopping us and saying that we must get the University's permission [to pass] is an additional way to delay and torture us. They knew only Al Najah University and we are from Al-Quds. Each day they create a new way to make it harder, and we are women not men, we can't stay out late when it is dark, between checkpoints alone, and the financial situation does not allow us to live close by our schools.

In other cases, soldiers forced female university students to take off their veils each time they crossed checkpoints, an act of coercion that vio-lated these women's religious beliefs. Such masculinist power games are not exclusive to the Israeli military. One clear example of such gender abuse occurred during the July 2005 elections in Qalqilia when the Islamic movement won the election. One of the first declarations of the political Islamic party was to order that women in Qalqilia wear the Hijab. Of course, this was a reversal of the Israeli military practice of ordering women to take *off* their veils, an irony often noted by the young women themselves (Shalhoub-Kevorkian 2007c, 2008).

Once again we have an instance whereby a contextualization within the specificities of 'culture' and politics leads us to observe the narratives and counter-narratives in play. Much has been written on the Hijab not just by Western Orientalists but also by Western feminists as well. The

Orientalists view it as yet another signifier of the 'mysterious' Middle East and the way in which the sheiks of their Arabian Night-imaginations control their women. The West, more often than not, also reads the veil as a signifier of oppression as part of an imagining of a more progressive social space wherein women are no longer required to be veiled. However, the significance of the Hijab as it plays out in the two narratives related here is much more complex than is allowed for by Orientalist or Western feminist interpretations. For it seems to me that veiled women are using their visibility in the space in which they find themselves as both creative challenges and as a means to unmistakably declare their presence. In instances when the soldiers humiliate female students by forcing them to take off the veil, the Hijab functions as marking the space of their presence while also declaring their opposition to occupation; as Siham said, 'the veil becomes our resistance'. Similarly, when they are coerced by masculine Palestinian authorities into wearing the veil, the veil also marks their presence – the veiled body is much more visibly obdurate, and it explicitly declares the women's presence within a masculinized political space.

NARRATING THE NATION: WOMEN AND THE MASCULINE HYMEN

I approach the connection between narrating the nation and women's activism/victimization in a manner that paradoxically walks between two polarized ideas, the spaces between allowing for various sites of survival. One pole of this polarity presents women as active agents having political agency, as advocating on behalf of their rights, and as participating in activism that brings social and political equality and transformation. This pole assumes that there is no gender discrimination, and does not lose faith in women's abilities to play the political game and to protect themselves and their society, their nation, land, families, bodies, and future. From this vantage point, women have developed various methods of participation, some of which are gender specific, such as being the invisible actor in the political struggle, or visibly participating in resistance actions, using weapons, organizing political activities, and participating in the decision-making process at the political level.

The other pole presents women as passive agents who need to be protected and controlled. An orientation from this pole calls for the patriarchal hegemonic actors in society to be on guard against any 'attack' against 'weak' women, that is, any attack that is understood to be primarily against women's sexuality and purity. Within this hermeneutic, any attack against the socio-political 'hymen' of the masculine powers might lead to 'social disorder'. According to this view, the masculine/patriarchal system has methods to preserve its 'virginity' and its authenticity, which at the base level is to say that it has methods to restore its 'hymen' through its military and masculine patriarchal power as well as through its power to articulate the nation. While the ongoing harassment and gendered violence on the part of the Israeli military must never be lost sight of, patriarchal powers internal to Palestinian society have exercised their own forms of gender control by, for example, imposing the veil (see especially Shalhoub-Kevorkian 2007c); the killing of women for so-called honour crimes; and imposing on a raped woman marriage to her rapist in the interest of 'family honour'. Within this polarity, women are required to be submissive and obedient and to behave according to patriarchal political orders.

Within these polarized perspectives, I have found that women have been able to create both a space and discourse of 'betweenness': a multiplicity of women's counter-discourses and counter-narratives. I approach Palestinian nation-building practices and women's activism and victimization simultaneously as liberating and confining. The analytical walk between liberation or creative agency and confinement, limitation or subjectivity will be discussed by examining the connections between feminism, women's activism, and nationalism. In building such an analysis, I elicit the multiple meanings and purposes to which the connection between nationalism and women's acts and agency are established. Such a connection may be seen as being reflected in the case of maternal activism and sacrifice – for example, the cases of mothers of martyrs and female political prisoners – both of which stem not only from the legacy and history of Palestine, but also from the hegemonic capitalist and masculine powers that hinder women in their struggle.

Historically, Palestinian women have been active agents in the social and political transformation of Palestine. Fleischmann (2003) shows how Palestinian women, although generally absent from the historical records, were nevertheless extensively involved in their country's struggle against colonialism and the Jewish settlement between 1920 and 1948. Their agency is evident in the holding of a national congress in Jerusalem in 1929, in meeting with government officials, planning and participating in demonstrations, smuggling arms, and participating in regional and international conferences.

Following the Nakba of 1948, the occupation of the West Bank and Gaza in 1967, and then during the First and Second Intifadas, Palestinian women responded to occupation, dispersion, and dislocation of their people while additionally asserting their own demands and asserting their critiques of the polity. For example, between 1968 and 1982 and more recently during the two Palestinian Intifadas, women have been actively engaged in the process of reconstituting the meaning and role of women in the process of national liberation and in nation-building. When they engaged in defence of their communities as fighters, frontliners, mothers, political prisoners, and in other forms of actual resistance and activism, they acted in reference to political colonization, hegemonic Orientalization, and culturally dominant patriarchy with all the highly charged symbolization of womanhood and gender roles within these processes. In spite of the latter, Palestinian women have managed to bring about a transformation of the significance of what it means to be a Palestinian woman as well as a transformation of the material roles that Palestinian women have historically played. Once again, while these meanings and roles are not outside of what may be culturally sanctioned, Palestinian women nevertheless managed to steadily and dynamically subvert the traditional and patriarchal meanings and spaces that women were allowed to inhabit as they created new spaces, roles, and meanings. For example, as Peteet has shown, the role of motherhood was challenged, accommodated, and reinterpreted (1997). As I see it, and as I have experienced in my own work with mothers of martyrs, in this particular arena of 'motherhood' women continue to negotiate between the various available options and continue to create counter-narratives of motherhood that challenge ongoing patriarchal notions while stressing mothers' roles in fighting oppression, inequality, and injustice.

Moreover, as a feminist who took a leading role in one of the strongest campaigns to challenge the existing legal system – that is, the Palestinian Model Parliament (see Abdo 1999) – I can also assert that women's political roles and their activism during and after the First Intifada constructed a new space for women's political validation and that the former became a basis of feminist demands for equal rights. The viciousness of, and statistical increase in, violent attacks by the Israeli settler state during the Second Intifada, which added to the international failure to stop the building of settlements and to prevent the continuation of atrocities against Palestinians, increased the lack of trust on the part of Palestinians, particularly Palestinian women, in the existing human rights discourses and the so-called 'peace process'. The ostensible 'war on terror' and the 'war against Islam' has led to the empowerment of fundamentalist groups that have called for a masculinized and militarized tactic of resistance, thereby further complicating an already complex social context. Despite all of these challenges, the gains that Palestinian women have made have not been completely eroded.

The transition to a highly circumscribed form of autonomy in the West Bank and Gaza during the 1990s was greatly complicated by the creation of the Palestinian Authority [PA] that was limited in its ability to govern by various political and economic conditions imposed by the Oslo Agreement. During this period, women activists (including the returnees – those who returned to Palestine with the creation of the Palestinian Authority) were appointed to political and official positions. New women's organizations were established to address both the political as well as the social and economic challenges facing Palestinian women. New roles arising out of this situation empowered as well as constrained women. Female roles were transformed in a way that empowered women's political activism but also in ways that challenged their socio-cultural and traditional ones. For example, while the 'mothers of the martyrs' were perceived as national icons, their symbolic and material participation in the varied, interrelated, and complex process of 'nation-building' was nevertheless not considered sufficient grounds for having gender equality between men and women. I argue that women's political role as icons of the nation was valued as much as their role as icons of cultural preservation. This represents a classic symptom of the in-between space of political action and transformation that I have been describing.

For women, coping with victimization as agency and agency as contributing to their victimization are both located in the interlock between the colonial project, harsh economic conditions, political violence, nationalism, political activism, state-building, religious beliefs and values, cultural heritage, and the prevailing constructions of femininity and masculinity. Femininity and masculinity are not premised on biological or cultural processes but rather on political, economic, and social experiences of oppression that generate many varieties of activism, including an anti-feminist one as when feminist activism begins to resemble the oppressor's actions and values. Women's activism and victimization are much more than what some in the Western media have called 'cultural primitivism' or 'political terrorism'. Instead, such activism represents a matrix of power that includes a political legacy, a history, a culture of oppression, and extreme violence and continuous conflict as well as capitalist power that ignores the voice of the Palestinians. Abuses inflicted upon women in this context represent this matrix and are socially and culturally produced and re-produced.

The voices of Palestinian women require us to raise the question of what happens to men and masculinity in societies during periods of war and violent conflict, that is, when the home and the homeland are violated. Cases of war and conflict in Rwanda, Sri Lanka, Kashmir, Afghanistan, Sudan, South Africa, Israel, Palestine, and Iraq, among others, have taught us that women's sexuality, bodies, and body politics become an acceptable location to negotiate notions of cultural authenticity, national unity, and religious differentiation. Moreover, we learn that local and international agents of social control actively participate in these negotiations and in the socio-political and economic struggle around them. Women's issues are made hypervisible during these debates in an attempt to make them 'Other' – thereby rendering them invisible and 'silent' – or by imposing on women the role of the preservers of the culturally, nationally, and religiously 'woman appropriate' status.

In examinations of the Middle Eastern context, researchers and historians have shown us that the preoccupation with women and family, with nation and society, can in part be accounted for by the encounter with Europe. Lila Abu-Lughod explains:

> In Turkey, Iran, Egypt, and elsewhere, the turn of the century was a moment of intense preoccupation with women and family – not to mention nation and society – in part because of the encounter with Europe, whether desired (as by reforms of Ottoman Empire), ambivalent (for the Persian-speaking areas), or imposed through colonial occupation (for many in the Arab World).

(1998: 4)

The exploration of earlier historical encounters, when ' "new" women and men were talking about remaking women' (1998: 4) and when there were calls 'for women's awakening' and 'the new woman' that were reverberating through the magazines, books, and speeches of the era (1998: 8), should not be divorced from the very complicated ways in which the local and global economy and political power affected the social and private spheres. In examining women's situation before, during, and after colonial struggles, one must take note and indeed foreground the fact that women were and are considered symbolic in terms of visualizing the emergent nation and society.

In the Middle East, the 'woman question' as it relates to the nation and the state has been discussed by various scholars. Deniz Kandiyoti's *Women, Islam and the State* (1991) emphasized the need to analyse the 'woman question' through the political projects of nation-states while looking closely at the way this 'question' is affected by the history of colonialism, relationships with the West, economic and class politics, and the role of religion (primarily Islam) in the formulation of law within the newly established quasi-states. Family law reform and women's rights in particular were central topics on the agendas of nationalist projects and of politicians and policy-makers. Examining the 'woman question' and the nation, therefore, allowed power holders to increase their control over local kin groups and leaders and to win the approval of international development agencies through these power holders' attempts to 'modernize' the indigenous populations. A critical feminist analysis of the implications of the project and politics of modernization has been fruitfully discussed by Mervat Hatem (1993), who suggests that one should be suspicious of such a project for it increases class inequalities while harming working-class and rural women. Thus, women's issues and women's and especially feminists' efforts were not simply objects of reform and political manipulation by men but were in addition ideological debates that enabled discourses about the connections between the West and the East and the local, the national, and the international. The very politicized and complex relationship between women and nationalism, between reforms for women and the politics of modernization, shrouded the situation.

Nationalists and other political players became anxious about outside interest in local women's issues. This anxiety raised new questions and critiques regarding the politics of modernity and the way it could be used to further control and oppress the new postcolonial state or the occupied Other. It also increased the fear of a backdoor re-colonization by the West while complicating the politics of East/West relations generally. The politics of modernization, colonization, feminism, and the new 'civilized' language of 'universal human rights' further made problematic the connection between women and nation. Empire's perceived need to 'liberate' the Middle Eastern woman and the understanding of the Hijab and the Burqa as signs of the primitiveness and backwardness of Middle Eastern society (of the South in general and women activists in particular) have compounded the struggles of women in the Middle East.

Discussions about women's roles in both the private sphere, as mothers and care-takers, and in the public sphere, as political and social activists, initiated what Sullivan argues are contradictory results different from the original intention: liberation of women (1998). As Abu-Lughod argues, the politics of modernization and the project of modernity and reformation in the Middle East affected the socio-political dynamic on the local and international levels. However, these new forms of modernization further domesticated and burdened individual women:

> the professionalization of the house wife, the 'scientizing' of child rearing, women's drafting into the nationalist project of producing good sons, the organization into nuclear house-holds governed by ideals of bourgeois marriage, and even involvement in new educational institutions – may have initiated new coercive norms and subjected women to new forms of control and discipline, many self-imposed, even as they undermine other forms of patriarchy.
>
> (1998: 9)

Historically, the Palestinians did not perceive masculinity as a quality that was either expressed by violence or imbricated in and through it. Palestinian masculinity was reflected in men's ability to protect the family and meet familial and social demands. These principles also applied to warfare:

> Palestinians did not directly conflate war-making activities with manhood. Indeed, under the Ottomans, Palestinian peasants tried to escape military conscription, finding little honour or future in the military. Masculine honour was more associated with one's cleverness in evading conscription ... Violence does index masculinity but not in ways often discussed in analysis of Western militarism.
>
> (Peteet 1997: 103)

As we can note in most of their political resistance activities, Palestinian men and women were more willing to die than to kill for the sake of acquiring their right to live safely and with dignity. However, even when armed struggle has been declared (such as in Lebanon between 1968 and 1982, and later, primarily during the Second Intifada), the space of combat and violence has not merely been a male-oriented space. The home, the school, the workplace, the hospital, the wedding, the Palestinian tradition of embroidery, attire, and religion all became sites of resistance. Women's bodies, homes, and lands became battlefields for both the internal masculine power and the external militarized political opponent. The continual violation of the space of the home – be it during 1936–9, in 1948 and then after the Nakba, or in 1967 during the occupation – through violent invasions of houses, house demolitions, bombings, sieges, and massacres, all these and more made Palestinians realize that the private home was not a sheltered place but rather the field of combat and warfare. Thus, women in their homes in camps, villages, and cities needed to act and react politically and militantly to ensure the safety and security of their loved ones. As one mother of a political prisoner stated, she tried 'to return the colours to the world', while a mother of a martyr said that she tried 'to give birth to hope'. To orient to their significant others in this way meant that women were acting against occupation and the military violence of Israel while trying to avoid opening another war front in the home, and so often choosing to adhere to the conventional masculine gender order of society.

VIOLATED MASCULINITIES AND FEMINITIES

How do women negotiate hegemonic militarism in conflict areas? How do they engage in building alternative communities within militarized masculinities? What happens when the emasculation of males and the violation of women become a method of controlling and desecrating the occupied Other, in our case the Palestinians?

In this section, I argue that Palestinian feminists and women more generally encounter a complicated process in negotiating their status and in attempting to position themselves within concepts of 'nation' and nationalist politics. The history of nationalism shows that nationalism has opened up new venues for women and has created possibilities for them to become activists and to raise their voices; but it has simultaneously also constrained their advancement given the limits of patriarchy, as the forces that bind women to nationalist struggles also bring with them forces that hinder their abilities and limit their options for self-determination. A question remains: how could the national struggle proceed in transforming its liberal values into reality – promoting justice and equality – while women were being denied a voice and a 'right to rights', as was and remains the case in Palestine? How much freedom does a particular nationalist struggle have to change and to challenge existing political and socio-cultural norms in the context of an increase in the power of economic imperialism and the increase in political Islam? How realistic is it to expect that the Palestinian national struggle could raise questions about women's rights and status or call for justice and fairness under the canopy of the 'war on terror' in general and the continued absence of Palestinians' right to rights in particular?

I believe that, in their quest for self-determination as a nation and a people, Palestinian women and men need to seek transformation from within to accompany the external changes that we are seeking. Yet, one cannot deny the effects of the political-economic and psychological systems of oppression that have made such progressive transformations almost impossible. The dilemmas faced by Palestinian women and the Palestinian feminist movement in dealing simultaneously with national claims, continual violence, and international neglect have placed women and the feminist movement in a very complicated position. National internal patriarchal powers were gravely threatened by the external patriarchal powers. The home as the homeland became a site of constant violation and emasculation. The nature of the colonial project and the repressive patriarchal techniques that preceded and then accompanied the political conflict beginning with the Nakba and the Naksa (the 'setback' – meaning the mass displacement and dispossession of Palestinians during and after the 1967 war) and then during the occupation and especially the two Intifadas has blurred the distinction between the home and the front. The ongoing violent attacks against Palestinians that resulted in the inability of the Palestinians to find a protected and insulated space even in their own homes, as individuals and as a collective, left most Palestinians with a sense of permanent insecurity. The attacks against the physical and social infrastructure and the social fabric has left the Palestinian male publicly exposed to an intense sense of vulnerability in the confrontation with colonial powers, states, soldiers, and settlers.

One of the many stories I heard was that of a close friend who was driving with her husband to his place of work. The Israeli military had set up a flying checkpoint. She witnessed a soldier pulling down the pants of one villager, leaving him naked from the waist down, a villager who was on his way to see his family, and holding in his hands two plastic bags filled with food for Ramadan. My friend got out of her car and started yelling at the soldiers. After almost fifteen minutes of pushing and yelling, my friend noticed that both her husband and their car had disappeared. Shortly after the police arrived as per her request for their presence, she called her husband who said: 'My dear, if I had stayed they would have pulled my pants down the way they pulled his.' This incident, like many others that we as Palestinian women have witnessed,

101

not only challenges social values and rules, but also adds gendered insults and social tensions to our injuries as feminist women seeking change in the midst of occupation.

The constant humiliation, the continual sense of social vulnerability, and the ongoing attack against the foundation of the Palestinian social fabric has increased gendered tensions but paradoxically has had the corresponding, ironic effect of adding to women's respectability and power. Palestinian women have played an active role in saving men from public humiliation, abuse, beating, and arrest at the hands of the occupying forces. These dramatic changes in women's roles have challenged and often overturned social roles, especially in relation to the home-feminine–masculine-front equation (see Peteet 1997). The renegotiation of the meaning of women's roles in the context of daily humiliation and military occupation, causing what Williams (1999) and Wing (2000) have called 'spirit injury/murder' (see Chapter 2), has taught me that putting forward a united gender front is the best way to confront such abuse. However, the transformation in roles was easier for women than for men – particularly those men who felt emasculated, infantilized, and humiliated by the occupation and who felt they had lost a degree of power through the transformation of roles among men and women.

Here I would like to present one additional case to exemplify the attacks on Palestinian masculinity and its ramifications. The first took place during the First Intifada in 1994. At that time, I was working at Bethlehem University teaching social work. It was also at this same time that we started the Al-Aman hotline. While I was talking about the importance of such hotlines, one of my students asked if I would be also willing to help abused men. Three days after hearing my positive response, he came to my office at Bethlehem University with Khalil and asked me to talk through the effects of humiliation with him.

Khalil sat for almost two hours and told me about himself, his family, and his inability to reach his place of work in Sdud (called in Hebrew Eshdod) due to the fact that the military forces refused to give permits to any of his village members so that they could commute to work. He explained to me that after seven months without any work and any kind of income, he managed to obtain a permit for himself and his seventeen-year-old son. Some other members of the village also managed to get permits and planned their first day of work with their Israeli employer. On that first day, while leaving the village, they were stopped at a military checkpoint where the soldiers ordered all the taxi passengers to disembark and stand on the side of the road. Khalil was the oldest passenger (at least he looked to them as such). He knew some Hebrew and tried to explain to the soldiers that he had eleven children at home who needed to be fed. He tried, to no avail, to make the soldiers understand the financial hardship they were facing. Then one of the soldiers told him that the only way the whole group would be allowed to pass was if he would bark. Khalil said: 'He asked me to bark like a dog, he told me "do like a dog does, do what dogs do."' Then Khalil burst into tears, and his words were filled with pain and anger. He explained to me how he barked so as to be able to pass the checkpoint and reach his place of work. He said: 'Do you understand the meaning of me barking, a man like me, barking in front of his own son and his fellow villagers?' All I heard from him afterward were the words 'inhaddet, hadduni, haddunni', which means, 'I was destroyed, they destroyed me'.

Although he managed to work that day and bring home some money for his family, later on he was often unable to walk or even wake up in the morning. He was in bed for four weeks, telling everybody that it was out of his hands that he could not get out of bed in the morning and that he was unable to do anything during the day. It was at this point that his nephew, my student and a former political prisoner, convinced him to come and see me. Both Khalil and my student felt that it would be easier to seek help from a female therapist than from a man. As his nephew stated, 'My uncle refused to go to any male doctors, he can't face men anymore, they burned him, they [he was referring to the Israeli military] knew where to hit us'.

Both Khalil and my student's stories take us back to Fanon's analysis of the effect of oppression on men as well as Wing's and Williams' conception of a 'spirit injury/murder'. Khalil's story is one of many experiences of humiliation and degradation that involves an attack on the Palestinian psyche. Khalil's reaction took the path of self-blame, resulting in severe depression and self-anger. For Palestinian men and women as victims, witnesses, and frontliners facing the occupation, the intense sense of fear, constant loss, and spatial unpredictability necessarily creates new men and women from their daily traumas. The reconstitution of the self through the enduring violence on the part of the occupier and fighting back either against oneself or against a less socially powerful Other, namely 'women', was and remains a gendered process that, not surprisingly, heavily impacted and still impacts the creation of new roles for women.

Women who protected other women while fighting back against the occupation also became 'new victims' when confronting in turn internal patriarchal abuse. In becoming the heroines who fought back, women were caught in the double bind of an ostensibly 'new morality'; they not only carried the liabilities of a 'national honour' imposed upon them – and as such were perceived as morally superior by being conceived as able to protect both their people and nation from abuse – but in addition they absorbed the abuse inflicted upon them by their own male counterparts, as convenient objects on which to vent male frustration. The shift in women's roles and the new expectations that resulted remained largely iconic, as women came to be perceived primarily as mothers or dutiful wives and daughters and as moral and material protectors of the nation. With the economic strangulation of Palestinian society, women also became major breadwinners for their families. Within the context of politico-economic violence and frustration, the patriarchal powers in society themselves experienced the vicious colonial attack against the Palestinian social fabric. They therefore not only refused to accept much progressive social change (especially when certain changes mirrored Western values that were oppressive to the Palestinian cause) but also started imposing masculinized 'protective' codes of behaviour upon the society at large. Therefore, when active and independent women acted in ways that 'deviated' from 'social expectation', the result was often social outrage. This in turn brought about more brutal methods of dealing with women, raising the level of violence against women even further.

Both violence against 'misbehaving women' and the new politics of morality were enacted in public and private spaces. Women were called upon to behave in a more 'decent' and religiously and socially 'appropriate' manner. While witnessing political violence and taking a role in fighting back was perceived as a form of political practice and not a private issue, women's response to patriarchal calls for an appropriate dress code, mode of behaviour, and Islamic education was also a political act of 'self preservation'. The militarized colonialism that wounded Palestinian 'Others' through its violent oppression turned out to have a devastating cost. However, the magnitude of this cost is difficult to determine as the situation is analogous to cases of child and sexual abuse in which the victim is burdened with having to prove her case based upon the oppressor's rules (see the similar argument in Williams 1999).

As we have seen, women during political unrest are often considered active political actors but also often help to define the moral and material boundaries of the nation being conceptualized – sometimes, unfortunately, with their own bodies and sexuality. In my research on the crime of femicide I have shown how all masculine powers – be these the police, judges, prosecutors, or family members – co-operate among themselves to 'solve' what is defined as 'crimes against morality and public order' while using women's lives and bodies to do so, and at their expense. Thus, the imposition of early marriage to prevent 'social scandal', the imposition of virginity testing to 'ascertain' the level of a woman's morality, the imposition of marriage on rapist and victim in order to 'protect' family honour, and outright killing of women in order to 'cleanse' violations of the latter are only a few examples of violence against women used to help heal the wounded masculinity of men and further empower the patriarchy.

The arrival of the Palestinian Authority in the West Bank and Gaza, the transitional period that followed, and then the current disputes between the various political and ideological factions, have affected the potential for women's activism and also made it both possible and impossible to address concrete policy issues such as the legal status of women in Palestinian society. The 1994 General Union of Palestinian Women (GUPW) 'Declaration of Principles', in response to the women's rights instituted by Arafat, demanded complete equality based on political, civil, educational, and vocational rights. The social policy of the Palestinian National Authority (PNA) was subjected to immense critique by women, by political, feminist, and human rights activists, and religious fundamentalists as well as by my fellow Palestinian intellectuals (for more criticism of the gender discrimination within the PNA, see Giacaman et al. 1996; Abdo 1999). The onset of the Second Intifada, the weakening of the Palestinian Authority, and the emasculation and compartmentalization of its leaders up to Arafat's death, the attacks of 9/11, which furthered the hegemonic attacks on Islam, all combined to increase the local popularity of political Islam. After the victory of Hamas in the last Palestinian election, gender relations were reconstructed and women's vulnerability to violence was increased. In November of 2007 the SAWA Coalition, an umbrella women's rights organization, wrote a letter asking Palestinian President Abbas to issue a presidential decree denouncing the crime of femicide, which are usually called 'crimes of honour'. The president's reaction was especially improper given the increase of the reported cases of the killing of women both in the West Bank and Gaza: thirty-four cases in Gaza and seventeen in the West Bank.

POLITICAL VIOLENCE, HUMAN RIGHTS DISCOURSE, AND NATION-BUILDING

Discussing violence against women in conflict zones, especially during periods of nation-building, requires a close examination not only of what goes on at the 'national' level but equally importantly at what goes on at the international and global levels, particularly the ways in which political-economic factors impede, aid, or mediate juridical and human rights concerns. The asymmetries of power between and within states, nations, and groups become highlighted as we invoke the various arenas of women's and human rights discourses. Thus, despite the fact that human rights discourse might seem more urgent given our globalized economy, in some cases, as with Palestine, this discourse has proven at times to be a source of repression and fragmentation of the local society and culture. The use of the human rights discourse can potentially allow for the application of international pressure to urge states to comply with treaties such as the Convention to Eliminate All Forms of Discrimination Against Women (CEDAW), but we know very well that such pressure is often dependent on the geo-political strategies of the specific states involved. Moreover, and as Sally Engle Merry argues (2003), the lack of enforcement mechanisms within the international human rights system to prevent violence against women or to punish such violence after the fact has led to its limited effect: 'Human rights are difficult for individuals to adopt as a self-definition in the absence of institutions that will take these rights seriously when they are claimed by individuals' (Merry 2003: 381). In addition, the adoption of a human rights discourse about a particular form of behaviour requires a wider understanding of individual experiences within their respective contexts. Sherene Razack (2002) has reported that in Canada the adjudication of claims of gender persecution in the cases of Third World women ended up promoting the interests of the First World. Razack has shown how Otherized women were successful in using the international human rights discourse only when they presented themselves as victims of their dysfunctional and specific patriarchal cultures and contexts. Hence, it seems that it is only through the use of imperialistic and Orientalist discourse that women outside the West are able to claim their rights. This approach results not only in the keeping of the exotic Orientalized woman at the margins, but more importantly in increasing their vulnerability – such as women living in conflict zones. The problem therefore remains of how to deconstruct and neutralize the historical and cultural biases (of the West in this instance) that come to contextually affect the possibilities for juridical relief in areas such as Palestine. How can we understand the functioning of gender, race, sexuality, and class in relation to internationalized human rights discourse within the specific contexts of conflict zones? Moreover, can we incorporate anti-colonial, anti-racist, and anti-sexist concerns within a human rights discourse that has generally claimed 'universality' by ignoring history, contingency, and the context of women in conflict zones?

What I am reflecting upon are the ways in which the international human rights discourse, particularly as it is applied to women, affects the relational dynamic between women and nation. The juridical language concerning human rights violations of women in conflict zones represents women as those who are raped, violated, sexually trafficked, undressed, veiled, killed for 'honour crimes', and so on, but all such representations are ultimately transacted through a purely voyeuristic, masculine lens. It seems to me that international organizations sometimes attempt to modernize the 'backward other' by presenting us with the First World's human rights discourse as a panacea for all our ills. Such discourse further accentuates the universalization of the notion of the so-called 'primitive' societies. Such a voyeuristic and essentially masculine lens further links women to heterosexual discourses of women as nation, as land, and as property (Layoun 1994: 63–75). Essentially, violence against women includes global, economic, and racialized violence and such violence further contributes to the construction of masculinity. At the same time as the violence is perpetrated against women, the human rights discourse is presented as an 'international protector', which is utilized, ostensibly, in the interest of women (see Grewal 1998: 502).

This need to protect the brown/Palestinian woman from the brown/ Palestinian man in turn awakens the internal masculine players, the 'nationalist protectors', who set out to save brown women from the white/Western man. We can fairly say that the globalized human rights discourse, with all its masculine power in reserve, collaborates with nationalistic discourses. The global power holders, the voyeurs, are always (re-)constructing their authority as rescuers, presumably functioning outside of history and economy. They view the violations of women's bodies and violence against them as the conduct and 'culture' of the 'Other'. The internal nationalist masculinity accepts the human rights discourse only when the perpetrator is an outsider, for if they apply it internally, it might turn out to be a suicidal act against the insider, oppressed 'Other' with his powerless status. Thus, when the abuser is an Israeli soldier in Palestine, or an American and British soldier in Iraq, the perpetrator is condemned and criminalized – at least, ideally. However, when the perpetrator is an insider, the crime becomes an internal issue, and internal sovereignty is not to be violated, especially when an issue concerns 'culture' and women. The demarcation between the public and the private, the national and the international, thus becomes essential. Ignoring the complexity of the positionality of the various masculine players, the refusal to look closely at the problematic power relations between global powers outside the nation, and the local context of ongoing oppression and despair ultimately results in the silencing of women's discourses about oppression and exploitation. Here, women as victims/survivors of political violence find themselves between two unequal masculine powers – the very powerful, imperialist, and militarist First World and the internal, relatively weak, patriarchal, and nationalist power.

The complexity of the situation and the diverse positionality of the players forces us to question the ostensibly 'neutral' discourse of human rights in order to better analyse the ways in which such discourses are utilized and play out during times of conflict. Such analysis takes us back to the basic premise of how the context of violent conflict is represented. Who is speaking for whom and how have they claimed such right of speech? What power relations enable them to speak for others? My queries here do not invoke the legal and political mechanisms and powers aligned with human rights discourses, for I believe that colonial oppression operates legally, using human rights discourses as a tool; rather, my analysis calls attention to the more perverse applications of such discourses.

In the first example with which I opened this chapter, the young girl Tamam stated that she carries in her backpack all the pain and the legacy of the Palestinian people. Furthermore, by walking the walk as a young Palestinian woman, her back also carries the politics of her identity as a national, religious, gendered, and ethnic entity that suffers from the effects of militarization and occupation. This young girl's narrative shows how her specific identity as a Palestinian affects her daily commute to school, her movement or restriction of her movement, her marriageability, her education, her employment, and her economic independence, to mention just a few aspects of her identity. In the violent context that is Palestine, the human rights discourse that is grounded in individualistic ethics and universalistic assumptions becomes very problematic. The human rights discourse requires her to refuse participation in resistance actions against the Israeli oppression – activities such as writing petitions, participating in demonstrations, attending political gatherings – for these can be construed as 'violent' and/or as 'terrorist'. The discourse impels her to refrain from confronting soldiers, challenging military checkpoints, or throwing stones when threatened by occupation forces. In addition, the human rights discourse might 'support' her by offering to help her if she challenges her family by refusing to marry at an early age, by documenting her failure to attend school at an early age, and even by defining her wearing of the veil as a tool of oppression. The mere fact of claiming that she should be protected when her individual rights are violated, when these violated rights are only those that are actions on the part of her father, brother, and family more generally, while refusing to protect her from violations on the part of external, economic, imperialist, and colonizing players, all too often ends up leaving her in a state of exile within her own homeland. By asserting her right as an individual, an autonomous being, she marginalizes and excludes herself from her context and often from her very identity as a Palestinian as well. Furthermore, this situation can result in the loss of her only support system, and given that the human rights discourse leaves her with very limited international protection, she can find herself in a very precarious position indeed.

The question remains as to why we should require women in such contexts to believe in the human rights discourse when it has failed them, their nations, and their societies for so long. I claim here, as Sherene Razack argues in her examination of the Canadian state's effort to combat domestic violence (1998), that our efforts – as feminist activists and as global and local activists – must begin with an examination of the effect of global, imperialist, economic power. Therefore, our efforts must begin with a closer look at the effect of white supremacy and an acknowledgement that every examination of violence against women is embedded within wider power relations and functions within political and ideological structures, not outside of them.

As illustrated by the narratives in this chapter, the symbolic and material status of women in general, the roles they define for themselves and are defined by, and the corresponding violence against women as a result of these shifting roles become part and parcel of the construction of social and political policy as well as the conceptualizing of a 'nation'. The simultaneous marginalization and centring of women situates them in a state of betweenness – a state that calls for constant negotiation between various masculine structures that are asymmetrical in terms of their power, but all of which are more powerful than any given individual Palestinian woman. By bringing forward Palestinian women's ordeals, voices, histories, and contexts, I locate the sources and origin of gender oppression. In this chapter, this archaeology has been conducted through the lens of 'women and nation' and women and nationalism. Here, I was concerned with tracking the discursive constructs of women and nations by listening carefully to women's voices and attending to their actions under military occupation and acknowledging my own subject position as a Palestinian feminist, therapist, and legal scholar. I contrasted women's voices with those of men to both articulate the relationship between women and nation-building and to realize a politics of contradiction, of 'betweenness', and a politics of exile in one's own home. One can make the argument that the project of the nation-state has subjected women to new forms of gender objectification, but there is also the argument here that this project has in addition opened up new possibilities for women's activism and autonomy – and thus, that nation-building and the nationalist project may have been at the same time both regulatory towards and emancipatory for women. Yet, one should not deny the fact that women and men in this specific historical and political context were and are discursively constructed to become the symbolic representations of their national and nationalistic causes.

This state of betweenness created a counter-space, a third-space that has been invisible to the modern, corporate eye and ear. Turning women's 'femininity' into a symbol to foreground Israel's colonial policies has relegated women to traditional gender-specific roles, but at the same time has included women in the national agenda – as agents of the revolution. Despite this schizophrenic state of 'betweenness', Palestinian women stood up against militaristic violence, dared to go beyond traditional boundaries, and created politics that challenged the national and international masculine agenda. They voiced their differences and they were keen to create social change for women in their nations in their own ways. Women spoke between and within this militarized context: daring to speak against the sexualization of women's bodies and actions, daring to be inside and outside their national and gender specific status, and daring to discuss the tensions that they experience – all this in an effort to counter the hegemonic discourse.

In a region that is occupied, policed, in a state of constant conflict, and controlled by myriad forms of colonial practices and masculine power, the effects of women's initiatives in the process of nation-building and 'nationhood' can often become obscured or overlooked. Compounding the issue is the fact that this is a region of the world where women are often misunderstood at best or at worst fetishized and condemned through Orientalist discourses – sometimes even by their sisters in the West. Throughout the writings in this volume, I have maintained that we need to argue for and activate a feminist criticism that takes into account particular specificities, including history, colonialism, location, culture, and the immediacy of violence and conflict. In so doing, a very interesting fact emerges: while the masculine powers in play are engaged in 'nation-building', the women of the region are also building 'alternative communities', often quietly and outside of public display or attention. Within the complexities of the public, domestic, and familial spheres, women have been quietly asserting their agency, their vision, and their quest for justice and autonomy. I do not think it is far-fetched to argue that the fact of their very survival attests to the success of these alternative spaces of being. These are spaces created out of the in-betweenness that has been discussed here, out of the scraps and fragments of a destroyed world, and out of the rubble of destroyed homes. In an essay in her *Feminist Contentions*, Seyla Benhabib advocates for a 'radical situatedness of the subject' (1995: 20), for only through such a consideration can we estimate the autonomy and rationality of the subject. What I have hoped to illustrate throughout this chapter is a material example of the kind of radical situatedness that Benhabib is arguing for. Once we take into account the array of forces – both internal and external – that affect the lives of Palestinian women, lives lived out in the midst of violence, we can see more clearly the alternative spaces these women are continuing to build.

CHAPTER 4

WOMEN FRONTLINERS IN CONFLICT ZONES: A GENEALOGY OF WEAPONIZATION

They used us as silah bashari *[as a human weapon] ... They asked the men to walk naked so as to be able to further invade areas, and then asked me and all the women in our neighbourhood to walk in front of their [i.e., Israeli] tanks, and walk them out of [the] neighbourhood. While men were watching ... the women became a new Zionist weapon to fight us.*

(Suraida from Jenin, May 2002)

When they invaded Jenin, they were using their amplifiers to scare us, they threatened to violate our honour. As in 1948 during the Nakba, they used women's honour to spread fear, but where are the Arabs, where is the world? Even our honour was used as a weapon against us ... but Umrna Ma Istaslamna *[we never surrendered].*

(Rania from Jenin, May 2002)

Soon after midnight. Those who were patrolling our village saw the Israelis come to us like rain. They flooded the village. They came from an entire circle surrounding us.

That night, my husband was working in the King David Hotel. I had my son, Mahmoud, four months old ... The attack began at about one o'clock in the morning. I was lying down and I was breast-feeding Mahmoud when I heard the tanks and rifles, and smelled the smoke. I saw them coming. Everybody was yelling to his or her neighbours, 'If you know how to leave, leave!' ... I had my baby in one arm, and I crawled on the floor against the wall until I could get down from the third floor and out of my house. I left with no shoes. I couldn't even get a blanket on my son ... We began to understand exactly what had happened in the village. We found out that they had asked people in each house to come out with a white flag. When the door would open, they would enter the house. They would search the women and steal their jewellery, drag their kids out and put the women and children in buses. My uncle's wife was taken by the Israelis when they came.

The males were killed on the spot. We used to breast-feed our children. But, to be honest with you, my breasts dried up from everything we went through.
(Aiysha Jima Zidan from Deir Yassin (1948), cited in Lynd et al. 1994: 24–5)

Over the years, as I was listening to or reading textual versions of the oral histories of Palestinian women, I realized that the word 'weaponization' has been constantly used by Palestinian women. However, the word itself does not appear in any formal studies pertaining to the occupation and militarization of Palestine. Perhaps the absence is explained by the fact that it does not translate well into English, or that the word seems awkward or contrived. Yet I realized that the words *bitsallah*, *yitsalahou*, or *silah bashari* – all variants meaning the treatment of women as weapons or human weapons – were much used by the women I came into contact with, and often appeared in the data gathered during my own research between 2000 and 2005; the words express the ways in which patriarchal forces use women's bodies as weapons in their wars or conflicts. But I also found similar perceptions among Palestinian women in historical material that quoted their narratives of the 1948 Nakba.

Within the women's testimonials heard throughout this chapter and in the epigraphs that open it are multiplicities of experiences and epistemologies, and in listening to these voices we are able to attend to a new perspective on the way women's bodies were used during the Nakba and are being used during the political violence of the current Intifadas. When these women share their experiences, although all speak in different voices and recall different moments in history, the implications in each case reflect the gender politics of the perception of women's bodies as political weapons. The political message conveyed in the articulation and use of such human weapons not only violates gender relations in the most horrific way, this use inherently violates the community and its sense of stability and control. A community's failure to protect those in need has direct impacts on socio-political relations and on the internal – local Palestinian – formal and informal systems of social control. Thus, the consequences of the weaponization of women's bodies reach far beyond the immediacy of the moment of horror, humiliation, or violence.

Palestinian women subjected to colonial edicts stipulating the guarding of their collective's national entity as well as their bodies and who are caught in the border zone between the Israeli military occupation and the matrix of their Palestinian national identities are the subject of this chapter. As with other chapters, this one presents women's voices as the main source of data for theorizing and discussing the effects of the military occupation and colonization in Palestine on women's bodies and lives; this chapter, however, investigates the *weaponization* of women's bodies and lives – by men, other women, or the women themselves. By weaponization I am referring to the ways in which the use of women's bodies to either 'fight', 'cope', 'revolt', 'protect', 'secure', or 'defend' fosters and further secures the boundaries that separate men from women, men from men, and women from women in the context of war and national and political struggle. Similarly, the militarization of women refers to the use of women's spaces, their time, and their assets for any form of militarized activity or action that has military value.

The feminist genealogy of the weaponization of women's bodies unravels the mechanisms of power related to these bodies in conflict zones. By invoking 'genealogy' in the Foucauldian sense, we trace the totalizing hegemonic discourses within historical knowledge that have shaped this knowledge with the goal of opening up emancipatory possibilities (Foucault 1980: 85). However, feminist genealogists have expanded Foucault's analyses and have emphasized the importance of rethinking history and domination, indeed, of history as domination. As Alexander and Mohanty have stated:

> The use of a word like 'genealogies' is not meant to suggest a frozen or embodied inheritance of domination and resistance, but an interested, conscious thinking and rethinking of history and historicity, a rethinking which has women's autonomy and self-determination at its core.
>
> (1997: xvi)

As such, Alexander and Mohanty add to the Foucauldian concept of genealogy the critical point of understanding it not just in individualistic or collective terms but also as a feminist political praxis for interrogating the 'social identities of women of colour, especially in terms of the formulation of international or global feminism' (1997: xv). By mapping out the present state of things and by making visible the effect of our history on our present, a genealogical approach enables a productive reworking of what we have so far perceived as accepted 'knowledge' 'about women'. A specifically feminist genealogy is a form of feminist critique that reviews and problematizes the most commonly held beliefs, thereby opening up space for possible change. Lastly, a feminist genealogical approach helps us free our analyses from ideological contamination by economic, national, militaristic, and state-oriented 'necessities' in order to open up to larger horizons of possibilities while delving into a critique that is ethical as well.

My particular genealogical approach researches the ways in which the transformation of women's bodies into weapons is not a marginal, irrelevant issue – perhaps something that obtains only within militarized zones – but rather is a core one in how this has been accomplished under colonial conditions and in conflict zones. Examining the way in which women's bodies and sexualities have been constructed in hegemonic discourse is a critical component of an understanding and critique of the process of Othering that women have been subjected to. Thus, by bringing into our narrative the voices of women who have lived and are still living under occupation, we aim to add an analytical depth in order to further our discussion of the history of the weaponization of women. Moreover, we hope as well to challenge the marginalization of Palestinian women and so allow their voices to reflect on their past and present – to reflect on the use of their bodies and sexuality within the context of war and occupation. Looking closely at the politics of the body enables us to interrogate the reasons behind the marginalization of these voices and the ways in which these voices can be productive in critiquing the complex power dynamics of the region.

Historically, women's bodies and lives have been used as commodities and also as frontline defences 'marking' the boundary between self and other. Facing a military occupation in which schools, homes, hospitals, and other everyday spaces of life become militarized complicates Palestinian women's ways of resisting coercion and the way patriarchal Palestinian powers act and react, for as we have already seen and will also be shown again in Chapter 5 in relation to the socio-economic and gender effect of the Israeli Separation Wall, in many cases Palestinian men have felt unable to protect and support the female population while at the same time they have come to exercise greater power over them.

Contemporary wars and violent political conflicts have changed in significant ways from the conduct of such actions in the past. Whereas in the past there were more clear demarcations between combatants and territories, in today's conflicts everything and everyone are transformed into a potential target. Furthermore, there is no difference between state-sponsored or non-state political violence in that both engage civilians to an unprecedented degree. This decentralized warfare often hinders efforts to remedy the harm inflicted on victims and, in my view, it should be an international responsibility to protect vulnerable and powerless groups. Women living in conflict areas and war zones struggle not only against an international silence while attempting to fight for their security, but also have to deal with silence on the part of their local and nationalist power holders who conduct a different kind of occupation by using women's bodies, sexuality, and lives to promote internal control over women.

Despite the vulnerability of women during political violence and war, the epigraphs to this chapter reveal women's strength in resisting colonization and modes of coping even within the constraints of patriarchal regulations, culture, and institutions. However, even given such strong will and creative intelligence with which to survive in a conflict zone, Palestinian women under political occupation are also operating within a complex and unpredictable socio-political and economic context that is ill-equipped to deal with women's growing needs as well as with their emerging strengths – as paradoxical as this may sound. They are demoralized by world politics and with their own internal (Palestinian) patriarchal system, but they are also disappointed with the emancipatory alternatives. While Palestinian women are seeking transformation of their own roles, which is difficult enough, they are also being required to accommodate the pre-existing machinery of colonization as well as the patriarchal rules that predetermine the context of their lives. However, they continue to fight and search for greater satisfaction of their needs or, in some cases, simply to be heard. Bereft of so much, Palestinian women are not willing to give up the social relations inherent within a collective society nor the sense of social, physical, and economic security afforded by their family ties, for their families generally (and often only ideally) remain as a calm centre in the midst of the chaos of their lives. Given such complex dynamics for simply carrying on from day to day, it was an experience for me to observe the engaged critique of the social fabric that these women are embedded within.

Palestinian women are facing two kinds of domination. One such domination is manifested in their political resistance to occupation and colonization and will be discussed in the first part of this chapter. The second is manifested in their resistance to the patriarchal social conditions in which men perceive women as the propagators of the nation and the preservers and reproducers of a cultural belief system that postulates women's reputation, purity, virginity, and sanctity as the symbolic cornerstones of the national culture. At the same time, the Othered body of the Palestinian woman becomes a promiscuous object that is open to attack, both internally (from Palestinian men) and externally (from Israelis), both literally and figuratively, when any act of rancour or abuse is left un-criminalized. Both Israeli colonial and international discourse around the so-called 'terrorist' other, combined with the national 'cultural preservation discourse' and its ensuing effects, have influenced the lives of many Palestinian women. The symbolic discourse of 'the terrorist other' and the militaristic values inherent within it not only affect policy-makers but also increases the state-sponsored violence and militarism of some Western nations. And the same discourse empowers and encourages internal masculine and patriarchal power holders to increase their control over women's bodies and sexuality.

BIO-POLITICS AND THE CONSEQUENCES OF THE BODY

It will hardly come as a surprise that during political conflicts the use of force outside all legality is quickly legitimized and that this force is more often than not turned against those bodies that are most vulnerable, namely, women and children. Giorgio Agamben draws attention to the difference in meanings between two ancient Greek words that describe life: *bios*, which describes the realm of political/legal existence, and *zoe*, which incorporates the pure, biological being. Agamben forwards the image and concept of the concentration camp as the paradigm of modernity and of political space as the point at which politics mutates into what he describes as 'bio-politics', since the camp is produced at the point at which the political system of the modern nation-state – which is territorially configured – enters into crisis (1998: 167–71). Beginning with Agamben's analysis, we can theorize the military occupation and the compartmentalization of the Palestinians in closed enclaves as being an extended concentration camp, as being an instance of what Agamben has called *homo sacer*, or 'bare life'. Agamben theorizes post-sovereign power (see Foucault 1998: Part 5) as being foundational to the emergence and practice of bio-power. The compartmentalization of Palestinians, the Israeli control over their time, water, electricity, and their economy more generally in a deliberate effort aimed at what Roy has called 'de-development' (1995), the incarceration of their president (in 2002) within a small area, and so on, demonstrate the racialized character of the Palestinian body, a body that is denied rights or liberties, and the 'legitimized' policies directed towards that body. Agamben has argued that the camp 'is the space opened up when the exception begins to become the rule' (1998: 168–9). By compartmentalizing people in small enclaves, by restricting and restraining them in their daily life, whether in terms of education, health, and protection, hegemonic power holders create a space beyond any juridical parameters ostensibly in order to remove any potential 'threats' from the social realm.

Ghanem, a Palestinian feminist, has employed Agamben's conceptualization of the *homo sacer* to illustrate how the (imagined) border of
the Israeli state came to signify a perpetual state of emergency, and how
'the border became the scene of life in the shadow of death, where the
Palestinian body was made by the Israeli authorities to undergo a transformation and become bare life, exposed and devoid of meaning, *homo
sacer*' (Ghanem 2003). Israeli policies – executed arbitrarily and capri-
ciously (consider, for example, the flying checkpoints) – have turned the
space of the Palestinian body politic into a naked body perpetually
vulnerable and open to attack.

In my usage here, bio-politics reflects the particular use of women's
bodies as weapons, what I am calling 'the weaponization of the body', as
an extension of the power of colonial and patriarchal systems beyond the
actual physical, social, and political control of material space that
colonization implies and indeed relies on. Within this dynamic, as we
have too readily witnessed in the recent wars in the Middle East, the
local powers speak in the language of 'nationalism', 'nation-building',
and the 'preservation of cultural authenticity', while the hegemonic
powers of Empire deploy the spectre of a discourse on 'terrorists' or
'terrorist nations'.

For Foucault, bio-politics begins during the eighteenth century
with the creation of regulatory mechanisms as a way to contain human
populations both taxonomically and epistemologically, commencing
with, as Foucault wrote in *The History of Sexuality*, their 'propagation,
births and mortality, the level of health, life expectancy, longevity'
(1998: 139). He notes that the invention of demographics (1998:
137) was an essential factor in the deployment of bio-power. Foucault
argues that modern sovereignty – as compared to the earlier rule of the
sovereign – does not so much exercise 'the ancient right to take life or let
live', but is instead synonymous with a 'power to foster life or disallow it
to the point of death' (1998: 138). Thus, the emergence of bio-politics
signifies the ability to display power over the life of the citizen even in
relation to the frequent bloody wars in recent human history; mass
slaughter, of other populations and of a regime's own population as
conducted by itself, 'now presents itself as the counterpart of a power
that exerts a positive influence on life' (1998: 137). Thus, human life, as
Foucault explains, is sacrificed through mass violence (1998: 137).
Looking at the deployment of bio-politics during political conflicts
and wars, one also needs to look at what I have here termed a feminist
genealogy of weaponization; this concept calls for a re-examination of

the ways in which we have hitherto conceptualized women and their bodies and sexualities.

Foucault has explained how the modern state can scarcely function without becoming involved with racism, which he sees as the break between what must live and what must die (2003). In constructing its fantasy homogeneities, the state becomes a harsh and punitive norma-lizing agent. In this regard, the state of Israel, as an occupier and colonizer, daily engages in a deadly power play based on the 'sovereign' right to kill and thus engages in a bio-political management of life. It is a power that is reliant on and is mediated by the total annihilation of what it considers 'other', achieved by sexual abuse and social exclusion through to mass murder. Faizeh, from a village close to Ramallah city, shared the following experience with us:

> It became so hard for us women, all of a sudden the occupying forces put up a checkpoint ... we call it *il-mahhasim il-tayarra* [the flying check-points] ... These checkpoints are not anticipated ... and we get so confused when we see them – one doesn't carry one's ID when walking in the field between my house and my grandparent's house ... This is exactly what occupation means ... A week ago, I was on my way to the University, when I came upon a checkpoint – and they undressed me and body searched me ... not only do I need to deal with the *sulutat Al Ihtilal* [occupying authorities], but also with a couple of *shabab* [i.e., young men] that started telling me that I shouldn't come late ... and when I argued with them, one of them told me that I had better find me an *a'aris* [a groom]. Those men looked to me, so weak when facing the soldiers with their big rifles, the unexpected checkpoints, and the constant humilia-tion ... and I became the only weapon that allowed them to feel in control ... Women these days do not understand where problems are coming from or how to handle these problems, the soldiers, the daily coercion, the men in the family, the society ... what we do is *q'immat il-nidal wal muqawama* [the height of defiance and resistance].

> (June 2004)

Faizeh's story exemplifies the way bio-politics plays out in the context of political conflict, the objective and subjective consequences for women living under occupation. Some aspects of Faizeh's narrative certainly address what we might think of as the obvious manifestations of an occupied and militarized space and the body located within it, such as the daily harassments or humiliations. For example, the flying check-points she mentions are constructed within minutes and appear suddenly, seemingly without reason, leaving women in constant uncertainty and feeling insecure and vulnerable. But what is more compelling for me about Faizeh's narrative is the way in which her words expose the socio-political fabric that surrounds the female body and the gender disruptions endemic to occupation and conflict. Faizeh, as with so many women trapped in the conflict, is put in a situation whereby she must negotiate not only the limitations imposed upon her own body and her time but also must understand the dynamics of the oppression of other bodies as well, even those that may lay further burdens upon her – such as the Palestinian men whose humiliation she also experiences, often at their hands, men who are ostensibly her protectors according to 'cultural values'.

The hardships endemic to the dynamics of a weaponized body are clearly understood by Palestinian women. They express the burdens of occupation not only through their own oppressions but also through reflection on the incapacitation of Palestinian males who constantly search for a way out of their humiliating existence, a search for personal dignity that often results in ironic and yet more rigorously oppressive acts committed upon the women. Khulood shared her story with us, a story that expands for us the ways in which women's social reputation is still greatly reliant on giving birth to male children – a way of ensuring that men remain in power. She told us how her marriage and reproductive capacity became the only way her father preserved his social power when all else, including ways of earning his livelihood, had failed. Khulood stated:

> When I had my first child, my father came to visit me. We had such a discussion about the hardships of the political situation (it took him two hours to reach me, and I live maybe ten minutes away in the car), the lack of jobs, the poverty, his inability to provide for his family, and his inability to continue seeing and facing the soldiers every single day on his way to his shop in Jerusalem. Then he said that the only thing that was keeping him strong was the fact that his daughters – we are three – have a good reputation, they all got married, and they all had male kids.

Khulood then stopped, looked at me and said:

> What a life … we women – our honour, our biological productivity – became the only weapon for men to *yitsalahou fiyu* [weaponize] themselves with … to protect themselves. So, the fact that I got married early, that I was honourable [she meant a virgin] when I got married, that I got pregnant right away … that I got him a grandson … is the only way to prove that he is a man. My father is all that we have left – for me and my sisters – in such hard conditions; I wish we could give him more.
>
> (July 2004)

120

As the words of Khulood and those of other women we listened to reveal, these women are able, remarkably, to build knowledge in moments of belonging and non-belonging and in the tensions inherent to a deep-felt sense of dislocation within their own land. Their narratives stress how their resilience in the face of occupation in some cases turns out to be a mobilizing force that nourishes them in their daily resistance.

But in other cases, the daily challenges hinder women's ability to address their own personal needs and can often result in the mutation of a valuable resilience into mere tolerance and acceptance. Overall, the tension that the voices of Khulood, Faizeh, Suraida, and other women reveal demonstrates the multilayered effect of the bio-political deployment of bodies in a militarized space. Such deployment clarifies how military occupation affects the economic stability, social security, and physical safety of the occupied. These narratives also illustrate the ways in which occupation and oppression additionally produce new modes of survival that also transform the beleaguered bodies of women into sites of productive resistance. To consider the weaponized bodies of women within the context of bio-politics provides an avenue for a more complex understanding of gender under the rubric of military occupation and nationalistic gestures, which I will examine in more depth below.

The analysis of the uses of the body and sexuality within the modern state in its construction of power in general, and women's bodies and sexuality during periods of violent political conflict in particular, is not a new subject of inquiry for feminist scholars. Farida Shaheed, a Pakistani sociologist and activist, has shed light on how 'culture, custom, outline the space available for a woman's definition of self, the cross-cutting factors she must daily negotiate in her actions, and the boundaries against which she needs to push for self-affirmation and change' (1998: 61). As repositories of the closely linked 'culture and customs', women are subjected to that which has been defined for them and then limited to 'appropriate' spaces with the result that they have few rights. In her study of black–white multiracial families in the United States, sociologist Heather Dalmage coined the term 'border patrolling' in order to indicate how people are socialized from an early age to know where 'borders' exist, the reasons why there is a need to 'patrol' those borders, and the consequences of attempting to cross them. In this sense, borders are cognitive and symbolic demarcations loaded with meanings and are an important site for power struggles. Borders created to protect resources such as goods and power are kept in place by laws, language, cultural norms, images, and individual actions as well as through interlock with other borders. In this sense, many types of borders exist, such as national, religious, political, sexual, gendered, and racial ones; all intersect with each other, and each has a unique history laden with power struggles (Dalmage 2000: 34). The concept of 'border patrolling' can be utilized to indicate how, in armed conflict, women's bodies and sexualities are the means by which familial control can exert, protect, and maintain the power of patriarchy through prescription of that which constitutes culture and customs. Women who 'cross' these preset borders are seen as subjecting themselves to violence and the act of transgressing these borders allows for violence against women to be normalized, produced, and reinforced.

There is a chilling resemblance between the treatment and control of women and the nation/land (Saigol 2000). While the political apparatus of nations (e.g., their international relations, citizenship rules, their waging of war, their governmentality) is constructed as masculine, the nation/land itself is feminized, (re-)affirming masculinity through the need to protect the nation and territories. The need to defend the nation from conquest and control is similar to the way in which women, their bodies and sexualities, are conceptualized, 'protected', and deployed as symbols (e.g., of 'virtue' and 'honour') of the nation. Thus, men's abilities and desire to possess, protect, and fight for the 'nation' is similar to how they control and treat their women. Therefore, women's bodies have become a contested site for nationalist sentiments and an affirmation of masculinity whereby male domination and patriarchal control are inscribed onto women's bodies the same way that land is fought for and inscribed with nationalist meaning.

Nira Yuval-Davis and Floya Anthias have identified five ways that women are linked as actors to the state and to ethnic/national processes:

1 as biological reproducers;
2 as reproducers of boundaries of ethnic/national groups;
3 as transmitters of cultures and agents of ideological reproduction;
4 as signifiers of national/ethnic differences; and
5 as participants in national, economic and military struggles.

(1989: 7)

Yuval-Davis and Anthias sum up the intimate relationship between gender and nationalism this way: women produce the nation biologically, culturally, and symbolically. Therefore, in armed conflicts, families may keep girls away from schools in order to 'protect' their virtue and family 'honour' and so ensure the purity of cultural continuity, in addition to more obvious concerns around immediate physical safety.

Women's ordeals in conflict and war zones, as seen in Chapter 2, show how violence against women becomes privatized as colonial powers and patriarchal societies enforce collective control over women's bodies and sexualities, turning their bodies into an instrument of war against society as a whole. In their introduction to *What Women Do in Wartime*, Turshen and Twagiramariya stated that the military-minded West and the weak state structure in Africa were the primary contributors to civil war in Africa (Turshen and Twagiramariya 1998). Where does such a war leave women? Sexual abuse against women in Africa and elsewhere once again attests to the increase in women's vulnerability in conflict-ridden areas and confirms the failure of the international community to protect the rights of women.

In my effort to share with readers the role that militarization has played in weaponizing women's bodies and terrorizing women's lives, I borrow from some paradigmatic historical and feminist analyses of women and militarization (see Cooke 1988; Enloe 2000). Based on their work, I argue that the need of militaristic systems to insist on the femininity of women, and the consistent stress placed on separate roles for women during political conflict and in times of war, indicates that militaristic powers need women's bodies, their social roles and femininity, in order to empha- size and empower masculinity or to construct hyper-masculine façades, or both. Thus, women's bodies are not only 'border patrolling' the internal equations and interactions between patriarchal powers but also are used by colonizing powers to threaten to either feminize or hyper-masculinize social groups. The irony of such situations is that within the dynamic of the militarization of the body and the land, both feminine and masculine become coeval terms dependent on a binary opposition for definition.

By complicating and nuancing meanings from the concept of the 'absent' or 'absence' (unless they are made visible or hypervisible to serve the interest of the powerful), I will focus on women's own voices and ordeals. The multiplicity of women's voices in reaction against militarization – that is, primarily reacting to the weaponization of their bodies – will be reiterated in the next section, particularly as these voices formulate a legacy of women living in war zones.

SPEECH AND SILENCE AND THE POLITICS OF NAMING

Weaponization is a particular form of violence against women's experience. The following quotations exemplify some of the gendered uses of women's bodies as devices of offence or defence. Nawal from Ramallah said:

Do you know why my father is preventing me from working, although I have a degree in nursing, and we are in a bad economic situation? Because he doesn't want to show that he needs us, he wants to show our neighbour that he won't allow anybody to use or humiliate his daughters. He always says that his daughters are very precious to him and that he is the man, the breadwinner. We all feel very sorry for him. These days ... nothing is left for men to show their manhood, and we women became *il-munq'eth il-a'atham* [the great saviour], their only weapon.

Here we see a woman used as a weapon to defend kin masculinity. Similarly, this is what Manal had to say:

Even when I cried ... and it was very hard to see your house demolished and your memories buried beneath the surface ... He [her husband] prevented me from crying ... He screamed at me, but he used my tears to protect himself. He used my reactions to hide ... and my tears were his weapon against fear ... and loss. He left the place and went out ... not because he couldn't handle my crying ... but because he wanted to join me ... but used me to justify his fear of losing control. What can I say ... when he totally lost control ... I was the only power left. My tears and crying gave him some power of what was left of his manhood.

Fardos from Huwarah, a village beside Nablus, provides an example of the weaponization of women in which Israeli soldiers assault women's experiences, thereby weaponizing them:

Could you believe that they used the bride on the happiest day of her life to hurt us ... Samaher, the bride, our relative, was in her white bridal dress, trying to pass [a checkpoint] to [go to] her groom in Tal. They used her, while she was in her bridal dress, to humiliate her family, mainly the men that accompanied her. All she wanted was to take her belongings, some Palestinian embroidery she and her grandmother prepared for her wedding day, two pillows that her mother specially prepared for her, a set of plates and cups ... but the soldiers confiscated everything. Her father tried his best to talk to them – he spoke some Hebrew – because he used to work with them. But they laughed at him, pushed him to the ground and one of the soldiers shot the pillows *marjaleh* [literally, 'manly power', but here with the sense 'to show off' or 'to show one's manly power']. Her father ended up crying in a loud voice and said to her: '*Yaba Ruhi Lajozek ... abuki battal Zalami ... Abuki Mish Zalami ... ruhi Yaba Alla Ywafe'e'k'* ['Go to your husband, your father stopped being a man, your father is not a man']. We all cried with him, cried at our situation ... They weaponized themselves with the young girl's happiness, with women's most happy moment, to degrade us.

May's statement provides us with another form of weaponization whereby women's bodies are utilized so that men could cross a checkpoint:

> In the checkpoints when men are afraid of the reaction of the soldiers, they ask us the girls to go first and try to pass through the checkpoint. If they – the soldiers – allow us to pass, the men follow us, if not … we start arguing and creating a fuss … we talk to them, explain, then scream, argue, push them, sometimes we end up crying and other time we keep arguing. We, the girls and the women, are the one's that are *bil-wajha* [in the forefront]. After all the hardships they [the Israelis] placed on us, we became the only *silah* [weapon]. So, when my father refuses to leave the house in fear of being humiliated, I will be asked to get him his cigarettes, not my brother. When he needs something from the neighbours, I am the one to go. But when my father needs to feel his manhood, he turns against me and my mother. They all use me … they all *bitsalahou fiyii* [arm themselves] with me.

These recent examples must be compared to historical ones; the following concerns the Tantura Massacre of May 1948:

> Before our eyes, they took a group of men away and shot them all except for one. To him they said, 'Go tell the others what you saw'. In their search for money and gold, they even went through the swaddling clothes of our infants, and when [a] little girl tarried in taking off an earring, a woman soldier ripped it off, and the little one began to bleed. There my grandfather, Haj Mahmud Abu Hana, sent one of his daughters to find him a shroud in 'Ayn Ghazal or Ijzim, for he sensed that his hour had come. She couldn't find one in either place and returned empty-handed.
> (Pappe 2001: 8–9)

I cannot help but feel that in the midst of destruction, these words take the fragments and pieces and rubble of homes and families and lives destroyed and reconstruct from them not only habitable spaces wherein families can gather, meals can be cooked, children fed, but also *new meanings* with which to continue living. As I have contended in my work elsewhere and also in various sections of this book, the politics of silence and silencing in conflict areas presents us with a complex dynamic. I bring these voices to bear on our listening, in the hope that these voices speak to us not only through words but also through the silences and the silent meanings between the lines. For when Nawal, through such an economy of words, is able to deduce not only her father's immediate pain and his brittle honour (which she is capable of restoring by obliging his expectations), we also note that she leaves herself out; the self that defines her, with *its* needs and wants and desires, is silent, and somehow it seems to me that that silence speaks as well and as loudly as her embittered yet passionate speech. Thus silence, keeping silent or speaking through it, emerges as a political strategy – not just a result of oppression – for both men and women.

The use of women's lives, bodies, and sexualities as weapons both to fight the enemy and to protect one's own sense of declining power during times of war is hardly surprising. But what is critical and consequential for us to understand is the ways in which such use so precisely invades the private sphere as well. And the words of these women echo with the labour and efforts and emotions of protecting the sanctity of their inner spaces, and by that I do not only mean the bedrooms or the inner recesses of a home but also the bodies and lives of these women themselves. It does not appear accidental that Manal's voice and words begin by describing her demolished house and what the rubble has *buried*. For in some sense, her words enact yet another ritual burial – a burial of herself. For however momentary or prolonged, her grief has to be buried: she must stop her tears which want to flow; she must stop them in the face of the demolished house, the buried objects and lives, in the face of her husband's screams because he can do no more. In short, in the face of utter futility, Manal buries her needs and thus creates out of her understanding an inner space. And perhaps this is only my wishful projection, but I hope this space of her own creation allows her, during her darkest times, a place of retreat.

In keeping with the spirit of this book, and while talking about feminist praxis within a global context in our case study of women frontliners in conflict areas, I first try to shift the units of analysis away from the local, the regional, and the national to the transnational in an effort to trace similar contexts across the world. Second, I want to understand the dynamics of inequality through women's perceptions, however such dynamics may be expressed: through horror, outrage, tears or even the silence I spoke of above. Third, perhaps bringing the discussion to a much more material plane, I want to examine these transnational relations in terms of women's oppression through economic, political, ideological, and historical processes that include race, colonialism, capitalism, and sexism.

During political struggles, the fact that women are considered the 'cultural bearers', 'mothers of nations', 'daughters of the state', and 'keepers of the earth' (Lentin 1997) exacerbates the existing gender inequalities of war-torn societies. During wars, the social construction of gender allows men to posture as if they are in control of the political and public sphere while relegating women to the private sphere (see, for example, Loraine Dowler 1997, who speaks about a similar dynamic occurring in West Belfast, Northern Ireland). Politically conflicted contexts often provide a ground for 'hypermasculinity' whereby men are transformed into 'superheroes' who are 'void of any emotions such as empathy, sympathy and compassion' and women are expected to play the role of sustaining the struggle by empowering and elevating the representation of manhood in a way that suits the struggle (Dowler 1997). The Palestinian case shows that while women have played a crucial role in being the mothers of martyrs and the protectors of the motherland, women have also found ways to subvert the dominant order and accentuate their agency all the while in many cases publicly proclaiming their power. During the two Intifadas, Palestinian women, as with their counterparts in many other conflict-ridden areas, have managed to transgress prescribed roles while searching for new venues and spaces through which to subvert the construction and representation of gender (Shalhoub-Kevorkian 2005c). But the paramilitary powers in Palestinian society, the militarization of society in the Israeli case (Golan 1997), and the continuation of violent conflict have reinforced and perpetuated the stereotypical role of women as subordinate and subservient.

VIOLENCE AGINST WOMEN: PERVERSE STRATEGIES IN THE GENEALOGY OF WEAPONIZATION

There is no better illustration of the precarious position of women during political conflicts than in the commission of strategic and state-sanctioned rape, one of the most horrific deployments of bio-politics. Not only actual rape and sexual abuse but also the fear of these acts often makes individuals and families impose prohibitions on young girls and women; prohibitions against leaving the house and proceeding with their normal, daily activities. Due to such imposed limitations on their lives, many women in Palestine end up getting married early or are deprived of an education as a result of fear of sexual abuse (see Shalhoub-Kevorkian 1994, 2005b). The history of the Palestinian Nakba is replete with cases of rape and threats of rape, an issue that contributed to many Palestinians abandoning their lands and effects out of fear of the violation of their honour.

Although Lentin has noted that it is remarkable that until relatively recently, reports of widespread rapes of Palestinian women by Israeli soldiers were rare (2004), Palestinian and Jewish historians have discussed many cases. In November 2003, the Israeli newspaper *Ha'aretz* reported a horrific case during the 1948–9 'war of independence' in which a troop of male soldiers gang-raped a young Bedouin girl before killing her and burying her in the sand (Lavie and Gorali 2003). Benny Morris, the 'new historian' turned apologist for the Israeli racial state, admitted that during the 1948 war, alongside the destruction of over 400 Palestinian villages and the expulsion of their inhabitants and alongside several well-documented massacres, rapes were a common occurrence. Most rapes ended with murder: 'Because neither the raped nor the rapists like to report these cases, we have to assume that the dozen reported rape cases are not the whole story, rather the tip of the iceberg' (Shavit 2004). Israelis silenced knowledge of these and later rapes because, according to 1948 veteran and peace activist Uri Avneri, rapes supposedly 'did not happen for *racist* reasons. Having sex [sic] with an Arab woman was considered *undignified*' (Lavie and Gorali 2003, emphasis added).

The feminist genealogical approach of this project attends to the way women's bodies and sexualities are abused when women are raped, imprisoned, forced to undress, and bodily humiliated, but also examines how so often women are unable to disclose such abuse. The collusion between the Israeli occupation and the Palestinian patriarchy reinforces masculinity and exploits traditional views of the importance of the 'virginity' and 'family honour' of girls, all the while silencing women and preventing them from disclosing their abuse. In addition to the voices of women living in war and conflict zones and their own individual and collective genealogies, I would like to consider women's political praxis as it is processed, utilized, and in some cases institutionalized within conflict zones. The use of women's bodies, sexualities, and lives as a weapon by hegemonic powers in political struggles, what I have called 'the weaponization of women's bodies and lives', assists us in marking the hidden weapons of wars and political conflicts, in particular the accelerated processes of gender oppression that re-colonization and occupation makes possible. My aim here is to bring the many voices of frontliners from the periphery to the centre of our analyses.

The sexism, racism, and classism inherent in many traditional forms of political and historical analyses often elides the kinds of gender discriminations that lead to the weaponization of women's bodies during political struggles. Bringing the voices of the women themselves to the foreground provides us with a better understanding of the historicity of the transnational, national, and domestic deployment of sexual politics.

By attempting to trace the genealogy of weaponization, I want to unearth the legacies embodied in the history of women's domination, commodification, and objectification as juxtaposed with the legacies of women's resistance, resilience, and agency. The use of women's bodies and lives and the racist/sexist construction of sexual politics during times of war is not a static tableau, but rather a continuously changing dynamic that is deeply affected by power politics, including hetero-patriarchal restraints placed on women's lives. Re-thinking history and historicity in a sexual politics that fights back within such a context aims at privileging the humanity and agency of the victimized, in this case primarily women's frontline activities. Thus, this approach hopes to make visible and intelligible the agency of women in conflict zones as we account for some of the ways in which female bodies and lives have been used to critique and resist as well as unavoidably reinforce hetero-patriarchal powers.

However, using the genealogy of weaponization to analyse women's experiences during political conflicts and war can be both problematic and liberatory. As Urvashi Butalia has stated:

> There is a difficulty that is attached to any attempt to document situations of conflict from within [i.e., from within that conflict]. For those caught in the maelstrom of the conflict the business of living is much more important than that of writing. It is for this reason that, despite many attempts, we have been unable to include these voices.
>
> (Butalia 2002: xxiii)

In an interview, Butalia related the fact that he and his brother killed seventeen members of their families – mostly women – in order to guard the purity of their religion and culture. It was his fear that women might be raped and possibly impregnated that made him kill them, as if their lives were disposable (Butalia 1997).

In an article called 'This Happened in Kashmir', Krishna Mehta shares the following testimony with us:

> we were asked to go out for a while; the raiders led us out of the room, along the river bank to Domel bridge. What I saw there I shall never forget. Before that I had only heard about the women who had jumped into the river; for the first time I saw the tragic spectacle of humanity surrendering life so willingly ... some women still stood at the edge of the bank with forlorn looks on their faces and a few others knee-deep in water. They threw their children first into the rushing river and seemed impervious to the shrieks and yells of their own infants. Life refuses annihilation. As their children floated down the stream their heads

came up, once or twice … The mothers looked on vacantly in front of them. Prolonged suffering had wiped out all colour and emotion from their faces. Then they jumped in themselves and it was all over in the twinkling of an eye.

(Mehta 2002: 23–4)

The abuse of women's bodies, sexualities, and gender roles is also apparent in Armenian history. As Adalian (1991) explains, the treatment of women differed from the treatment of men. Women lost their lives in transit and, before their tragic deaths, many suffered unspeakable cruelties and sexual abuse. The most common method of suicide chosen by these women was by drowning themselves in the Euphrates River. In fact, this practice was common enough that several survivors related the words of a song which was sung in the orphanages that included the lyrics: 'Virgin girls holding each other's hands, threw themselves into the River Euphrates' (Miller and Miller 1999: 103). Thus, out of fear of gender-related abuse, primarily in the form of sexual abuse, women often make the very tragic moral choice of killing themselves or their children, or both. Miller and Miller conclude by saying: 'Suicide is always morally ambiguous, but the extenuating circumstance and the deportees' complex motives preclude indiscriminate condemnation of the choices that they made' (1999: 105). The use of women's bodies and lives as weapons by women themselves in conflict zones, although infinitely complex in multiple ways, provides some women with new means for resisting oppression.

One might argue that suicide is not a survival strategy, but as one observer has stated: 'the solution of suicide, when once discovered, seemed to all to be the most efficacious' (Mehta 2002: 24). Armenian women's need to prevent any violation of their sexuality and integrity and the requirements of gender roles made many women take very drastic decisions to safeguard their ethnic group and/or nation. The story of Shaheg, an Armenian woman, is only one of many:

One of the leading women named Shaheg, perceiving that the Turks and Kurds were getting ready to seize and ravish them, called the other women and said: 'Sisters, our husband's are killed, and you know what is in store for us and our children. Don't let us fall into the hands of those savage beasts, we have to die anyway, and can die easier, and without being defiled first, and perhaps tortured. Let us go to the precipice and jump off'. So saying, she took her baby on her arm, ran to the rock, and threw herself over. The others followed her.

(Gaidzakian 1889: 224)

Scenes of Ottoman soldiers wrenching babies from their mother's arms, cutting their throats while the mothers were pleading, boiling them in kettles and forcing their mothers to eat the flesh, cutting open women about to become mothers, and pouring boiling water on them are constantly mentioned in literature regarding the Armenian massacre. Gaidzakian, in a discussion of Armenian history between 1894–6, explained how 'The handsomest girls and young matrons were not murdered, but worse; each one was kept as a spoil of some Turk or Kurd, who carried her to his house and made a slave and concubine of her'. Thus, gender differences during the Armenian massacre and genocide was also apparent, for as Sanasarian stated, many girls and young women were taken away from their families to serve as slave-brides (1989: 449–61).

The use of women's bodies, sexuality, and roles as mothers and girls to humiliate the ethnic group to which they belong is apparent in many historical events. Women were not only used by men; Goldblatt and Meintjes, in a discussion of the South African case, point out that women also participated in violence or practiced institutionalized violence, inflicted torture on imprisoned women, organized prostitution for men, pumped water into women's fallopian tubes, and applied electric shocks to women's nipples. As the authors concluded, women's views regarding violence against women is not monolithic, and many women supported apartheid, racism, and violence believing that these were necessary means of maintaining order (1998). Similar examples are reflected in the case of Abu Ghraib, where women used their power in order to physically and sexually humiliate men. By doing so, they emasculated male enemies by trying to feminize them while turning themselves (as women) into the masculine other – and turning themselves as American soldiers into hyper-masculine power holders.

The need to emasculate the 'other' was also apparent in the former Yugoslavia. Rada Boric quoted a Zagreb journalist and leading feminist who told him: 'A raped Croatian woman is a raped Croatia' (1997: 39). Here was a mystic unity of women and the country identified through her body. Once again, the nation's identity is established through women's bodies. The consequence of equating the raped woman with the 'dishonoured' country is that all members of the 'enemy' army are viewed as rapists – not just those who started the war, the politicians, the generals, and the exponents of systematic rape in aid of 'ethnic cleansing'. 'There are no individual culprits, but the whole nation, including its women, is culpable' (1997: 39). Thus, the construction of femininity and masculinity combined with the cultural codes of honour and shame in many instances contributed to the alienation from society of women who were raped. When Bangladeshi men were incapable of 'protecting' their womenfolk from being raped by Pakistani soldiers, the men found ways to erase the memories of their failure to 'protect' and to ensure that the 'impure' women remained silent and invisible. The perception of raped women as 'contaminated' by the enemy is also found in Rwanda, Bosnia, Bangladesh, the Sudan, and in other cases. With these cases we again see women's bodies constructed as a gendered arena that sets boundaries of purity, nation, identity, honour, and so on. In the conflict in the Sudan, 'Men's ownership of women's sexual conduct positions women as the first property to be attacked and violated ... Violations of other property may be rectified, but the damage to the owner caused by the violation of "his women" cannot be' (Abdel-Halim 1998: 91).

A historical review of rape, in different locations, among different ethnic groups, and in different historical periods shows that it has been committed for various reasons, including boosting the soldiers' morale, to keep combatants in a fighting mood, to increase hatred of the enemy, and to increase men's sense of entitlement and superiority. Hague Euan deconstructed how masculinity provided the basis for genocidal rape in Bosnia-Herzegovina, stating: 'all rape is an experience of power, domination, degradation, and humiliation, wherever, whenever, and whoever commits the crime. Whether raping a woman, girl, boy or man, the rapist takes a position of power, subjugating the victim' (1997: 50). All these reasons and others transform politically conflicted areas and war zones into legitimized spaces of rape. The political and social license to rape, gang rape, and to commit sexual abuse and torture terrorizes both women and their societies, forcing people to flee their homes and to leave their families. It destroys their potential for reproduction and interrupts the ethnic continuity of communities (for a broader discussion, see the various articles collected by Turshen and Twagiramariya 1998). Treating women's bodies and perceiving their roles as reproductive machines was also evident recently in Darfur (in the Sudan), just as in other contexts. The political motive of the violence against women in the context of war and violent conflict can therefore never be divorced from gender or criminological and victimological analysis.

Women's bodies, their way of dressing, and their very lives were used by American power holders and politicians during the war on Afghanistan and the invasion of Iraq. Afghani women's wearing of the veil was used by the hegemonic imperialistic power as a *causus belli* in order to 'liberate' them from the internal oppression of the Taliban, while 'Iraqi oppression', including the rape of Iraqi women by Saddam Hussein and his supporters, was also used as legitimation for the attack on the Iraqi nation. The use of women's bodies in the crimes of rape during political conflicts, the need to raise the issue of such crimes as required by the moment yet to be silent about them when 'politically appropriate', is embedded in the social construction of masculinity or in the threat of losing such masculine power in a hyper-masculinized context of war, or both. The Guatemalan case provides us with a good example that highlights for us the way state-sponsored rape was silenced during the recent civil war. Julie Hastings, in her ethnographic research on Guatemala, challenges the claim that it is only the local culture that silences survivors of state-sponsored rape, arguing instead that it is national and international forces that depoliticize rape and silence rape survivors (2002).

A woman's body becomes an object that is rendered into a landscape for men to conquer. Without disregarding the obvious implications of the rape of women as a weapon of war, I am suggesting the alignment between the pre-existing notion of women's bodies as both the symbolic and privileged sites of articulation of the nation as well as the site and the landscape upon which national conflicts are played out. As Kaplan and Grewal succinctly state in their discussion of rape in Kashmir: 'the discourse of rape is acceptable to nationalist discourse only when the perpetrator is an outsider' (Grewal and Kaplan 1994: 502). Given Grewal's observation, the particular suppression of knowledge of instances of rape or sexual abuse by internal patriarchal powers is easily understood, since such disclosure both symbolically and literally disrupts the borders created in a conflict both by the invader and the invader's victims.

Additionally, the control over women's bodies and the violence enacted upon them through rape and other war crimes also targets women's reproductive abilities and their perceived power as the link of 'continuity' for an ethnic or religious group. Flora Anthias and Nira Yuval-Davis have discussed population control programmes that targeted women. For example, they have shown how Nazi ideology, which rested upon the so-called 'superiority' of the 'Aryan' race, targeted the 'inferior Jewish' Other by sterilizing women and murdering men and women (1992). The Chinese government in Tibet has also been engaged in a mass sterilization campaign against Tibetan women. The Jewish Israeli situation has shown not only that the state's population policy militarized the Jewish woman's womb but also that Jewish women have not been passive recipients of such 'biological destinies'; rather, they have been used within the dynamics of eugenic reproductive policies aimed at combating the enemy (Sered 2000).

The case of the Armenian women who immolated themselves and their children, fearing rape and torture, the case of the Kashmiri women who committed suicide to prevent further atrocities, the case of raped women in the former Yugoslavia, of women under Nazi occupation, in Rwanda, the Sudan, and the case of the Korean comfort women are only some examples of the reinforcement of the construction of women as boundary markers and as bearers of a nation's construction of its own cultural purity and the corresponding engendering of the notion of 'family honour'. Thus, without a bio-politicizing of our analyses of the use of women's bodies with all the attending complications that such an analysis entails, one cannot comprehend the political efficacy of crimes against women or investigate the representation of women's bodies and lives in such politically intense contexts. I believe that one cannot attend to women's testimonies about war, hegemonic violence, gender legacies, and agency without also bringing women's bodies into the discussions. Bringing women's bodies and lives into analysis via their voices and testimonials aims first to borrow meanings from a political identification of women's shared history of repression. The centrality of women's voices in the analyses also shows the centrality of women's own repressions of their political objectives and agency as well as the freedom from such repressions when women resist being a tool of internal or external hetero-masculine nationalist narratives, narratives which are particularly forwarded during times of war or crisis. The question remains: how do we restore women's history without doing further injustice, or victimizing them yet again, by submerging the multiplicity of their voices into a false univocality? How do we bring women's voices to the forefront in a humane and just manner?

Literature on violence against women (VAW) has articulated certain common principles that have sometimes resulted in policies that take an optimistic view regarding the amelioration of such violence. However, despite innovations in analysing and reacting to issues of women and violence (Strang and Braithwait 2002), recent debates continue to show that as we harness new possibilities to address VAW, we should take into account – among other issues – the socio-political and religious contexts of a specific society during a specific period of time in which the violence occurs (Dadeghi-Fassaei and Kendall 2002). It is by no means a surprise that societal customs, rituals, regulations, and laws are often designed to be used as a tool to control women's sexuality and so preserve the existing divisions of power in gendered, socio-political relations. Thus, in studying and working with oppressed groups, the challenge is not only to analyse the structures of oppression but also to take into account the political and social contexts that activate, encourage, and mediate those oppressions.

Using as a focus the phenomenon of imposed virginity testing (IVT) and femicide – both of which are commonly used in Palestine to 'investigate' crimes of sexual abuse – as a focus, one could examine the interaction between medical and juridical discourses within the specific political legacies and culture of the region in order to study the power dynamics at play that often further oppress the victims of abuse. The issue of 'perception' that I am raising is an important one, since our examination reveals that both formal and informal systems of thought come into play in the investigation of sexual abuse. It bears repeating, as I have stated in my previous work on this topic, that even the insistence on the forensic in the investigation of cases of sexual abuse is laden with ideological, political, and cultural expectations that obtain within that ideology. In this regard, my general objection to relativizing (and thereby dismissing) the problem of sexual abuse as apolitical in the OPT and in other Middle Eastern countries through the invocation of 'culture' or 'tradition' becomes even more acute. I am arguing that the cultural specificities of sexual abuse – while they must be accounted for – *do not* supersede the political. By understanding interconnections between the cultural, the traditional, and the political, I intend to examine how agents of social control react to sexual abuse in the context of being Palestinian, bearing in mind that since 1948 Palestinians have been struggling against the Israeli occupation and the ways in which such ongoing political struggle often paralyzes social institutions and adversely affects the legal apparatus (Bisharat 1989), often at the expense of women, resulting in further oppressions (Shalhoub-Kevorkian 2003a). My own research indicates that this has been the inevitable and repeated pattern due to the continuation of occupation and *despite* the arrival of the Palestinian Authority within the OPT following the Oslo Agreement (Shalhoub-Kevorkian 2003a, 2002; see also Abdo 1999).

Ostensibly, IVT is a contemporary medical and legal practice that aims at the provision of an 'expert's' medical testimony based on 'evidence' for the resolution of sexual assault cases, and/or when the patriarchal structures and customs in place dictate the use of the test. As we shall see, the results of such an examination, as shown in my previous studies, are not just a matter of clinical concern, but are in some cases a matter of life or death (Shalhoub-Kevorkian 2002, 2003a, 2004a). These are procedures that turn women's bodies into a new weapon that define and verify the 'culturally' sanctioned borders between what is or is not reputable behaviour in the women's sphere. The phenomenon of the IVT necessitates that we study the culture, the politics, and the systems of power (including the legal and medical systems) that are brought to bear on women who claim to have been sexually abused. It is critically important to think of the IVT process as 'phenomenon' which by definition suggests a nexus of various factors that come into play, stressing and fracturing the cultural/political foundations of the region in various ways.

Ilkkaracan has argued that 'the practices leading to violations of women's sexual rights in the Middle East and the Maghreb are not the result of an Islamic vision of sexuality, but a combination of political, economic, and social inequalities through the ages' (Ilkkaracan 2002: 754). Expanding upon Ilkkaracan's statement, I argue that practices leading to the violation of women's sexual rights in the Palestinian context, as in many other conflict or war zones in the world, originate in more than just political, economic, and social inequalities and can be traced beyond the specificities of 'culture' to more genealogically verifiable gender-related insecurities, colonial crimes, and national traumas. In addition, the nationalist movements and ideologies that accompanied the foundations of the nation-states in Middle Eastern countries pose additional contradictions and challenges to the dynamic nexus of perceiving and conceptualizing 'women and nations', and these internal tensions have had their effect on the Palestinian national and women's movements (see Sayigh 1994; Peteet 1991). On the one hand – as shown in Chapter 3 on feminism and nationalism – national needs and challenges promoted women's participation in political life and thus required a change in their gender roles. The Palestinian national movement, as Sayigh states,

> has encompassed varied and contradictory discourses on women and gender, attempting to steer a middle course between active and symbolic forms of mobilizing women. For women, national mobilization began almost with the beginning of British occupation, was relatively self-initiated, and has always contained elements of indigenous feminism, however suppressed by nationalism's priority.
>
> (1998: 167)

Yet, from another perspective, women were and are considered the standard bearers of the nation, nothing short of national icons. This seemingly symbolic turn in fact led to the emergence of new, materially viable strategies to control women.

A considerable body of existing literature has convincingly shown that in the Middle East, North Africa, and the Muslim world more generally, women's sexuality is perceived as something that must be controlled by both the family and tribal and formal state apparatuses (Mernissi 1982; Abu-Odeh 2000; Ilkkaracan 2000). The concept of 'virginity' is a patriarchal construction that encourages the keeping of younger women under male control; the constructions of women's 'virginity', 'chastity', and 'purity' claims to 'preserve family honour' and reputation in the period of life before women get married. Thus, breaking these patriarchally sanctioned conventions entails a masculinized punitive reaction, be it IVT, imposed marriage to a rapist, institutionalization, incarceration, and even the extreme commission of a sanctioned femicidal 'crime of honour', what I have elsewhere termed femicide (Shalhoub-Kevorkian 2002, 2003a).

To follow up with our intent to utilize a genealogy of weaponization, there is a corresponding need to trace the historical roots of IVT. Therefore, it is important to bring out the reasons behind the rise of the phenomenon in the Palestinian context. The Palestinian Nakba in 1948 greatly agitated the nexus of issues that allowed for the conceptualization of 'family honour'. The Zionists employed various methods to facilitate the eviction and displacement of Palestinian populations, including sustained abuse of women's bodies that in turn caused symbolic attachments to those bodies, making them iconic avatars of purity and 'family honour'. Researchers have indicated that women's sexuality and bodies were specific targets used to expedite the Palestinian expulsion in 1948 (Nazzai 1978; Sayigh 1981; Pappe 2007). Writing on the Tantura and Qula massacres, Pappe (2001), and Slyomovics (2007) have documented the use of different forms of sexual harassment, molestation, and rape. The testimony of my mother, who left Palestine in 1948 with her three children, indicates that the stories of rape and the sexual abuse of women in Haifa City actually caused families to quickly abandon their villages and towns. As she stated: 'The invocation of the proverb al-ard qabl al-'ird ['land before honour'] was meant to encourage people to stay rather than to leave, despite the stories of sexual abuse that were spread'. Thus, tracing the signification of virginity and the preservation of one's honour in Palestine – indeed, *as* the preservation of one's honour – through to the contemporary period in Palestine shows that the contemporary meaning is overdetermined as compared to the earlier Israeli colonial period; the meaning of virginity is now more than merely the patriarchal or cultural and includes larger nationalistic, historical, political, and economic referents. Further, we must not get caught up in the apparent anachronism in my mother's statement that the slogan was used in 1948, contrary to Hasso's assertion that it only became popular after 1967 (see 2000: 495). My mother's statement *epitomizes* her experience (see on this Fogelson 1989), and indeed I argue the experience of many women in 1948 and after; assuming Hasso is correct, any attempt to disqualify her statement from the historical record would be to miss her point entirely and at the base level would be to *compound the violence that was done to her experience.* Rosemary Sayigh, in discussing how gender norms became nationalized, has said the following: 'As to honour, I say that if our Palestinian society has managed to preserve its unity, it was on this basis: Migration and refugee status usually lead to unemployment, and to girls going out to seek work, whatever it may be. As for us – and I consider this something to be proud of – the Palestinian family has preserved its tradition in spite of social liberation' (Sayigh 1998: 169). We must also see Sayigh's statement as applicable to my mother's voice.

Sayigh foregrounds how displacement and exile created social, gender, and economic insecurity in the context of constant political hardship. These hardships jeopardized the material and metaphoric aspects of the sexual culture and rituals of Palestinians on account of the attacks on the actual physical body of the citizens, particularly women, in addition to attacks on the national body contextually engaged in political struggle. The fact that Palestinian families used traditional means of preventing sexual abuse against women (such as limitations on women's mobility) in turn allowed for and indeed resulted in nationalized forms of greater patriarchal control. Today, the phenomenon of imposed virginity testing is an artefactual residue of this history and is much more than a medical or juridical procedure initiated in the quest for justice after the commission of a sex crime; the very application of IVT is *itself a crime.*

Concepts of virginity and perceptions of women's sexuality thus exceed patriarchal or familial power over women's bodies and sexualities and come to occupy a much larger social sphere wherein 'virginity' becomes another instance of the woman's body weaponized and re-shaped into a tool of political control. What I am emphasizing here is that any discussion of women's 'virginity' and 'honour' in the Palestinian context cannot be divorced from historical, political, social, and economic contexts that mediate gender relations and sexual rights, as is the case in any society; patriarchal notions are not a phenomenon exclusive to what has often been invoked with regards to this issue as 'Palestinian culture' with all the Orientalist implications of such statements. Given all this, it is hardly surprising that the complex and intricate connections between the need to control women's bodies and women's sexuality through politically sanctioned medical, legal, and medico-legal practices has yet to be properly and fully explored.

Women's sexuality has been historically conceptualized as dangerous, evil, polluting, and nothing short of an omnipotent and boundless energy (Mernissi 1975; El-Sadaawi 1980). Our discussions and the ongoing process of social activism regarding the transformation of the status of women in Arab countries shows once again that despite the willingness of Arab and Palestinian human rights and women's organizations to bring about change, the fear of being 'Westernized' through values connected to the oppressive colonial legacy is still very pervasive. We can approach our understanding of the body in culture by conceptualizing the connection as an initial oppositional binary between the sanctioned conformities of public culture versus the private female body and the ways in which the legal and medical apparatus of the quasi-state attempts to nullify that opposition. Once again, the practice of the IVT is a particularly efficacious site to examine this struggle.

Just as gender-biased social customs and rituals are often translated into laws and regulations that are used as political tools to control women's sexuality, modern medicine and its applications are now also being used as methods of control (Nandy 1998). In Palestine, political unrest led to the transformation of 'traditional' systems of social control into *weapons* of political anti-colonial struggles. This unrest also affected the Palestinian legal system, turning it into a hybrid of Ottoman, British, and French colonial laws, Jordanian and Egyptian laws, and Israeli military orders, all in addition to Islamic religious tenets. The Palestinian catastrophe in 1948 followed by the Israeli Occupation that was resisted by various means has effectively militarized the environment for Palestinian women (Shalhoub-Kevorkian 2003a). Palestinian women's virginity and sexuality became hostage to a legal, medical, social, personal, and systematic power which rendered them more unequal than they had been in the past and with the prospect of violence in their daily lives (Shalhoub-Kevorkian 2003a; Daly 1994).

In discussing the sexual harassment and abuse of Palestinian women, the related use of the virginity test, and any corresponding applications of the juridical, one needs to examine political–legal apparatuses and power as well as what I am calling the 'parallel' legal system which was constructed to address the needs of a stateless society that required some kind of social regulatory control aside from colonialist law. The parallel legal system is manifested through circuits of power that constitute the tribal – such as the extended family system, the religious system, and prevailing social customs and sanctions that are used to ensure social stability and security. This is a system found primarily in patriarchal societies (Wing 1994). The parallel legal system has its own written and unwritten laws and codes, its own hierarchy of forums, and is practiced by specialized males (and some women) holding privileges of class and social status within a context of occupation and national resistance to foreign invasion (Institute of Law, Birzeit University 2006).

The historical role of the tribal system has been continuously adjusted and adjudicated within the historical context of occupations by the Ottomans, British, Jordanians, Egyptians, and Israelis. These occupations have resulted in greater prominence being given to tribal laws and have specifically served to aggravate issues of gender, sexual politics, and sexual abuse. It also affected the concept of 'privacy' and the ways in which one demarcates a private realm; all these became part of the tribal, *hamula* (extended family), and kinship systems. Colonizing powers manipulated tribal and kinship systems by allowing them compartmentalized power over their domestic private spaces, thereby transforming women's lives into a site of control. This historical legacy, which gave rise to tribal and familial controls, continues to deeply affect women's socio-political and cultural roles. Over time, inflexible and binding rules were created to control female sexuality, mobility, and indeed the ways in which a woman would come to conceptualize her future. Femicide and the imposition of virginity testing in the Palestinian context was transformed from a traditional method of social control to a weaponization of the woman's body to soothe the psychic and material fears of the emasculated and colonized male (Shalhoub-Kevorkian 1999a, 1999b, 2003a). There is perhaps some bitter irony to be found in the fact that artefactual residuals or survivals from a prior colonial legacy mutate to newer forms of oppression under continuing colonial control. Correspondingly, laws and the juridical system in Palestine have been deeply affected by imperialist and colonial policies. In fact, the juridical arena is one of the main areas where colonial strategies have most clearly infiltrated native culture and left their mark without much resistance.

However, criminal laws regarding sexual abuse in Arab countries in general and Palestine in particular, despite the colonialist legacy and political unrest, are undergoing a process of transformation. Yet the reluctance to criminalize certain acts – such as marital rape, the giving of exemptions or reduced sentences for so called 'crimes of honour', the practice of de-criminalizing rapists when they 'accept' the decision that they must marry their victims, and the continual privileging of testimony by men in such cases over the statements or claims of women – still makes socially sanctioned injustice legally acceptable (Wing 1994). The tendency to de-criminalize some acts while omitting others from the scope of the law has enabled further societal control of women's bodies and also furthered the ability of those in power as a result of colonial legacies to define what 'appropriate sexual behaviour' is – most notably for only one segment of the population.

Not surprisingly, for Palestinians the ongoing military occupation and the lack of trust in the formal Israeli military system have enhanced the role of the existing tribal system which is seen as an internal power that resists occupation (see Bisharat 1989). Customarily, the tribal system has handled land and social disputes as well as the mediation and conciliation of sexual abuse cases and 'honour'-related issues. The power of *urf*, or 'customary law' (that is, any type of non-legislative law in a tribal society), dates back to pre-Ottoman times but is still used by Palestinians to resolve conflicts outside the formal civil courts, particularly with respect to the rights of women, and so is derived from the patriarchal system in which women's roles were limited to the private sphere of the family and her principal responsibility therein of nurturing and protecting her family honour and reputation (Wing 1994).

In 1993, after the signing of the Oslo Agreement, the Palestinian Authority came to the West Bank and Gaza and began organizing its forces so as to administer and control the legal system. This development has affected the dynamics of power between the formal system of law and order and the informal, parallel tribal legal system (see Wing 1994). No studies to date have discussed the connection between the two systems of law enforcement and how the existence of both has affected their mutual evolutions. It is fair to say that while the newly established Palestinian National Authority (PNA) legal system was busy organizing and empowering itself during a period of state formation, it preferred to leave the so-called 'women issues' – the personal, the familial – in the hands of the informal tribal system to which such matters had always been historically allocated. Since the process of transforming power from the tribal to the formal legal system was not an easy transition for the tribal (*hamula*) heads and other notables within it, the Palestinian Authority was willing to give up or share part of its power with informal social control agents. The process of negotiation is clearly revealed in President Arafat's appointment of tribal notables as official advisors to the newly established Palestinian Authority (see Abdo 1999). Although both systems have worked hand-in-hand to promote social stability, their co-operation with regards to gender related issues, such as the sexual abuse of women, discriminates against women and further oppresses them (Shalhoub-Kevorkian 2000). Moreover, the resulting judicial system became a patchwork of secular, Islamic, Ottoman, and tribal provisions that lacks harmony or consistency (Al-Rais 2000; Dara'awi and Zhaika 2000), a condition that is clearly apparent when this system deals with the abuse of children and women while turning the rule *of* law into rule *by* law.

The transformation of women's bodies into a site of resistance, a site that simultaneously also requires protection, is also evidenced in the way virginity and female sexuality has been conceptualized and deployed, as I have been arguing in this section. Historically, developing a system of control over the politics of sexuality and 'virginity' and over women's sexualities and sexual rights has been a matter of course. Women's bodies were weaponized and disciplined within fundamentalist prescriptions as repositories of sin as well as of purity and a culturally sanctioned morality. The control over women's bodies has always been reflective of the power struggle between men and women via the medium of the family (not always at the initiative of women), religion, legal systems, and through other social 'experts' and institutions. Women's bodies became the location of conflicts between those in power, regardless of whether that power was manifested and expressed in economic, ideological, or patriarchal terms. This power struggle and the ongoing political violence have turned women's bodies and sexualities into a new site for both political disempowerment and empowerment. Both militaristic and patriarchal power holders obtained and claimed their power through narratives which constructed them as protectors, saviours, social and economic supporters, and so on. In so doing, they created new 'objective' mechanisms of control through 'scientific' and 'legalized' methods such as imposed virginity testing, 'honour crimes', and so forth.

CONCLUSION: OVER MY DEAD BODY

In looking at women frontliners in conflict zones, we learn that agency and victimization are interchangeable, for within women's victimization the conceptual parameters of agency are also clearly present. And women's bodies, emotions, tears, education, time, acts, marriages, and love lives can all potentially become sites of resistance. Thus, power mixed with powerlessness and moments of resistance cannot be separated into discrete analytic elements that render a site of helplessness. The only totality that remains harsh and apparent is the occupation and the oppression of the occupier.

The question remains: what should women do during times of violence? What are the best 'moral' or political responses? Personally, I listen to the voices of Palestinian women and see how questions of morality and ethics become troubling almost to the point where they cannot obtain as valid. How can one formulate 'rational' narratives and hypotheses, or propose 'rational solutions', when rationality died a long time ago for these women? The use of women's words, tears, bodies, and spaces to heal the wounds of an emasculated manhood was not comprehensible to me until I heard Manal's voice – her requiem to her house and her memories, but at the same time her construction of new insights and visions. Her testimony transmits to us a responsibility to protect and preserve her role as a frontliner.

While thinking about the narratives in this chapter, I realized the need to look with a disorienting vision of the present, to raise the compelling and profound and surprising insights into the complexity of women's relation to the historicized present that necessarily succumbs to gendered and infinitely complex spaces. To understand what women's voices are saying, we must explore certain questions: what are we made to witness, to see and understand? Are we looking at the reproduction of events? The discrete power of words alone? The philosophical arguments endemic to such a complex network of issues? Women's creativity? The ability of women to engage, despite the continuous disengagements of their daily lives? The truth? The capacity to transform pain and loss into power? One thing is clear to me. Such questions have given me the chance to witness trauma, to observe the way it was constructed, to record it, remember it, and perhaps eventually, to formulate from these voices productive theories concerning the violence perpetrated upon these women with the goal of gender emancipation, without which human freedom is not possible.

Listening to the voices of Palestinian women in my clinical interventions as well as while I was conducting my studies, I came to the realization that women *always already* knew how they were used as weapons – not only to fight the other but also as boundary markers. They understood that they were being used as the 'border' of a space that is occupied and that has no definitive or recognized borders, that they were being used as a weapon for their community when the community had lost almost every weapon with which to survive – used as a site of struggle, a space of resistance.

To prevent further violence against women, it is necessary to look beyond the impact of the Intifada on women, and so to look at the complexity of the intersection between power and powerlessness, between oppression or occupation and liberty, between shock, trauma, and paralysis, but also to include agency. Contexts of war and political violence leave women with one and only one goal; as one woman put it in my presence: 'How can I return the colour to the world?'

This chapter has shown the ways in which the politics of sexuality entered the political, the socio-cultural, the physical, and the psychological body. As Sayigh has stated, 'History surely affects narration of the female self, repressing or liberating the expression of gender-specificity and sexuality, as well as influencing the way women reflect and appropriate gender norms, rebelling against some while speaking for others' (1998: 182). The voices heard in this chapter were voices of women suffering from sexual abuse in Armenia, Darfur, Bosnia, and elsewhere in addition to voices of Palestinian women documented during the Nakba and during the second Palestinian Intifada. In the latter case, women's critique of the use/abuse of their bodies and sexuality were temporally inflected with the collective political values of the Intifada, a collective struggle that was more tolerant of bodily oppression directed from within and towards the domestic sphere. The question remains whether the bio-politicization of both women's bodies and rights will allow for the promotion of women's rights and transform them to meet women's feminist goals and national aims. As Sabbagh noted in *Palestinian Women of the West Bank and Gaza*, the consistent attack of the globalized capitalist media further simplifies the very complicated conflict over the female body in the midst of crisis and jeopardizes women's abilities for transformation (1998).

In terms of theory, one should first remember that the examination of crimes against women cannot be divorced from the larger political and cultural contexts within which such crimes are embedded. Thus, narrowing the analyses of crimes that are related to the weaponization of women's bodies to merely victimological, criminological, legal, evidentiary, medical, or individual/psychological dimensions strips away the larger contexts of oppression and domination in which such abuse occurs. The intersections and interconnections between women's rights as circumscribed and reflected in the bio-politics endemic to military occupation and the local, military, or international policies that are often engendered by such occupation urgently calls for the posing of more challenging inquiries. Scholarship and research in this case needs to grasp the nettle that weapons of wars are gendered and sexualized and that crimes, medicine, law, and militarization are integrally connected – and therefore these sites must be incorporated within our critique as sites of struggle.

This chapter has shown how national history has entered the most private sphere of the domestic domain, the realms of bodily security and sexuality, to bring about the weaponization of women's bodies and consequently their lives. These strategies of weaponization have been engendered by military occupation and through other political power holders both from outside and within the women's own social structure (for more detail, see the essays in Sabbagh 1998). The voices of Rania, Suraida, Khulood, and others attest to the fact that one cannot see the internal Palestinian reality without looking at the force and power responsible for women's ordeals. I bring forward these voices here to escort us in our efforts to look closely at the way women's bodies, lives, and destinies are part of the warfare, part of the battlefield – not only the local Israeli–Palestinian struggle but also the one in the international arena as well. We must trace the effects of military power (both hidden and in plain sight) that is used to oppress and dominate, that infiltrate both body politics and the actual physical body of Palestinian individuals, most particularly Palestinian women. I therefore argue that in the Occupied Palestinian Territories, as in many other militarized areas, every act is affected by, is dependent on, and is mobilized by militaristic values. The militarization of both the private and public space increases the vulnerability of both men and women and further entrenches and emboldens the patriarchy.

The intricate nature of the issues at hand requires me to keep refining the ways in which I reflect on the complexity of what I have called the weaponization of women's bodies. In some instances, as I listened to these women, I tried to embrace them in an acknowledging exchange and silent understanding of women's inherent subalternity while taking account of the individual and multiple epistemologies expressed through their voices. At other times, I tried to understand the ways in which they negotiate their status within the structures of oppression and how they deal with the constant challenges facing them.

In the various narratives and instances of the abuse of women's bodies throughout the nation's history – during the Intifada and in the crimes of domestic violence, including IVT and femicide – we learn that despite all the political and patriarchal regulations imposed upon women, their activism and their 'will to resistance' has never abated. Their agency and emancipatory activism have been utilized in actions, in silence and screams, and more. In this book, it is not assumed that Palestinian women need to speak the hegemonic language in order to be considered emancipated women. Their acts of resistance, their resilience, and survival within the contexts of occupation and a legacy of loss are a testimony to their status as liberated women. The multiple discourses of Palestinian women reflect the meanings of their status and positionality as frontliners, as the weapons, as the gatekeepers.

The discourse on weaponization is part of the general configuration of the historical legacy of the region; a discourse that nevertheless puts forth solutions and alternatives to oppression that are not readily available, that in some cases do not yet exist, but are created, innovated, and generated. This unavailability of alternatives is not often discussed, nor is it confronted. The fact that women are used as weapons against the masculine powers is not always very visible. Nor is it very often acknowledged that the young girl May is getting her father his cigarettes because she is the only one who can do so. Her body, her life, her education, her tears, and so on are all invisible weapons that must be confronted, both theoretically and by women in Palestine themselves. It brings forth evidence from their own suffering, with their own words: it brings their own truths.

The value of their frontline activities, of the effect of weaponizing women, situate women who are in conflict zones and regions of war in a space whereby they are society's children and men's protectors who should also be protected by the same individuals they are protecting. They are the weapons used by military forces to further oppress the occupied. They are the weapons that arm the community, but these weapons are also devalued, marginalized, controlled, and oppressed by that same community. Their weaponization and oppression intersect and is located within their liberation, emancipatory actions, and activism. Their agency grows out of victimization and their power grows out of their powerlessness. They are de-sexualized when weaponized and over-sexualized by the occupier to dehumanize the occupied, and yet they can also be sexualized and eroticized when weaponized, as in the case of Kholood. Their wombs become the protector of manhood and masculinity, their hymen becomes the protector of men's honour, but by having such powers, by in a sense being that power, they are also demonized. The womb is not a workshop that produces children, it is the power of sexual politics, it is social power, political power, but it is also the reduction of women to sexual objects and to the machinery of purity, reproduction, and honour. The womb, the body, gender, class, and sexuality all implicate and adjudicate the relationship between the domestic and the political economy to produce the subversive power of women's resistance and frontliner acts.

What women frontliners have remembered or can risk remembering, what they have recorded, what they have narrated, what they have used to justify their struggle, what forms they use for political mobilizations, are in many cases paradoxically contingent, but they are also grounded in women's legacies and contexts and strategized accordingly. This chapter has illustrated how Palestinian women under military occupation have in many cases needed to strategically adopt the national discourse to accede to patriarchal demands and to seek refuge in an internalized and localized cultural history in order to survive or in order to prevent the invasion of their own bodies and sexuality. Similar trends have been found by Heng, who shows that feminism under threat will at times strategically assume 'the nationalist mantle' (1997) or seek 'legitimation and ideological support in local cultural history, by finding feminist or pro-feminist myths, laws, customs, characters, narratives and origins in the national or communal past' (Alexander and Mohanty 1997: xxii). The ways Palestinian women have found for dealing with the omnipotence of the powers around them is unique as compared to women's struggles in other parts of the world, in that Palestinian women are aware of their nation's legacy and history of oppression yet are able to innovate that legacy into new strategies for survival. In addressing the question asked by so many Western feminists, 'Why can't Arab women be more like us?', Sabbagh has figuratively responded by stating that: 'the question also implies the recommendation that Arab women should jump out of an airplane without the benefit of the parachute' (Sabbagh 1996: xv).

In a society living under conditions of constant political violence and dislocation, where both men and women use their very bodies as a mode

147

of resistance to the extremes of martyrdom and/or suicide to raise their claims for national rights and in their quest for freedom – bringing pain and loss to many Israeli and Palestinian families – within such a space, the body of the man and the woman is not simply a metaphor but a political reality. Since it has been often argued that the physical presence or loss of the body is necessary in the quest for national justice, within these narratives it is not surprising to find that the physical body easily mutates into the national body as it is perceived as serving the national cause. Once again, it is not surprising that in a space of perpetual displacement, the value of the national body exceeds the value of the individual, physical body. Yet the value of the discrete, physical entity that is a body, when violated by the opponent, is easily conflated with the national body and makes its claim for protection and preservation. Thus, even within these equations of the individual and national bodies, of bodies nationalized, we can see that the relations of power which transact the body are infinitely complex. Perhaps the narrative equations between individual and national bodies seem simple because they must be reductive in order to serve a political purpose; the true complexity of the transaction would defer any action indefinitely as a matter of rational discourse. But as I have been arguing, neither the body nor the nation can be contextualized in rational ways within an irrational situation. The body is the power, but the body is also used against the assertions of the military occupation, the economy, sexual pleasures and rights, family rights, and so on. Martyrs who use their bodies in an act of power politics are also using them against the right of their own community and their loved one's celebration of their individual lives. The body is as much used against the martyr's own children, family, parents, and significant others as it is used against the opponent.

Each move by one adversary was equally answered by another. However, what strategies of power do women or feminist and human rights entities have available to seize power? Nothing is more material, practical, physical, and corporal a reaction to the hegemonic attack on the body – than by using the body and the struggles for power in which it becomes implicated. In a seemingly endless reproduction of Foucault's power/knowledge nexus, power over women's bodies and sexualities in fact constructs the destiny of such a body. The power structure of each side in the struggle requires politico-military forces that constitute themselves in an internally organized manner, with mechanisms of hierarchies and organization of power perpetually at play. 'Humanized militarism' and 'science' – particularly medicine and law – represent a politicized science that plays a political role in the effects of power they propagate against official power holders (as when medicine works against the state, or against women). When Foucault studied madness and incarceration, he enabled us to trace the constitution and deployment of the punitive apparatus. Here in this book it was necessary to understand the history of socio-political control over women's sexualities and how the current highly complex relation to power and force (be these medical, legal, or other) has conjoined into a punitive apparatus to 'deter' and prevent further abuses of women in the name of 'protection'. The weaponization of the rationalized body through abuse, harassment, and attempts at 'protection' (be the latter through actions of the Israeli military or those of Palestinian patriarchal actors) shows how intellectuals, politicians, and people of science provide the instruments of 'analysis' that yield the results that they desire.

It would appear that the final outcome of the politics of the body within revolutionary strategies for the acquisition of more strength in the power struggle can be ultimately reduced to the challenge and defiance – and indeed the politics – of saying to the oppressor: 'Over my dead body.'

CHAPTER 5

SPEAKING TRUTH TO POWER: VOICES OF PALESTINIAN WOMEN FACING THE WALL

The colonial world is a world divided into compartments.

(Fanon 1963: 37)

Firyal (eighteen years old):

> Do you know what *shatat* [displacement] means? Do you know what it means to me to line up each and every day in front of the checkpoint awaiting [the Israeli occupation soldier's] approval, so as to pass and go to school? Do you know what it means as a *ka binet* [young woman] to stand in line on your way back from school each day, enduring harassment by soldiers and taxi drivers, seeing your teacher humiliated, your brother beaten, and your father looking like an idiot, searching for a new lie to convince the soldiers to give him permission to reach his shop in Jerusalem? Do you know what this Wall has caused me, how much pain it has brought to people I love, how much land and wells it has grabbed from my family? Now the Jews live outside the Wall, walking freely in our streets, enjoying our land, drinking our water. They built it to live! To have more freedom, and [to enslave us more] ... But you know what? They are the slaves and we are the free people. I still do what I want to do, reach school, write on the Wall, drive the soldiers crazy and, as long as I can still sing for Palestine, I remain free.

Rabab (nineteen years old):

> They classify us like animals, I have a blue Jerusalemite ID like my mother, but my brothers have a green ID and the rest of the family has an orange one.[1] We were all born in the same place and house, in the Old

---

[1] Jerusalemite Palestinians carry colour-coded identification cards. Those considered to be residents of Jerusalem by the Israelis are issued blue cards while those without carry either orange or green ones that indicate that they are ex-political activists/prisoners or residents of the West Bank

City of Jerusalem, but ended up having different IDs, with different colours. Before the construction of the Wall, those IDs prevented my family from meeting at family gatherings or reaching schools or health clinics. For each of us has a different status. But we always managed to sneak out through side roads. The different ID colours created so much tension and envy in the house, we call each other names based on the colour of our ID. We fight based on it, and I was beaten so many times by my brothers because I can reach my college in Jerusalem while they are imprisoned in Abu Dis [a Jerusalem neighbourhood where the family resides]. Now, with the construction of the Wall, we live in a ghetto, we all call it Abu Dis Ghetto, a ghetto funded by America to save the Jews from Hitler's ghettos. Even when it comes to choosing a husband, I refuse to marry someone who carries an orange ID. Why should I live all my life in a cage, in a ghetto …?

May (nineteen years old):

The Wall was built to slowly bury us; I can tell you that it buried all my dreams and wishes. It turned me into a robot. Yes, I sneak out sometimes and manage to visit my uncle's family, and the soldiers don't notice. I climb sometimes from the back road, and manage to reach my school faster, but without my parents' knowledge – for if they knew, they would go crazy. The soldiers shoot right and left, and I could easily be killed – I wish. I try to get good grades at least, to make my parents happy and keep them from depriving me of school. They are also tired of worrying each day an additional worry. We inside the Wall feel like we are in a zoo, in a cage, I sometimes feel as if we all live in a collective grave, a new kind of grave where people die slowly, a slow death.

Telling the stories of women, opening new venues to voice the unheard, provides us the opportunity to see how these voices are constructed, produced, and reproduced through the gendered political geography of the space that the voices inhabit and arise out of. The narratives cited above are taken from focus group meetings in 2004 with young Palestinian women (aged between seventeen and twenty-one, from Jerusalem and its surrounding areas), who either dropped out of high school or who graduated but could not enrol in a university. Participants were all taking a one-year diploma course in order to obtain semi-professional employment, such as secretarial work and bookkeeping.

and Gaza Strip respectively. Those with blue IDs are served by the Israeli health, social security, and other state systems, while the rest are not entitled to any Israeli medical, educational, legal, or social services. Many women and men who were originally Jerusalemite are not allowed to carry a blue ID. Moreover, holders of blue IDs are allowed to be physically present in Jerusalem; everyone else needs to obtain a special permit issued by the Israeli military system.

The focus group discussions, which took place as incidents of political violence were daily occurrences in the OPT, allowed me to look closely at the way young women perceive the gender effect of spatial violence and, in particular, internal displacement, dispersion, the construction of the Israeli Separation Wall (ISW), house demolitions, land grabbing, and more (Shalhoub-Kevorkian 2005c, 2007b).

As in Firyal's opening words on abuse, the word *shatat* (Diaspora, exile, dispersion) was used by many women in the groups who articulated the ways in which the occupiers' spatial policies (re-)create Israeli policies of power, producing yet another kind of oppression. The young women constantly discussed how their mothers and other female relatives and friends were prevented from reaching final exams, health clinics, and hospitals in a timely fashion. They testified as to how women's health was constantly jeopardized, and related the stories of many women who miscarried because they could not reach health professionals in time or who never made it to the clinics because they lost track of their children at checkpoints. They told of how the limitations imposed by the Israeli Separation Wall (ISW) prevented them from finding adequate employment. And they spoke of how these limitations in turn caused the men in their lives to become more authoritative around, protective of, and fearful for the women, and how such 'protective' measures, ironically enough, often expressed themselves in aggravated violence against females.

The voices of young Palestinian women set up a relationship between identity and space, as reflected in issues of gender, race, class, and culture. The voices of May, Rabab, and Firyal, like those of many other young women I heard, allow us to take a close look at how the effects of colonial power are played out as a series of engagements between space and gender. Looking at the intersection between space and power, with space itself acting as a marker of the power struggle and the knowledge mirrored by geo-political realities (such as the ISW and checkpoints), helps us understand how gendered spatial politics confines, defines, and yet mobilizes women. Firyal for one discussed her fears of being sexually harassed and abused by the soldiers. She showed how, for her, the space of occupation became sexed and raced; her background as a young Palestinian woman was expressed by her as a young Palestinian woman as a subject of constant internal displacement. To live in a space that has been materially transformed into a 'zoo', a 'cage', or a 'collective grave', as the women put it, and the manner in which such spatial designations are particularly restrictive from a gendered perspective, is part of the racist policy of the occupiers. However, as ironic as it may sound, the way Firyal for one experienced her displacement and located it in the disruptions endemic to the ISW actually transformed both her imprisonment (as she is caught within the confines of the Wall) and her own body into concrete sites of resistance and sources of freedom and liberty.

But the voices of women participants also compel us to examine our own investment in the epistemological and ontological tools we use to unlock the meanings of what the women have to say. My methodology in this regard stresses the centrality of the first-hand testimony that these women provide. In my estimate, the effect and importance of such seeing to gender and feminist studies – particularly in the production of transnational feminist studies – cannot be overstated. However, it is critical to remember that what such witnessing also reveals is not only what was actually seen, but by implication, what is not seen, what we have *not been allowed* to see, and thus what we need to look at again, in a new way.

This methodological approach, as well as my use of the historical legacy of the Palestinian Nakba, is based on the reaction of Nuhad (age seventeen) within a focus group. When I told her of the proposed aim of my study, of learning from young women about the effect of the ISW, she reminded me of Ghassan Kanafani's story 'Returning to Haifa'. Kanafani tells of a frightened couple who fled Haifa during the Nakba in 1948, leaving behind their five-month-old child. After the second dispersal in 1967, the couple returned to Haifa to find that their son had become an Israeli soldier who refused to recognize them and who was fighting against his *fida'i* (revolutionary fighter) brother on the other side of the border. Nuhad explained that if she and her family did not fight the effects of the ISW, they would end up facing the same tragic fate as the couple in the story. Her reaction made all those present in the focus group dig into their own histories by relating stories told by their parents and grandparents. The discussions revealed that they vacillate between their determination not to forget the past – including, of course, the displaced and refugee status of their predecessors – and the ever more burdensome present in which new losses are created every day.

Analysing women's voices leads us to focus on their priorities for survival because these voices are at once personal and subjective. Additionally, it would be fair to say that these voices inscribe the very body from which they arise, since they inevitably reflect the ideology of the militarized space – a space that the body is consigned to occupy. More importantly, we seek to move beyond the mere spatial rhetoric of colonialism and occupation and look at the way we conceptualize and analyse notions of space, place, placement, and displacement. In other words, I want to identify the epistemologies we use to negotiate the complex alignment between space and oppression. Space not only shapes our identity but also contributes to the way we come to know who we are – through such familiar, if ultimately vexed, concepts such as 'home' or 'homeland' – and further embeds these concepts in a gendered matrix. What is important to understand about the Palestinian situation in particular are the ways in which this identity formation operates out of an oppositional binary: for the formation of the gendered racialized Palestinian Other helps to sustain the fantasized subject position of the 'superior' Israeli and the corresponding political powers accorded that fantasy subject.

How is the spatial policy – both in general and in the way it is reflected in the ISW – articulated through its various components, such as class, race, and gender? How does the presence of the ISW create and sustain the racialized Others it needs in order to continue to be built? And how does this classed and racialized space affect gender relations and the ensuing gender violence? This chapter aims to track the dynamics of an occupied space within the context of state occupation and violence. However, in doing so, I elaborate on a case study that specifically investigates the construction of the ISW in order to learn how it both symbolically and materially reproduces gender marginalization and oppression.

Applying spatial theory to an analysis of sites of resistance in politically conflicted areas, as in this case study of the ISW and other oppressive Israeli spatial policies, can be beneficial in uncovering hidden power relations. Space is here perceived as not only a material landscape but also a linguistic and symbolic one, replete with concepts of memory and historical legacies as well as the internalized landscapes of female subjectivity incorporating the sexual, the maternal, and the feminine. The question of inquiry here is how concepts of the spatial have been politically and culturally constructed within the specific historical contexts and legacies of Palestinian women, and particularly how such configurations are gendered and affect young women. We will explore the structure of occupation through a set of complex and intersecting spaces and their corresponding temporalities, including the myth of 'secure spaces' or the notion of a 'security barrier' – as presented in the Israeli and international media. Distinguishing between different kinds of spaces such as the ISW, demolished houses, patrolled streets, military checkpoints, and other invaded and violated locations will enable us to explore the paradoxes and complexities of Palestinian women's experiences against the background of hegemonic texts.

ISRAEL'S SPATIAL POLICY: WHAT IS THE ISW?

Israel's daily geo-political and spatial restrictions have deeply affected the everyday lives and welfare of Palestinians in the OPT, in all their economic, social, health, and political aspects (Dugard 2004). For example, the Israeli military has destroyed more than 5,200 Palestinian houses since 1999, rendering 25,719 Palestinian women, men, and children homeless (B'Tselem 2005a, 2005b, 2005c; Al-Haq 2004). Palestinian homes are destroyed as punishment for 'terrorist acts'; Israeli troops often storm homes at night with dogs, randomly shooting guns at walls, windows, people, clothing, and furniture (Elfstrom and Malmgren 2005; Al-Haq 2004). Houses are also destroyed and land is grabbed due to 'military necessity', such as when these homes fall within the planned location for the ISW; in 2004 alone, 1,399 Palestinian homes were destroyed for such 'military purposes'. Since 2003, more than 696,700 dunams (174,175 acres) have either been completely enclosed by the ISW or effectively annexed by Israel because the land falls on the wrong side of the Wall. This land accounts for 12.4 per cent of the total landmass of the West Bank (B'Tselem 2005d; Al-Haq 2004; PENGON 2003). As is the case with homes destroyed as punishment or collective punishment, families living in homes destroyed out of 'military necessity' are given about thirty minutes to gather their belongings. Obviously, this occurs under great duress, often in the middle of the night, and with soldiers threatening to shoot into the houses, to set houses on fire with children still inside, and with the threat of rape and the practice of other forms of terror and intimidation (B'Tselem 2005a, 2005b, 2005c; Elfstrom and Malmgren 2005; Al-Haq 2004; PENGON 2003).

A recent UN report (OCHA 2007) on the humanitarian situation in the OPT points to the harsh impact of Israel's spatial policy – primarily as reflected in construction of the ISW, the creation of gates to control and restrict movement, and the requirement that some Palestinians repeatedly obtain short-term permits to reach their own homes – and the effect of such restrictions upon access to jobs, schools, and services. The report shares the advisory opinion of the International Court of Justice (ICJ) rendered on 9 July 2004 that the construction of the ISW and its associate spatial regime are contrary to international law.

Furthermore, on 20 July 2004, Resolution ES-10/15 of the UN General Assembly called on Israel to comply with the legal obligations identified in the ICJ advisory opinion. The Norwegian Refugee Council Report (21 June 2006) emphasized that the Wall is leading to additional displacement of tens of thousands of Palestinians. The UN Office for the Coordination of Humanitarian Affairs (OCHA 2003) estimates that close to 680,000 people (about thirty per cent of the Palestinian population in the West Bank) will ultimately be directly affected by the ISW. Concerns were also raised in the international community about further internal displacement.

According to the Israeli human rights organization B'Tselem, the geographical space occupied by the ISW is 60 to 100 metres in width and 66 kilometres in length. The Wall is three times as long and twice as high as the Berlin Wall. Its cost is approximately USD $2.5 million per kilometre, for a total of two billion dollars. The estimated population affected by the Wall is 250,000 people in eighty-one community enclaves, with 210,000 people in East Jerusalem separated from the West Bank. In addition, 402,000 people have lost access to the outside world, having been cut off from their schools, jobs, health care, and families (2005d, 2005e). As to the land itself, B'Tselem states that 951,000 dunams (238,000 acres), constituting 16 per cent of the West Bank, has been affected, turning 1.7 per cent of the land in the West Bank into closed military zones. In the West Bank city of Qalqilia, for instance, 40,000 residents are imprisoned within the boundaries of the Wall in what the Israeli court has called 'suffocating rings'. Entrance to Qalqilia is controlled by eleven manned gates that are open for general use for a total of fifty-five minutes a day. As throughout the OPT, Palestinians over the age of twelve must obtain permits to pass through the gates for whatever purpose. There are twelve types of permits – for farmers, medical personnel, teachers, and so on. Permits are valid for only a few months, for particular gates, and for certain times of the day (2005e). Without a doubt, the ISW has affected the poverty level in the West Bank.

The radically racist nature of this spatial policy was exposed by Mark Lavie on August 2005; he reported that the ISW 'in the Jerusalem area is meant to ensure a Jewish majority in the city and not just serve as a buffer against bombers', as Israeli Cabinet minister Haim Ramon acknowledged. Similarly, B. Michael, from the Israeli newspaper *Yediot Ahronot*, explains his perception of the ISW in no uncertain terms:

Three thousand kilometers of barbed wire have been stretched along the 'first phase' of the 'separation fence'. Three million meters. Equal to the distance between Israel and Switzerland. A lot of 'separating' can be achieved with 3,000 km of barbed wire: separating livestock from their owners, olives from their harvesters, vines from their pickers, a doctor from his patients, a worker from his place of work, a teacher from his students. Especially the farmer from his land. Only one kind of separation will not be obtained by thousands of barbed kilometers: separating the suicide-bomber from his victims. He – as we have learned from the State Comptroller's report on security procedures – will continue to reach his objective. The fence will supply them with the infrastructure of despair and loss of hope, and fortify hatred, frustration, madness.

About 200,000 people live in the immediate vicinity of the northern part of the fence. Hardly any of them have not been hurt by it. The entire town of Qalqilya, with a population of over 40,000, is hermetically sealed off. Only one gate connects it to the world. Tulkarm is cut off from the west by a wall, and from the east by closure checkpoints. Eighteen villages, with all their inhabitants, are completely surrounded with barbed-wire fences. Their residents live in a genuine pen. Three thousand families (at least) have already been separated from their lands. The 'farming gates' which they were promised do not exist. About twenty-five wells have been destroyed, another fourteen face destruction. Thirty-six wells have been separated from the communities that used their water. These wells would yield 6.7 million cubic meters of water. This is the secret of the Wall: not security, nothing like it. Not war against terrorism, war against reason. A slow-motion *Nakba* [catastrophe]. Gradual strangulation. An evil illusion that an entire people can be made to surrender and become a nation of slaves, to make Sharon's and Mofaz's wet dream come true.

(Michael 2003)

CONCEPTUALIZING 'SECURITY REASONING' IN A MILITARIZED SPACE

The occupation of the Palestinian territories is not limited to military control of the land, as it essentially entails the colonization of all economic and physical means of survival. Daily humiliation and harassment, as well as constant displacement and eviction, have been imposed on an entire people. The history of this occupation includes the theft of territories followed by the implementation of legislation and policies designed to impose the rule of the occupiers.

One powerful method for militarizing space and imposing dominance on it is the use of 'security reasoning' to legitimate the action of soft hegemonic power holders – like the 'security reasoning' that the US has used to provide a justification for the invasions of Afghanistan and Iraq. Israel's adoption of this approach has resulted in a deep intensification of the policing of Palestinian spaces and has resulted in the granting of sweeping power to the state, the military, and the police to attack any site, any person, any icon, and to punish suspected 'terrorists'. With 'security needs' so broadly defined, Palestinians can be arrested, attacked, dislocated, and destroyed. Security laws and regulations, enacted to help the Israeli state sort out who is a 'terrorist' and which space could potentially destabilize Israeli society – and so create 'national insecurity' – have jeopardized the security of Palestinians. Such 'security reasoning', combined with the historical colonization of the land in Palestine (see Abu Sitta 2000), has given rise to a racialized structure that includes the militarized use of grabbed land (see also Ghanem *et al.* 1998; Zureik 1978; Shehadeh 1998; Rouhana 1997; Kimmerling 1983).

This 'security reasoning' has brought about the socio-economic exclusion of Israel's Other and has resulted in the formation and imposition of economic, political, legal, and spatial racial discrimination against Palestinians who reside in socially and physically isolated spaces, lacking economic stability and long-term jobs, enduring continual loss of land, homes, and loved ones, and suffering through social instability. The structural growth of socio-economic exclusion at the local Palestinian–Israeli level, combined with the hegemonic use of the logic of exclusion and 'security reasoning', have fanned violent resistance on the part of the occupied, this in turn increasing the Israeli use of and flexibility in defining 'security reasoning' – and ultimately has resulted in the emergence in Israel of what Bonaventura de Sousa Santos has called 'social fascism'.

Sousa Santos explains that the emergence of social fascism in the current world does not mean a return to the fascism of the 1930s and 1940s:

> Unlike the earlier one, the present fascism is not a political regime. It is rather a social civilizational regime … it trivialized democracy to such a degree that it is no longer necessary, or even convenient, to sacrifice democracy in order to promote capitalism … We are entering a period in which democratic states coexist with fascistic societies.

> (2002: 453)

I borrow Sousa Santos's concept to reflect on the unique 'democratized' Israeli fascism that is apparent, among other policies, in its creation of ghettos. Thus, the use of various spatial policies, including the construction of the ISW, not only causes the physical and social exclusion of the Other, but also creates a spatial division between 'secure zones' and insecure, demonized, ghettoized ones. The hegemonic claim about the need for such zones constructs a discourse in which secure zones are under constant threat from the ghettoized ones. Such insecurity gives Israel and its international allies the 'right' to use all means to 'defend' their zones. This situation creates and manipulates the sense of security and insecurity – of both Palestinians and Israelis – and results in chronic anxieties vis-à-vis the present and future stability of the colonizers. In that sense, the justifications underlying this social fascism are similar to Hitler's arguments about the threats to the German *volk* in prewar Europe.

This spatial-ghettoized fascism embraces (in one way or another) the four main forms of social fascism that Sousa Santos discusses: the fascism of social apartheid, parastate fascism, the fascism of insecurity, and financial fascism (2002: 452–6). Such spatial-ghettoized fascism creates a context whereby the might – and not the right – control even the smallest spaces, such as domestic or personal space. As we will see in this chapter, being under the domination of such spatial fascism results in Palestinian men and women learning through their inability to counter the influence of the occupier that the Israelis are in control. They become conscious that the 'security' of Israelis and the knowledge regarding the rights and wrongs they produce in relation to the political conflict possess a value superior to their own in the eyes of the hegemonic Western Empire. Israeli women in this context are used by the hegemonic power as justification for the implementation of their gender-specific imperial role in the home and without, while Palestinian women are to be acted upon through the colonial project as boundary markers (see Chapter 3 of this book for more detail on women as boundary markers), marking the difference between the Israelis' superior 'security' value and the Palestinian Other who should be ghettoized in order to make secure such superior values.

In exposing the spatial fascism imposed on the OPT, in understanding its history and origin, the following section aims to track its gender effect through exploration of the historical and political legacy behind it. This is followed by an analysis of the gender formation of such racialized spatial politics. My focus on spatial-ghettoized fascism is automatically a focus on class and gender hierarchies as well, for such racial hierarchies come into existence through capitalism and patriarchy. Using an interlocking approach that considers how race, class, and gender affect spatial politics and policies requires a closer examination of the globalized racial capitalist policies that manufacture difference and separation in the service of the powerful. While the following sections examine both postcolonial contexts and current occupation and colonialism, an inter-locking approach as called for by Jane Jacobs requires closer attention to how spaces are 'mapped together' (in Razack 2002: 16). Adopting Jacob's argument, Sherene Razack refuses to accept monocausal explan-ations (such as those that arise from 'security reasoning') and proposes that analysis give greater attention to 'interlocking systems of oppres-sion' (Razack 2002: 16). Razack explains:

> Two steps mark our interlocking approach. First, we examine how the systems mutually constitute each other, an analysis aided by Jacob's advice to map how spaces are linked. Second, we pursue how all the systems of domination operate at the local level, a task facilitated by attending to material and symbolic constitution of specific spaces. Our goal is to identify legal and social practices that produce racial hierarchies.
>
> (2002: 16–17)

I adopt here Razack's interlocking spatial approach in order to uncover the racialization of the Palestinians. To understand spatial-ghettoized fascism in the OPT (including the construction of the ISW), we must talk about the mobility/immobility of women in these militarized spaces; about the economic status of women and violence against them under these circumstances; about secure and insecure spaces that increase women's vulnerability to sexual violence; about the isolated and excluded spaces that favour a particular system of control. More importantly, we must look at the way all of this combines to impact gender relations. Thus, a spatial analysis helps us understand the interlock between history, politics, gender, space, race, occupation, capitalism, law, and international globalized power games. Men and women come to know themselves, their roles and power through their gendered body and spaces. Understanding how gender roles and bodies are produced in spaces and how spaces racialize bodies entails an inter-rogation of how subjects come to know themselves in and through spaces, within multiple systems of domination.

THE HISTORY OF DISPLACEMENT

Not surprising given that the ramifications of occupation have been so prevalent in Palestine, the historical narrative of the region has invested the concept of 'space' with multiple meanings. The Zionist (and later Israeli) racial policies of transfer and expulsion of Palestinians and the various crimes of ethnic cleansing have their historical origin in the late 1800s. Ben Gurion summed up the intent of Zionist policies in 1936: 'With compulsory transfer we [would] have a vast area [for settlement] ... I support compulsory transfer. I don't see anything immoral in it' (cited in Morris 2001: 144). The Israeli propaganda efforts that have created the view that Palestinians abandoned their homes of their own volition has come under close historical scrutiny. According to the Israeli historian Benny Morris,

> Ben Gurion clearly wanted as few Arabs as possible to remain in the Jewish state. He hoped to see them flee. He said as much to his colleagues and aides in meetings in August, September and October [1948]. But no [general] expulsion policy was ever enunciated and Ben Gurion always refrained from issuing clear or written expulsion orders; he preferred that his generals 'understand' what he wanted done. He wished to avoid going down in history as the 'great expeller' and he did not want the Israeli government to be implicated in a morally questionable policy ... But while there was no 'expulsion policy', the July and October [1948] offensives were characterized by far more expulsions and, indeed, brutality towards Arab civilians than the first half of the war.
>
> (Morris 2004: 597)

Israeli author Simha Flapan, in his book *The Birth of Israel* (1987), explains how Ben Gurion's ultimate aim was to evacuate as much of the Arab population as possible from the Jewish state. In doing so, he employed various means, such as the destruction of whole villages and the eviction of its inhabitants. Benny Morris relates how, by mid-1949, the majority of 350 of the Arab villages were either completely destroyed or partly in ruins and uninhabitable (Morris 2004). However, even though the historical record has been set straight, the Israeli establishment still refuses to accept any moral or political responsibility for the refugees (see, for example, Peretz Kidron quoted in Said and Hitchens 2001). Although the first UN General Assembly resolution pertaining to Palestine (No. 194, 11 December 1948) affirmed the right of Palestinians to return to their homes and property, and while similar resolutions were repeatedly passed no less than twenty-eight times since first date, Israel has negated the possibility of return and has systematically and juridically made it impossible, on any grounds whatsoever, for Arab Palestinians to return, be compensated for their lost property, or live in Israel as citizens equal to Jewish Israelis before the law (Said 1980).

Sami Hadawi (1979) discusses the issue of flight, arguing that Palestinians fled out of real fear of a repetition of the 1948 Zionist massacres and, as such, flight is not legal ground for denial of their right to return. Clearly, when civilians are caught in combat zones, they understandably panic. International law prohibits the confiscation of homes and property by an occupying power.

The long history of displacement and dislocation of Palestinians began in earnest with the UN partition plan of 29 November 1947 meant to divide Palestine into two states – one for the Jews and the other for the Arabs. Israeli historian Illan Pappe discusses the Lausanne Conference of 1949, describing how on 12 May of that year the UN's Conciliation Commission for Palestine (UNCCP) reaped its only success when it induced Israel and Arab states to sign a joint protocol on the framework for a comprehensive peace. Israel for the first time accepted the principle of the repatriation of Arab refugees and the internationalization of Jerusalem. Pappe shows how Israel agreed to these principles as an exercise in international public relations and under pressure from the United States, having signed with no intention to live up to the agreement (1994). The catastrophe continued to unfold. Although the UN passed a resolution in 1948 to create a United Nations Relief for Palestinian Refugees (UNRPR) agency, it was only in December of 1949 that the UN took decisive steps by passing General Assembly resolution 302 (IV) establishing the United Nations Relief and Works Agency for Palestinian Refugees in the Near East (UNRWA). The UNRWA had the mandate of taking over the operation of more than sixty refugee camps from Jordan, Syria, and Lebanon, with said operations commencing in May of 1950.

Israeli spatial politics, as evident in its ghetto fascism and the internal displacement of Palestinians, is closely linked to Israel's continuing strategy of *hidden* displacement which is manifest in acts such as the invasion of cities, house demolitions, and the construction of the ISW. Further, the establishment of the Wall and the house demolitions that have accompanied it have induced a variety of migratory patterns – individuals have moved once or more, displacement has been of short or long duration, and movement has covered short or great distances.

MILITARIZED SPATIALITY AND GENDERED SPACES

[M]any of us have dark moments of hopelessness and despair. We know that under the spreading canopy of the War Against Terrorism, the men in suits are hard at work. Our strategy should be not only to confront Empire, but to lay siege to it. To deprive it of oxygen. To shame it. To mock it. With our art, our music, our literature, our stubbornness, our joy ... and our ability to tell our stories. Stories that are different from the ones we're being brainwashed to believe.

(Arundhati Roy 2003: 108–12)

Power is dynamic and multiple, but it is also muscular and masculine. In his analysis of power, Foucault argues that power is not opposed to freedom, and that freedom is not freedom from power. Freedom is a potentiality internal to power, even an effect of power. Power produces the possibilities of action and the conditions for the exercise of freedom. Thus, the point made here is not that remapping as an analytical strategy is resistance, or that remapping *is* a form of resistance, but rather how such remapping affects women's agency. Maps are our ways of projecting power onto our human and physical landscapes. The question remains as to how the symbolic world constructs the conditions of its own moral and political agency.

The first issue that strikes any researcher studying the effect of spatial politics on Palestinian women is the physical compression of families and communities into separate, limited, and constantly 'guarded' spaces. Living in such a space means being under the constant legal, social, religious, cultural, and economic control of the colonizer's state and politics. Women's spaces in relation to their health and their social, educational, and economic needs are supervised (to say the least) by the discriminatory system of Israeli law and order. Militarized intervention in space challenges gender roles and invades women's private places. Their lack of privacy and the restrictions on physical space prevent women from being physically sheltered. Their private lives become transparent and are policed by the colonizer's political apparatuses as they become more visible to that colonizer's security and surveillance forces. They face tremendous violence, humiliation, and harassment. At the same time, they need to cope with Palestinian men's fear around the challenges and hardships that the militaristic context imposes on men. The situation is additionally complicated by constantly shifting lines of demarcation drawn by the racial politics of the colonial power that lead to the 'demapping' and 'remapping' of women's routes to school, home, relatives' houses, health clinics, and other places of daily life. The unpredictability of changes in laws and rules – that determine which houses can be demolished, who carries what coloured ID and what privileges are offered to those who carry the 'right' colour, and whether or not a permit is required to pass a checkpoint – are dramatic and in some cases overwhelming, adding to the chaos of displacement and dislocation.

Attacks on domestic space have had tremendous implications for Palestinians in general and Palestinian women in particular. Policies imposed as the result of the doctrines of 'no safe place' and 'security reasoning' increase women's lack of safety even in their own home and private space. In many instances, during home invasions or house demolitions, family members have been prevented or unable to protect their own children or themselves from the Israeli military. The voices of the women I have heard (and their photographs, as we shall see below) reflect how they feel homeless in their own homes, lacking the security that every human being deserves. The constant fear and insecurity on the part of women residing in their own private domestic spaces has led them to believe that their children are not safe either inside or outside the house. The sense of safety, belonging, and privacy that a home generally affords has been turned into an arena to display the power of the occupying state. As Maha put it: 'They poisoned the water in our wells and uprooted my favourite trees, and grabbed my land and my grandparents' land, the only place I used to go to when I needed to cry, to shout, to rest, to pray'.

Women with whom I worked in my voice therapy groups who are related to political prisoners explained to me that the intent of the military occupation was to destroy Palestinian homes by increasing the number of Israeli settlements – Israeli housing projects built on Palestinian land in the occupied territories. Hafiza stated:

> Every day I wake up, I find out again and again – as if I refuse to believe it – that I lost my home following the arrest of my two children, but I also see the new homes built for the Jewish settlers. [Seeing] their homes being built in a modern way, with large gardens and playgrounds for their children, while my children are either in Israeli prison or here, in this *khusshe'h* [a small, roughly built, unsanitary room] that the members of the camp were able to give me following the demolition of my house – it kills me. So, the *khusshe'h* is my home and my children's home.

Hafiza's attempts to deny the loss of her home have been made harder and more painful through witnessing the construction of new Israeli homes. She asked the same question over and over: 'We are imprisoned in our own homes, and they are free to move. Why do they consider us animals and only themselves as human beings?'

By living and working in the area, I have learned that the trauma arising from imprisonment, house demolitions, restricted movement, constant fear, displacement, injury to loved ones, and daily loss have negatively influenced the ability of Palestinians to preserve family ties and connections and at the same time has shaped how the people deal with military practices and the countless acts of violence that prevent them from living a normal life. Both a reliance on family and the awareness of a national legacy of oppression have promoted the need for *sumud* (steadfastness) and 'togetherness'. Mothers of martyrs, for example, repeatedly discussed the loss of their children and homes in metaphoric terms as a vessel, one that carried the varied meanings of home and family: the rituals of cooking food, meetings, maintaining social ties – in short, the home as a vessel of unity, love, care, and hope. The loss of their children evoked memories of being refugees during the Nakba in 1948 (Shalhoub-Kevorkian 2003b), taking them back in history to other narratives of loss, and making them cognizant of the recurrence of loss in the present.

The women's narratives repeatedly revealed their understanding of how Israel's practices of attacking the family's unity and its sense of privacy and integrity were deeply embedded in complicated systems of political oppression and military occupation – a multi-level system that operates through the powerful support of hegemonic power and a mobilization of an international machinery of control mainly in the US. The women fluently discussed international politics, especially referring to America's blind support of Israel. Such practices have also become apparent in studies of wars, primarily the effect of war on women (see Enloe 1983, 2000; Goldstein 2001). Women's constructions of their narratives of displacement were such that attacks on families should best be understood as part of a larger repertoire of hegemonic militarization over the Palestinian and the Muslim Other. Women analysed the wider process of attacking the family unit and family members as a way of undermining the stability of the social fabric. They traced the entire process, from the destruction of a family's home to experiences of night raids, beatings, imprisonment, and shootings of family members, to the constant trauma and helplessness of not being able to safeguard one's family.

In my work with mothers of martyrs (Shalhoub-Kevorkian 2003b) and my clinical work with women of all ages, I have discovered how they portray a ritualized military routine that sends a symbolic and practical message to all Palestinians: 'There is no safe haven'. Such a clear message was sent, for instance, during Ariel Sharon's entry into the Dome of the

Rock (Haram Al Sharif) – an act that triggered the onset of the Second Intifada in late September 2000. This means of oppression, involving an incursion into a sacred place, was an attempt not only to subdue a rebellious population but also to minimize the ability of Palestinian men and women to protect their own. Violation of religious space is considered by Palestinian women as a violation equivalent to the invasion of familial, domestic space. Whether such attacks are aimed at religious sites (spiritual homes), schools and universities (educational homes), or private homes, all ultimately constrain and burden women. The need to protect and preserve the home has turned some areas into political and ritualized spaces that are markers of something greater than an individual loss; they become sites of a collective loss and symbols of resistance and political struggle. As Um Riad stated:

> I wake up each day, and before I go to pray, I open the door between my bedroom and my son's room [i.e., the son that she lost]. I look at the floor, he was the one who put the nice tiles on the floor. He is the one that made us all feel that this is the family home, he turned the house into a beautiful, elegant *raqi* [house], in the midst of all the messed up houses in the Old City of Jerusalem. So, I bend down, kiss the floor, and put my cheeks on the floor to feel his hands. I feel his hands, I even see them sometimes. If you only knew how much I miss him.
> (a portion of this quotation appears in Shalhoub-Kevorkian 2003b: 400)

Through my research with young women focusing on the ISW, I learned of the effect that separation from family homes has had on their feelings of belonging. When discussing the effect of the Wall, these young women constantly reminded me that what I see is not what they see. Nawal's statement that 'Only when you see the ISW from my window will you understand its effect' led me to give women cameras to photograph the Wall from their own point of view and with their own eyes. I asked them to write a caption under each photo, to help me know what they want me to see or understand, to know what they saw, thought, or felt when they looked at the pictures they had taken. The following are samples of their work.

Figure 2 shows a mass of rubble – demolished houses in front of a young woman's home – in preparation for further extension of the ISW. Siham, the photographer, said the Wall 'darkened' her life, turning her house into a dark, dirty, imprisoning space. Her caption stated: 'You defiled our environment, darkened our life. When will you get out of our way?' While Figure 3 shows a green field and trees, a scene of peace and

Figure 2 Siham's photograph.

Figure 3 Iman's photograph.

serenity, the ISW is present, peripherally, at the far end of the frame, indicating the way its construction separates the land from its people. Iman, who took this photo, wrote: 'Even heaven is not a place to be in, if those individuals [we care for] are not there.' She was quoting an Arab proverb used to convey the notion that we are social people and that we need each other's company.

In looking over all the photographs taken by these young women, I was struck by the absence of the photographers in the sense that they did not arrange to have themselves photographed in the sites they wanted to capture. In almost every case, the centrality of the images revolved around the spaces of their lives: whether ruined spaces that were nothing more than piles of rubble, or peaceful, verdant spaces where trees are growing and the sky is serene; they are nevertheless landscapes that carry the effects of the political struggle juxtaposed with gender meanings. Besides sharing these photographs with me, the young women also hung them on the walls of their classrooms so that they could be seen daily, as if the photographs themselves, however metaphorically, reclaimed the space that had been taken from them. The act of taking the photograph, of daily confronting the loss in the classroom, is also an act of healing and a reflection of agency. It should be noted that a certain emptiness in the photographs is haunting; it is as if no one lives there anymore, if by living we mean a life with depth and breadth of emotion: joy, sorrow, family gatherings, laughter. In these photographs, the silence and the screams tell a story of *shatat* – dispersal.

These means of speaking out against the ISW – the focus group dialogue, the photographs and their captions – help young women to talk back to the hegemonic powers that allow its construction. The ISW has become the primary signifier of a continuing oppression, part of the daily reality of trying to pass the barriers and checkpoints of the Occupied Territories. By concentrating on the voices, the photos, the sites, and the words of the women themselves, we extend our analyses to the 'presence' of the historical setting. Salwa, who took the photo in Figure 4, provided the caption in English (rather than Arabic): 'To be Continued.' When I asked her to explain her remark, she said: 'You plan to show the photos to people in the West, and write about them in English, and I want to say to everybody that, no matter how much they keep oppressing us, we will continue our resistance.'

The words and photos of young women caught in the frontlines of daily confrontation reflect a growing awareness amongst Palestinians of both the power and weakness of resilience as a method of survival. As Nawal's

Figure 4 Salwa's photograph.

narrative reveals, these women are aware of the complex nexus of issues that the Wall signifies beyond the obdurate barrier that it presents. Nawal's epistemological as well as ontological analyses of the symbolic and political message of the ISW made her refer to 'a million walls':

> It is not that we face a Wall, but walls ... just think of the fact that the Wall is built by Palestinian workers who need to live and bring food to their children, think about the fact that Qrei' [an official and former minister of the Palestinian Authority] is the one selling them [the Israelis] the cement for the Wall; think about the Americans who are supporting Israel financially and morally in the world. They give them guns, and help them kill us, do you think that it is only this one wall? So many walls. My father is a wall, my school principal is a wall that is blocking me, our society builds a wall, a prison only for women.

THE GENDERED DISCOURSE OF *SHATAT*, IDENTITY TRANSFORMATION, AND AGENCY

The socio-political effect of hegemonic spatial policies is closely and inseparably connected to the psychosocial dimension of loss, homelessness, and displacement, which raises a number of important questions (Shalhoub-Kevorkian 2005c, 2007b). How are women's life choices shaped by internal displacement, eviction, forced migration, demolition of living spaces, and loss of land? How are they affected by economic hardships resulting from the loss of job opportunities and by an increase in the poverty rate, particularly the feminization of poverty? How has spatial racism impacted women's education, making it difficult to reach their educational institutions and often causing them to 'drop out' – or more accurately, be deprived of education? In what ways has this racism altered and/or transformed women's social support networks, disturbed their mobility and domestic spaces, and impacted the social fabric of communities? In short, how has spatial-ghettoized fascism and the doctrine of 'security reasoning' affected the lives of Palestinian women, particularly those who are most vulnerable – women from a lower socio-economic level; women who do not carry an Israeli ID; young women; and women working outside the home?

Edward Said has remarked:

> The exile knows that in a secular and contingent world, homes are always provisional. Borders and barriers which enclose us within the safety of familiar territory can also become prisons, and are often defended beyond reason or necessity. Exiles cross borders, break barriers of thought and experience.
>
> (Said 2002: 365)

Although Said is specifically referring to Diasporic exile, the experience of exilic homelessness are reflected in the voices of the young women as they speak out against the ISW. Firyal said:

> Do you know what it means to be m'shatateh [dispersed] in your own home? When you leave, not knowing whether you will be able to come back? When you will be back? And how? At the checkpoint, I feel like I am uprooted, At home I feel unsafe.

Similarly, Shaden wrote:

> We were refugees, but my family managed to work hard and bought a piece of land and built our house. All my uncles built their houses in this area so as to be together and so not to feel that we are refugees anymore. Now, the Wall will divide us again, our house will be on one side of the Wall and my cousin's will be on the other. My other uncle's house is under threat of demolition and so we hired a lawyer to prevent it. Now all the family money and savings will be collected to pay the lawyers to fight Israel in the Israeli court. My grandfather said that he might need to sell one of the family houses to fight them in court. My main fear is that we will lose the case, and then our house, and become refugees again.

As Firyal and Shaden have voiced, there is no point of departure that Palestinian exiles can return to. The experience of living as refugees under occupation has predetermined women's lives, and they must find new points of reference other than those that inscribe a stable origin. Shaden's experiences reflect this ambivalence: 'Being at home doesn't mean you're at home. Look from the window and you see the Wall; you realize that no one in this house is safe. My home, my land, my school, and life became unsafe.' Through Shaden's narrative of displacement, we understand how experiences are deeply rooted in a sense of place. To be separated from the persons or locations that one loves or knows most intimately is to experience loss. Similarly, Firyal's concept of *shatat* requires imagining distance in less binary and more complicated ways. Young women discussed the fact that whether distant from the Wall or close to it, it nevertheless carries one meaning and reflects one interest, which is the interest of the dominant to turn all the spaces of the Other into unsafe terrains.

The discourse of exile in the words of the women was subsumed under the broader historical discourse of *shatat*. But this historical and contemporary *shatat* became both a source of power/knowledge and a source of the legacy of loss. Even more, the current *shatat* both generates creative methods of mobility and imposes burdens of restricted mobility. The current *shatat* is often experienced by the young women as a split domain – one that inspires freedom from occupation, even while one is trapped in both the spaces and narratives of displacement. To move from one place to another means having the social and political power to do so. The question asked by many of the women was, in Fahima's words:

> How can a young woman move from her home to her school without being in danger? How can I visit my grandmother in Jerusalem without having to undergo body searches and humiliation by the soldiers, without fearing being shot, for only yesterday they killed three school children? I am a woman; why should I leave the house under such conditions?

Fahima's words clearly reveal that restrictions on mobility have specific impacts on women and burden them with further gender discrimination. Thus, the term *shatat* becomes more 'inclusive' in that it is strongly related to economic, gender, and political power embedded in spatial dominance. Spatial changes and policies – the ISW, house demolitions, restrictions on movement – have created unsafe spaces, although some are safer in their lack of safety (or given their lack of safety) than others. The need to challenge such unsafe spaces has made young women realize the limits of such spaces, which has also meant that they are neither insiders nor outsiders and that they have the power to push limits and create new, safer spaces. In a sense, the constancy of *shatat* contributes to certain transformations of identities to the extent that experiencing dislocation, eviction, and forced migration requires the development of new internal co-ordinates in order to navigate gender effects. Women facing occupation and political conflicts also faced the need to be involved in the double project of empowering their own identity while simultaneously deconstructing the logic of the oppressor's identity.

The most important transformative experiences were clear even in the midst of varied and often contradictory choices the young women had to make. As Manar said:

> But you know, despite the Separation Wall, the checkpoints, and the daily coercion [*qahar*], in my village in Kufur Aqab – where most school-girls need to pass through the checkpoint each and every day ... we are more interested in going to school, attending colleges and universities and educating ourselves.

Others echoed Hadaf's sentiments: 'My sister decided to quit school ... she can't handle the daily fears ... and now she is nineteen years old with responsibility for two babies, a family, and no house' (she lives with her in-laws). And Sharifa stated: 'I want to complete my studies and find a job with a good salary, this is the best way to live an honourable life, if I will be allowed to do so.' Unfortunately, the construction of the ISW in Al Dahia neighbourhood ended up preventing Sharifa from completing her studies.

The story of nineteen-year-old Byan, who lives in Sheikh Sa'ad, a village that has been virtually enclaved since the construction of the ISW (see B'Tselem 2004), is telling. Because of the Wall, her father was unemployed as the restriction on his movements made it impossible for him to continue working in Jerusalem. This situation has affected Byan's future: despite her high grades on the *Tawjehee* (final high school exams) and her acceptance to Al Quds University, she decided to accept the first marriage proposal she received. Furthermore, her engagement made her look for more short-term educational opportunities, and she ulti-mately decided to enrol in secretarial school at the YWCA:

> The *shatat* of my family, and the economic hardships following our constant migration [some of the family members held Jerusalemite IDs while others did not] led to me become a secretary for a physician in our

village instead of being a physician myself. My grades – if we lived in normal conditions – would have allowed me to be the first female physician in the family, but now I minimized my dreams to fit the situation. Because I am a young woman, with no income, I am part of a family that is suffering financially and mainly because I am Palestinian with an orange ID, although I was born in the Old City of Jerusalem in my grandparent's house.

Byan's identity is unclear and occluded; she was uprooted and could not return to Jerusalem, even though she was born there. She did not 'legally' belong where she was, due to the constant state of forced migration and the imposed restrictions on her mobility. Accepting an early marriage proposal 'helped' her, as she said, to find some peace and safety. But when I met her again (seven months after her engagement), she expressed her disappointment:

> I am not sure where my home is anymore. Jerusalem is my home, the village is my home, and now I need to move to Hebron to live with my fiancée's family and turn it into my home, I really do not know where my home is, I feel like a nomadic Bedouin.

Byan's constant discussion of her *shatat* reflects her feeling of exile in her own homeland. Mixed with her constant desire for a sense of belonging, her feeling of exile situates her and many other young Palestinian women like her on the edge, at the outer limits. The search for a home with borders, for clear maps and a permanent legal status so as to be safe and secure, is juxtaposed in these situations with women's location and gender status inside and outside the bordered space. The women are constantly in search of a space that can be clearly mapped, where a visible social and legal order is apparent.

The lack of a definable space to call home means death to some – as Samira stated: 'We are locked in a prison … as my friend said, in collective graves' – but, interestingly enough, this metaphor also engenders power, resistance, resilience, and agency. The young women's stories of young Palestinian women and men who committed suicide to make their voices and nation's claims heard turned the incarcerating spaces into sites of resistance and liberation.

While the deep-rooted legacies of loss understandably create a sense of hopelessness, the feelings of *shatat* raise women's awareness of the importance of finding a safe haven. This knowledge combined with the actual need to create such a secure place encourage the young women to search for housing options and to read analyses of invaded Palestinian spaces; doing so makes them feel responsible for finding solutions, and this responsibility in turn leads them to be more active and more resilient. We should once again remember Tamara, who told me that she carries in her schoolbag her nation's losses, pain, and the need to maintain the struggle in addition to her school materials. Other students related how they would sneak behind checkpoints, meet in remote areas, challenge soldiers, and perform many other innovative actions that created counter-spaces of safety to challenge the sites of incarceration.

In my encounters in the Jenin refugee camp after Israeli incursions, the sight of women recreating a home from the rubble was not uncommon (see Shalhoub-Kevorkian 2004b). Women I met with were reorganizing their homes and sleeping quarters for their children and neighbours and cleaning up the debris. I found one woman turning a half-demolished room into a home, transforming a long bedcover into a missing wall. I witnessed another making a bed for her newborn daughter from plastic pots cut in half cushioned with material; she used the high ends of the pots to hang a piece of cloth so as to protect the baby from flies and mosquitoes. I vividly remember seeing another woman, sitting on the remainder of what used to be her balcony, looking at the scene of the destruction of the camp, while she carried two plates in her lap and prepared dinner for the family. The fact that their homes had been attacked by bombs and air-to-surface missiles and were partially or completely destroyed did not stop them from immediately creating what they could from the debris in order to house their families and begin again.

Looking at how the politics of location and dislocation impinge on gender issues, challenges, and risks calls for new feminist analyses of place and displacement. In this respect, the women's own analyses of their situation have immeasurable value. Their ability to eloquently discuss the economic, political, and social aspects of their situation and to consider its local and international context points to their power as oppressed people to function as critical analysts of their world. Their constant search for answers – 'Why me?' 'Why us?' 'Why should I suffer so much?' – focuses on the realization that it is the women themselves who end up suffering and losing the most and who make the most difficult compromises.

In various focus groups, many young women shared the legal hardships they face. Siham related her concerns about the fate of her sister who had married someone in the West Bank. She explained that her sister was facing legal problems because she could not file a complaint against her abusive husband in the West Bank, as there is no legal system there that functions on a permanent basis. The court is constantly shut down due to political problems and the recurring Israeli closures of the area. Siham said: 'If the judge is unable to reach the court, how can we ask my sister to fight for her legal and religious rights?' The young women discussed the many legal issues that face women, such as obtaining their rightful inheritance, the right to live free of abuse, and the right to obtain a permit to access their lands. Manal explained that her mother was filing a request to gain her inheritance rights, but her uncle's influence in Hebron led to the court dismissing her case through a claim that the court was unable to meet due to the political situation. Byan concluded: 'When it comes to women's rights, no one is able to help.' These women are not only raising legal issues but are also searching non-stop for new legal and extra-legal solutions. One woman requested the intervention of tribal heads in order to obtain her inheritance; another turned to a Jewish Israeli lawyer to pursue her right to prevent the demolition of her home.

To cross a spatial border and challenge hegemonic oppression potentially emancipates the oppressed through the use of his or her body and life as a way of voicing their condemnation. The observations of the young women are grounded in a real sense of, and sensitivity to, what it means to be a woman living under military occupation. By telling their stories of past and present oppression, they aim to recover their own views as well as resist all that is manifested in Israeli techniques of occupation. Crossing the ISW and passing the checkpoints is an insurgent subaltern activity that goes beyond the quotidian resistance of displaced and imprisoned people. These are the survival strategies of groups and communities enclosed in enclaves, a discourse that focuses on the heroism of daily survival, what the women call *nidal* (struggling). The young women's declarations of the need for constant *nidal* created the desire and even the responsibility to transgress. Daring to reclaim the right to re-map the hegemonic map – although potentially placing personal security at risk – seemed for many young women safer and more honourable than the alternative of not doing so.

The creation of counter-spaces and counter-discourses to talk back to hegemony was apparent in the challenge not only to external militarized power, but also to internal patriarchal authority, primarily with respect to the tension reflected in relations between men and women. For example, in the early stages of the current Intifada, Palestinian women were perceived by Palestinian men as less vulnerable to Israel's physical, political, and legal abuse. This created a situation wherein women became more mobile and able to support the family economically, socially, and politically, while men were the targets of restrictive spatial policy. Having to deal with the Israeli state and other agencies expanded women's gender roles and functions; it actively involved women with national and international NGOs and thereby extended their gender spaces. Women explained how such hardships and additional demands mobilized them and enhanced their membership in public and political space – making them more visible but simultaneously also more vulnerable.

Many women discussed how construction of the Wall has increased the sense of loss of control that their male family members were already experiencing on account of the occupation, and how such loss is correspondingly expressed in the men's need to preserve their power through traditional, religious, national, social, and familial patriarchal methods. Limitations on mobility and militarized spatial policies are accompanied by daily mistreatment and humiliation, emasculating men in public and private spaces. As we have seen, such emasculation engenders frustration, anger, and aggression on their part which in turn contributes to increased violence against women. This has significant symbolic and ideological ramifications that add to emerging tensions over gender relations and the re-negotiation of gender roles in connection to spatial politics. The increased need to preserve patriarchal power is accompanied by women's need to challenge, tolerate, and/or cope with both internal and external hegemonic powers.

While Israel's militarized spatial policies create confusion and fear, paradoxically they also promote women's agency. Siham stated:

> This Wall will always remind me of our resistance, of our screwed-up reality, of our past, of their fear. Each time they build it higher, my grandmother laughs and tells the soldiers who are sitting all day long beside our house, that the more they do things, like walls, curfews, closures, violence, the more we know that they are scared of us. Do you know why are they scared? Because they know that we are *as'hhab haq* [the ones who have a just cause]. I sit, listen to my grandmother, and laugh with her ... but I also know that my present, my ability to move, visit friends, or go to University will be negatively affected by the Wall. So, yes, I laugh at the Wall, but I also cry so much, it scares me so much, it will block my future.

Nawal, one of the other focus group participants, asked her: 'So why do you laugh?' Siham replied: 'What else can I do but laugh at them and laugh at myself?' Nadia replied: 'Are we going crazy ... they drove us crazy, they caused us the Nakba and constant loss.'

The words of these young women show us how spaces are political products that sustain social and economic hierarchies and organize the socio-political and gendered fabric of life. Young women discussed how unemployment and poverty led many young women to leave school and work in low-paying jobs. The effect of spatial politics that further empower the powerful and further oppress the already oppressed is clear in their stories about Palestinian women who needed to work as housekeepers for Israeli settlers, the very people who are depriving them not only of a decent income but also, as Manal said, 'of having a roof above our heads'. The paradox is that such women are considered very lucky, for at least they are able to help support their families even while they are forced to perform 'undignified' work for the occupier. They are praised for being able to accept personal humiliation in return for economic independence and the ability to live in a dignified manner without having to receive help from others. Despite the blow to body and spirit, despite imprisonment of themselves and their families, they still survived.

The multilayered discourse of *shatat* reveals how the women carry within themselves a multiplicity of voices which enable different ways of looking, knowing, and assigning meanings to their contexts and experiences. Their narratives and photos show how they negotiate the multiplicity of power plays, manoeuvres, and illusions, how they challenge many issues and are not entrapped in socio-cultural ascriptions. The play of their self-images as freedom fighters and frontliners, as agents of social, political, economic, and cultural change, as mobilizers of political transformation, and even as those who preserve their 'cultural and religious codes' reflect an ongoing process of self-identity which must be encouraged, as Palestinian women seek to escape the homogenizing images promoted in official Western discourse. The young women's words, writings, and photographs form a counter-discourse that seeks to escape the replication of the oppressor's mode of thought and power.

SEXUALIZED GENDER SPACES

At the intersection between militarized spatial policies and gendered spaces also lies the politics of sexuality. In her discussion of a different context, Evelynne Accad has stated: 'If an analysis of sexuality and sexual politics would be truly incorporated into the revolutionary struggle in Lebanon, nationalism could be transformed into a more viable revolutionary strategy' (1990: 38), adding that: 'It is also evident that sexuality often works together with what may appear as more tangible factors – political, economic, social, and religious choices' (1990: 44). Similarly, Rubina Saigol discusses women's bodies as arenas of violent struggle:

> An important part of nationalism in South Africa has been the way women and their sexuality are treated as the symbols of culture, tradition and home. In a situation of national conflict, this leads to the women of the enemy being forced into a similar symbolic role. This is why while violence during communal, ethnic, and international conflicts is directed against everyone, women are violated in a sexually specific way, that is, they are raped. Not only are they raped, their bodies are marked in particular ways that are meant as reminders of their being women, the honor of the community/nation.
>
> (2000: 116)

Violation of the security of the body and the ensuing scenes of verbal and physical abuse tend to be sexualized and directed particularly towards women (see Al-Haq 1988: 40–1) as part of a strategy to upset the equilibrium of the domestic space and to sexualize its gender roles. Studies on Kosovo, for example, showed that those who suffered sexual violence were forced to live not only with the psycho-emotional effects but also with the social alienation and stigma (McKay 1998); my studies in Palestine have indicated that fear of and actual threats of sexual abuse have endangered the well being of young women (Shalhoub-Kevorkian 1994, 1998a, 2004b).

Gender-oriented victimization is well reflected in the words of Umm Riad of Jenin Camp who shared the following:

> I did not know how to handle so much pain. Every hour we heard a new story, a new rumour. It was terrible; we were thirty-six people in one room that barely could take six or seven people. We were unable to breathe or move, unable to talk most of the time, unable to cry, unable to look outside.
>
> Three weeks after she delivered her first baby, my daughter-in-law still had heavy bleeding because we never managed to take her to the hospital – the political situation prevented them from leaving the camp – and her health was in bad shape. She was with us in this small room, with three other women who started menstruating and four children with diapers. The room, the smell was very bad. We were unable to open a window or a door, and going to the bathroom was a very risky task. The smell of the blood filled the room, and the old man [i.e., her husband] got very upset, and decided to ask all menstruating women and children who urinated on themselves or who had diapers to sit in the corner. On day eight I also started menstruating, and sat with the group of

filthy woman and children, the group that cried the most, cursed themselves the most, I personally knew that being a woman is a curse, but
never imagined how much of a curse it is.

(Shalhoub-Kevorkian 2004b: 74)

In listening to Palestinian women discussing the effect of militarized
space on their bodies and sexuality, I repeatedly heard two main concerns: sexual harassment and abuse, either by the military forces or by
Palestinian taxi drivers. The young women referred to crimes of abuse on
the part of Israeli military personnel during body searches at gates or
checkpoints. Fadwa, for instance, spoke of her experience:

Two days ago, it was around 6:40 a.m., and I was on my way to college.
While I was standing in line waiting for my turn to be body searched, I
heard the voice of another Palestinian girl crying loudly from inside the
tent [the military had built tents to allow women to undergo body searches
without exposure to the public]. I got so scared, and looked around for help.
Only men and young girls were lining up, I couldn't find a woman to help
me help her. When she came out, she looked so afraid and *maswoo'qa*
[traumatized]. The girl told me not to allow them to body search me, for the
person conducting the search was not a women, but a man. See, they [the
military forces] have found another way of humiliating us.

Samaher echoed Fadwa's story:

I had a similar incident. I will tell you what happened to my cousin
Suhad, on one condition: that you don't tell anyone in here. I do not
want my father to stop me from going to college. A month ago, while it
was raining very hard, my cousin Suhad was trying to pass through a new
checkpoint that the Israelis had just put up in front of our village. They
were searching everybody, men, women, children. They had a place at
the side [i.e., of the checkpoint gate] for body searching women. When it
was Suhad's turn, the noise from the rain was so bad, and one female
soldier came in and asked her to take off her veil and gown and stand
there in her underwear. Then she left and told her she would be back. She
waited for almost ten minutes freezing from the cold, and all of a sudden a
male soldier came in and wanted to search her. She didn't know what to
do – she started screaming at him, pushing him with both hands, asking
him to leave, and then started putting her clothes back on. She got so
upset and angry, on that day she told me the story, and both of us decided
that we are going to join the *tanzim* [referring to one of the Palestinian
political parties] and get revenge for what they are doing to us. If she had
not defended herself, the soldier could have raped her, and with all the

noise that was around and the fact that it was early morning, no one would ever know. I am telling you [she bursts into tears]; it was the first time that I thought seriously of blowing up myself and many of them.

The young women also discussed how soldiers invade the privacy of women during night raids. Women related how they had been undressed by soldiers in front of their children and male family members, and how they were continually touched in abusive ways.

Discussions with the young women brought out shared feelings of anxiety and of the need to preserve oneself but also reaffirmed a shared sense of belonging and identification as Palestinian women that transcended specific narratives. It opened a new matrix of meaning, a sense of national belonging and a willingness to sacrifice one's body for the sake of resisting (*muqawameh*) and fighting back. Women's bodies became symbolic of Palestinian status, a status characterized by inequality, marginalization, and exclusion. Women also noted that the sexual abuses engendered new forms of religious, patriarchal, and political ideologies aimed at 'protecting' Palestinian women, and these new ideologies often manifested themselves in the denial of the women's full access to education, a workplace, social events, and political activism. However, once again, the dynamics of such abuse also yielded a sense of solidarity among the women that provided fertile soil for political mobilization.

In other cases, however, the 'protective' inclinations of the patriarchy increased women's vulnerability and empowered men to enforce arbitrary measures as they saw fit to further marginalize the female body from the social matrix. This is clearly apparent in the phenomenon of *zaherat al fordat*, the problem of the Ford taxi drivers who abuse women forced by circumstances to ride with them (the need to drive through various hilly, mountainous, and otherwise risky roads requires large vans, known as *fordat*, as they were manufactured by Ford). Restrictions imposed by the construction of the ISW and the attending military roadblocks and checkpoints have called for the rearrangement of the Palestinian system of transportation. Palestinians from all walks of life need to find new means of reaching their schools, workplaces, and other destinations, including the use of back roads so as to be able to avoid checkpoints. This stifling situation, exponentially aggravated by the building of the ISW, has turned taxi drivers into experts on the geography and topography of the area and on the ways to avoid military roadblocks, gates, and checkpoints. They play a valuable part in avoiding contact with the

Israeli military as much as possible during their travels. Abu Fadi, a cab driver from the Ramallah area, used to take me through fields, driving between olive trees and homes, to get me to the Family Defense Society in Nablus.

The young Palestinian women that participated in my focus groups shared their ordeals with taxi drivers. While some are helpful brothers of Palestine, like Abu Fadi, others took advantage of the isolation of the back roads and other routes to harass and even rape women. Ayshe shared with us the story of a teenager who was locked in a car for hours and sexually abused by several drivers. Fayha'a told us of a pregnant woman who was raped by many drivers, for they knew she could not get pregnant by them. Others discussed the way Ford drivers drove them around remote areas for hours trying to seduce them into performing oral sex. The stories about these drivers were varied, and referred to rape, sexual advances, gang rape, forced oral sex, harassment, and abductions in order to get money from women's families – even stories of young women who fell in love with and consequently suffered abuse from the Ford drivers – and in certain cases, married them as second wives.

By examining the ideologies, rhetoric, and militaristic social interactions through which this interweaving of spatial occupation and gender/sexual abuse occurs, we can see how the personal is political and how personal power cannot be excluded from the politics of power, particularly the politics of occupation, where space becomes a symbolic and material manifestation of that power. These stories illustrate how the physical space of the region – the checkpoints, roadblocks, and the rambling, continuous barricade of the ISW – has subsumed roads, fields, homes, villages, and boundaries as masculine political capital. As the intersection of the political, gendered, and spatial meanings of occupation, the ISW as a boundary in space is also a place of gendered abuse, a realm of contradiction and frustration. It is a marker of what it means to be a woman living under military occupation: a limited space of constricted borders. The irony of the fact that local communities are dominated by men – that these men are also abused and harassed daily beside the ISW and at checkpoints – only increases the complexity of the intersection between spatial politics, women's sexuality, and the emergence of new forms of resistance.

As Abu-Lughod notes, forms of resistance are useful means of diagnosing the location and structure of power. She reverses Foucault's proposition that 'where there is power, there is resistance' to 'where there is resistance, there is power' (1990: 42). As I have noted throughout this book, the gender and sexual abuse collectively experienced by Palestinian women, abuse particularly aggravated by the ISW, has become a basis for political mobilization, identification, and resistance, even in the midst of their need for constant self-protection. Power, as Radhika Mohanram has noted, is spatially organized (1999). These courses of action are about the production of identities – dominant ones and subordinate ones in specific spaces. The compelling question is how we might interrupt the production of dominant subjects. As a researcher and feminist, the question is how to document and understand racial formations and the production of identities in specific spaces. In exploring these questions, we examine 'the uneven geography of capital investment, legal and judicial regulatory regimes, as well as the various territorializations and deterritorializations of spaces which occur through protest, violence, ironic artistry, or simply dwelling in place' (Jacobs 1996: 10).

CONCLUSION: LIBERATING GENDERED INCARCERATED SPACES

This chapter wove together various strands of research that encompass theoretical premises and the specific voices of women to forge an analysis that draws from both the local and the global – from place to space. We examined the relationship between identity, nationhood, and space – what is imagined or projected onto specific places and bodies and what is being enacted there. The question has been raised: how does an identity of dominance keep the racial Other in general, and women in particular, in place? And how does place become race and gender? By exploring the racialization and genderization processes that are directly experienced as spatial, we hope to further understand the ideology of occupation.

In pursuing this analysis, I was confronted with several hard questions: how do we interrogate our own ways of looking? How do we regain control of dominated spaces, and how does this allow and motivate the confined Other to resist compartmentalization? When we examine space and spatial politics, how do the concepts of security and 'secure zone' shift or dissipate?

Any analyses of women's agency during times of conflict become more intricate when the process of spatial dominance and the material and symbolic meaning of the actual space of the Other further increase gender discrimination. Behind the building of the Wall is a racialized ideology that is spatially mapped onto the land itself. This ideology cannot be ignored in class, race, and gender analyses. This symbolic construction of racist separation through the very concrete Wall aims at Apartheid and as such at the reproduction of marginalization and the marginalized Other. The politics of place, as reflected in the construction of the ISW, shows how the right to mobility is reserved for Israeli-Jewish women. Such women have what Mohanram calls strong passports, while the Palestinian women have weak ones: 'Women with weak passports are normally confined within their borders' (1999: 82). Nonetheless, women frontliners have decided to continue their daily lives, their schooling, and their work despite spending hours at checkpoints, being searched and humiliated by the military forces. Yet at the same time, the economic and political violence has increased gendered classism and racism, increased women's poverty, insecurity, and vulnerability to patriarchal violence, and silenced their voices. Such silencing is exacerbated by abuse directed specifically at women, such as sexual violence (Enloe 2000: 248; Machel 2001).

In listening to the voices of these Palestinian women, sometimes reviewing and revisiting, if through memory alone, the scenes of destruction they have witnessed in various locations throughout occupied Palestine, one realizes how significant are issues of gender, space, and the pervasive sense of Otherness to a woman's own acts of agency. Confronted by spatial racism and oppression, they create new spaces of belonging that are remarkably not solely about individual restoration but rather also about healing the community.

What is the price women pay to reconstruct a liberated space in an incarcerated context? Some Palestinian women find the quest for such independence, given the conditions in which they live, to be a weakness, a selfish act that brings only loneliness for the already marginalized excluded. Others prefer to withdraw into the totality, the collective, and at the same time into the self. Women's ways of challenging the various systems of dominations, as portrayed in the repeated attacks on private and public space in the name of 'security reasoning', in many cases empowered their wills again injustice. The racialized nature of this fabricated security threat created the conditions whereby women spoke counter-discourses to hegemonic ones. These women frontliners understand their actions for what they are – political resistance. They refuse to let the West 'culturalize' their acts as merely the nurturing instincts of the less-civilized, less-liberated Arab woman. Nurturers they are, and I do not think any of them would wish to refuse that label, but if feminism accepts that the personal is political, then why can't acts of nurturing, particularly collective nurturing in the face of disaster, also be political acts?

In the absence of resources and globalized support, Palestinian women shared with us new epistemologies that created an atmosphere of sharing the *shatat* but also preventing it from hindering their acts. Their gathering of the displaced by offering various counter-discourses in the community is built on their accounts and future lives. Women have constructed new counter-discourses and counter-spaces to cope with the constant and unpredictable changes affecting unemployment, their lack of physical safety, their social and economic insecurity, restrictions on movement, and so on. Some of those counter-discourses are apparent in women's constant efforts to maintain gendered traditions, such as early marriage or adjusting their educational goals or place of work. Other counter-discourses are based on historical legacy and premises. By invoking the historical and political legacy of displacement and loss, women-oriented counter-discourses manage to turn loss into a source of power and encouragement. Women use the nation's history to lift their own personal and their family's morale. This encourages them to keep up their daily activities, such as going to school, finding a job, coping with imprisonment and loss, and moving to a new location to better deal with new restrictions. Additional counter-discourses are more transformative and innovative, creating counter-spaces to the ghettoizing ones through women's actions, reactions, and proactive activities.

The literature on women in war zones generally attempts to reveal women's victimization in contexts of conflict, particularly in the private sphere. This chapter, in contrast, has shown the confluence of the private sphere and the larger political and politicized space beyond. Women's modes of resistance and coping reveal their efforts to preserve their families and communities. Their investments in the re-creation of the 'safe haven', in empowering the victimized, and in protecting society from a descent into despair, calls for a new feminist perspective into victimization and agency itself.

Some of the participants in our study looked at violence against the occupier as a mode of facing abuse and raising their gender role in society. This is a very serious issue that needs nuanced and sustained study. Women are fighting multiple struggles, both internally and externally. They fight against tradition, but when the occupier chooses tradition as a weapon of attack, many women revert to defending it, for it then becomes conflated with a sense of home and identity. Thus, many who are fighting neo-colonial occupation find themselves pushed towards fundamentalism.

How can we stop Empire from growing? Perhaps a way to begin is by rewriting our histories, documenting our memories, exposing the world to the cruelties of Empire, and reinventing civil disobedience in the way that the Palestinian women have been doing – whether this be through the continuing struggle to live, by taking photographs of the ISW that declare their vision of it, or by ululating in opposition to the soldiers. Perhaps we can begin by saying that Palestinian acts of resistance are not 'terrorism' but rather the privatization of war. I here return to an earlier question: what are the concrete effects of such spatial political restructuring on the raced, classed, nationalized, and sexual bodies of women – in schools, on the street, in the workplace, in neighbourhoods, prisons, and social and political movements? How do we recognize gendered effects in militarized spatial politics? And how is all this related to the changes faced by women in the public as well as in the private space?

One of the most commonly found analyses that links the centrality of gender to spatial politics attempts to connect gendered spatial politics to questions of subjectivity, agency, and identity with the political state's economy and – I add – militaristic values and violence. I argue that there is a need to rethink patriarchy and hegemonic masculine power in terms of imperialism and nationalism, and to re-theorize the gendered aspects of colonization in relation to the political occupation. In so doing, we can focus on unpredictable sites of resistance and their effect on the global imperial power's efforts to restructure local gender roles. Empire's restructuring of gender roles actually increases the centrality of gender in the local, global, and imperial restructuring of gender. As Mohanty has stated (and many feminists have echoed): 'the reorganization of gender is part of the global strategy of capitalism' (Mohanty 2003: 245). In the Palestinian case, women's bodies and lives – particularly women from lower socio-economic strata, internally displaced women (IDW), and those who have suffered greatly from political violence – are used and abused by hegemonic masculinities and patriarchies. The rise of religious fundamentalism in conjunction with conservative nationalism in reaction to Israeli spatial politics and the global Empire's capital and cultural demands has transformed the policing of women's bodies, movement, and lives into an additional war front. The policing of the bodies of the poor and internally displaced who are imprisoned behind the concrete Separation Wall brings the intersection of gender, race, occupation, and capitalist interest to the centre.

185

By focusing on the importance of locations and placements, we also complicate the meaning of the way we look at space and place as sites not only of boundary crossing but also of boundary making that produces and re-produces gender roles – and gender violence as well. I have shown how the occupier's settler-colonial plans do not exist outside history, place, and politics, and how the Palestinians in general and Palestinian women in particular are mired in social and political forces. By carefully examining the words and photos of the young women who have shared their stories, we reveal the ways in which women's bodies are embedded in the histories of space and place: 'Place', according to them, is their 'woman's place'. This place affects women's ways of building their identities, identities that are neither unchanging nor static. The narratives of women confronting the ISW portray how 'women in place' create their identities within an oppressor's culture.

CHAPTER 6

RUMINATIONS AND FINAL THOUGHTS: WOMEN IN-BETWEEN

As a child growing up in a Palestinian family, I always wondered how my mother, my mother-in-law, and all the women I encountered had managed to endure all that they had experienced. Looking at Palestinian women today, including my own daughters, I realize how the generations that came before us prepared us for our current ordeals. The everyday struggle to survive the violent effects of the colonial-settler project and the constant political hardships that Palestinian women face – keeping their families and the social fabric intact, facing displacement and dislocation, enduring abuse – have enabled women to construct counter-spaces that allow them to survive and to envision that they might some day attain the justice they have so longed for.

While writing the concluding remarks that comprise this chapter, I became aware of the irony of the power vested in written texts as also a place of struggle and the meanings that may accrue to such texts. The menace of the Zionist war against the Palestinian entity, the courageous acts of the frontliners, the massacres, the Nakba, the Naksa, the constant battles – these have formed my background as well as the framework of my present existence much more so than the daily activities of family life. My aim in this concluding chapter is to attempt a summary of the archaeology and technology of domination primarily through the lens of my own experiences and reminiscences. Furthermore, as I have attempted to show through the voices and actions of women in this volume, hegemonic power always harbours the potential to be disrupted and undermined by human agency – with regards to the specific narratives in this volume, the actual and potential force of disruption of women's

187

agency and their constant search for justice. Challenging power and the politics of domination reveals not only the operations of that power on the mind and the body but may also, as I have been arguing, provide individuals with the power to re-invent their self-identities whereby together in groups they can contest the material and discursive practices that oppress us. It is by taking a position between the possibilities of visionary thinking and the innovative practices of Palestinian women that I am able to claim the authority of my own experiences and thus claim myself as part of the collective, name the violence that has been committed upon us, and offer my interpretations as I move to conclude this book. My radical standpoint and the 'politics of my space' are what have given me the voice with which to transgress and move 'out of my space' in a movement pushing against oppressive boundaries that are established by dominating powers. It is the 'politics of our stolen spaces and stolen time' that has given women in conflict zones, as much as it has given us Palestinian women, the power to pull down colonial boundaries and create new choices, realities, and locations.

EYES AND NO EYES

The voices of the women shared in this book are included not merely to share strategies to enable negotiations or transformations, or to share learning about how to survive or to better their world. More importantly, what these women have shared represents an opportunity to engage in social praxis through the constant surveying of social powers while learning how not to take those powers for granted – instead, there is an opportunity to realize how social movements and differential modes of oppositional consciousness can be enabled by the very powers of oppression themselves.

Recently, these voices loudly spoke to me when I dropped off my partner at his clinic in Esaweyyeh, a Palestinian village in Jerusalem. I was stopped by a squad of soldiers who had constructed, within four minutes, a flying checkpoint that was not on the street when I first drove in. I was ordered to line up against a wall, in public, in the cold, with a group of Palestinians who were trying to leave their village and go to their schools, workplaces, health clinics, and so on. We communicated to each other without words, through facial and hand gestures, and eyes that were asking 'When will this uncertainty be over?' In silence we helped each other to find our place within the confusion of militarized space as we were forced to co-operate with the soldiers. We were angry, yet not surprised. After all, for a long time now we have been witnessing the way in which our spaces continue to be sites of brutalization and how the supposedly safe road that leads into and out of the village can be suddenly militarized. The soldiers ordered the men to line up on the left side of the street while women were lined up on the right side. Our bodies were used to draw lines between men and women and also between the ones with power – the soldiers – and those lacking it – us Palestinians; but our minds and souls created a new kind of solidarity – a collective marginality that survived the coldness of the space and weather.

The soldiers drove their two jeeps closer to us, the women, while they sat in them with their rifles pointed towards us. The men were asked to put their hands on the wall and they were searched one by one by the soldiers. We women were asked to move three metres south of the jeeps; the soldiers wanted to make sure they could see us clearly. It was cold, I was leaning on the wall behind me, very upset; there was too much uncertainty, I was going to be late for work, and my warm coat was in the car (since they had stopped me and ordered me to step out of the car without allowing me to take my coat). Um Ahmad, a woman of perhaps fifty years, who stood tall beside me without leaning on the wall, asked me whether I was really cold (I was shivering) and whether I had or needed a coat. When I told her that it was in the car, she called the soldiers and requested in Arabic that we be allowed to go get the coat. Her voice made him jump, and using his weapon to confront us, he screamed that we should go back and stand closer to the wall. He feared our Arabic language; he feared Um Ahmad's concern and courage. Um Ahmad did not fear him, she knew already that this detainment would continue for a long time, and she took the lead by telling a school girl to take out her books and study, by asking a young mother to breastfeed her crying baby, and by asking me to speak again to the soldier about getting my coat and perhaps allowing the young mother to sit in my car in order to breastfeed her baby.

Within ten minutes, the scene on the road that leads to and away from Esaweyeeh was changed. New meanings were added to that location and to our wasted time, new solidarity and relationships of love and care were created, and new ways of fighting back had been invented. Between my ability to speak Hebrew and Um Ahmad's organizational skills, we were able to create a counter-discourse and a counter-space to the militarized ones, ones different ones than those that reside in the place where meaning is unstable, without anything to anchor it. This scene of humiliation, intended to divide women from men through the performance of a masculine military ritual also aimed to demonstrate to the Palestinian men and women their 'impotence' in the face of such humiliation and so show us the 'omnipotence' of their military power. The entire scene made me realize how meanings are within the eyes of the beholder, and my eyes saw much more than those who were trying to oppress us were able to comprehend. Those of us lined up against the wall as Palestinians created other meanings, implications escaping any finality and able to evade the contours of the power around us. The oppositional and largely unspoken language of struggle that we created as Palestinians in our own space, on our familiar village road leading to work, to school, to health clinics, to life, created multiple and liminal meanings that escape the eyes of the occupiers.

The objectification of myself that I experienced when told to line up, in the cold, while stripped of my voice and dignity, made me dig back into my memories and forward in searching for a way out, while at the same time living the moment of Um Ahmad and the men and women around me with the love and solidarity that was created. Forced to stand in the street, leaning on the freezing wall that rendered the whole world concrete for the moment, under drops of rain, I suddenly heard another woman standing beside us saying: 'Thank God that it has started raining, it did not rain this year and we need the rain. People will remain ill if it doesn't rain ... Thank God, thank God.' Her talk about the importance of the rain in reducing our suffering shifted the militarized context in which this humiliating incident played out and allowed for an explosion of other meanings, meanings that normalized and humanized the situation, such as the sudden thanks sent up to God for the rain that would ensure the harvest, and thus our survival.

This incident, as with many others, brought me back to my constant reapportioning of my spaces, my boundaries that I engage with. On that day at the checkpoint, we Palestinians worked out ways to realign our oppositional powers. Standing at that makeshift checkpoint, I understood in a visceral way yet again how women's agency is contingent and spontaneous, in keeping with their constant struggle for freedom, their commitment to do the right thing. As I have attempted to relate through my recounting of this incident, living under occupation affects time and memory in strange and unexpected ways. Moments float free of their confines and attach to other fragments of time, half-remembered, half-anchored in a different time and place, bringing with them their accompanying emotions but also recollections of acts of resistance and triumph as well. I think of other stories and memories that float like strands in a collective pool of time and history. I hear now in my head my mother's stories, almost like a chant, repeated many times, picking up a thread in time; she would go on to other things, and then return to pick up the thread again, laying down another stitch in the tapestry that she wove for us.

My mother told me many stories about the way women were affected by events before the Palestinian Nakba of 1948 and the time following it. In transcribing a tape-recorded interview with her in June 2006, she told me about her grandmother:

> She was a very wise woman. During the 1930s, she used to read the newspapers and would tell us about the world. Once she explained to me that some [locusts] were eating the plants. We were all worried that the Zionists would bring more and more locusts to eat the plants, and so force us to leave the place. She was very wise. She had a long fight with my father, she wanted me to finish my school and get education. All the girls in my school managed to graduate, what we used to call in French breve.

Sometimes she would look away, as if in the hazy distance she could see the scenes replaying, or so I think. She would then come back to the present moment and continue:

> My father used to work with the *thuwa'ar* [the revolutionaries, the rebels], they used to carry guns and defend the country. Jews used to kill Arabs and Arabs used to kill Jews … My father was working hard to free Palestine; he was very active gathering activists in our house and in planning their activities … that was during the 1930s … I think that one of the reasons that my father wanted me to marry early was his fear of the Jews … we actually needed to move to Acca from Haifa out of fear of persecution.
>
> When I was in Rahbat Al Nasreh school in Abbas/Haifa, I was around ten or twelve … we were very afraid walking in the streets The British used to support both Arabs and Jews, one day they used to work with the Palestinians and another day with the Jews … My friend Nahi and her sister used to pick me up and walk me to school … they used to shoot people while they were walking. People used to be shot to death in the streets and we were so afraid … girls were more afraid than the boys …
>
> After I got married – I was only twelve years old – my parent's house was in Al Mukhales Street … We had a large house, a big hall and five rooms. I was with my son Toufiq … they killed a Palestinian, and threw his body in front of the house … then we decided to leave the house and move to my grandmother's house.

In 1948 ... they [the revolutionaries] would stand in line beside the fence ... I used to give them ammunition; I even carried weapons and shot at them [i.e., the Zionists] many times ... My husband [at that time] used to prepare them [the freedom fighters] and we worked together to defend our land. There were big [containers] ... and we were behind them trying to protect our country, our land ... My husband was a soldier in the area; he was high-ranking [officer] ... he was around twenty-eight years old. All the men and women were involved in defending our homes and our children. Your own father Jamil was also involved. He directed the activities in Haret il Kanayes, which is today called Stanton. Your father and my ex-husband were all fighting. Sima'an, my ex-husband, used to bring the ammunition and hide it in an outside storage room. There was a long fence in the German Colony where I was living. The Jabrah Jammal family also left, they fled the area, but they left before us and told us to use their house while they were away. The Jammal family had two girls; their parents were afraid and worried about their daughter's honour, so they left. The Palestinian soldiers used to blockade the area and prevent the Jews from passing. So Jews were in one area and Palestinians in the other. I was very afraid; I was around fifteen years old, with three children ... When we left, when we fled the area, the Jews were shooting at us all the way. I couldn't even say farewell to my own family. We left Haifa in a small boat filled with many people, all Palestinians. I did not take anything with me, no food, no clothing, no money. I just left.

The stories of the killing in Il-Mijedel and other places frightened all of us and made us run away. So many people were telling stories regarding massacres. They [the Jews] started massacring Palestinians in villages, so we in the city were afraid and started leaving our homes, believing that they would soon come and kill us all. We were not sure who was killing us [i.e. at the time], the British or the Zionist Jews ... at that time we did not think about it ...

How did we decide to leave? It was early morning. I could not sleep because of the shooting. No one was left in the building ... those who stayed went to the convent of Dir Mar Elias [Stella Marris]. My husband [at that time] told me that the Jews in the Haganah [the Zionist army] were looking for me, and that we must leave. I walked with my three children towards the sea, and maybe fifty or sixty people were in it. We went to Acca, there were plenty of cars, service, taxis, and with other people who had fled from their homes. The ride in the boat was so bad, children were crying, people were vomiting, we barely made it to Soor [a city in southern Lebanon]. We arrived at Soor exhausted ... it was late at night. We rented two donkeys for transportation, the kids were crying, we needed food. On our way to A'q'tanit, the village of my in-laws, I ended up knocking on some families' doors asking for milk and some food for my children. I told the people there that we were refugees from Palestine, the

Jews had kicked us out, and we needed food for the kids. I felt so humiliated, but had no other choice but to beg for food.

We reached A'q'tanit at 4:00 a.m. We were so tired, for the children were on the donkeys sleeping, but both my husband and I were walking all the way. All the way, both my husband and I were crying at our fate and about life, how we lost everything. He felt so humiliated. I felt so bad for the men; they were really in a bad way, walking with their heads down. They tried so hard to protect the land, we women tried so hard to confront, to resist them and face them, but the British army helped the Jews ... we tried our utmost.

We lived with the whole family, with Samir Elias, Zahieh, and Izabel and George, and I came with my husband and children. My mother-in-law used to cook for all of us, and I used to collect firewood and drew water from the spring. Although the whole family was born and raised in Haifa, they all immigrated before us, found a house in the village (which was my mother-in-law's brother's house) and stayed there. My father-in-law was working for the British Mandate, and my husband also worked as a labourer for the British army. But during the *Thawrah* [i.e., the Arab Revolt] and before 1948, they all participated in protecting us from the killing and threat of the Zionists. When the Der Yasin and Mujedel massacres occurred, we began running away by sea, to Soor in Lebanon and from there to Beirut. My uncle Naemeh and Afif also fled Haifa, and during the war in 1948, the Nakba, they left all they had in Haifa, their shops, their houses and by sea they went to Beirut. Our financial situation was manageable in the beginning, but with the deterioration of the political and economic situation, and the fear of the unexpected, my husband felt the need to go and look for a job in Beirut. I stayed three months, maybe four with my in-laws, and then moved with him to Beirut.

I lived with my husband and my three children in Beirut Al-Ashrafiya, in a small room underneath the stairs. My neighbour Mary allowed me to help her as a tailor. I used to shorten dresses, fix clothing, and tailor new clothes, just for the sake of having an additional income and so find a way to feed my children. Our financial situation was bad and we as Palestinians were not wanted in Lebanon. The Lebanese people used to be disgusted when they met a Palestinian, and would stand far away from us. My cousin Michel, who lives now in Orange County, could tell you so many stories about the hardships he faced after they all immigrated to Lebanon. Life was very hard, we were not in our country, we were not wanted by anybody, our economic situation was very bad, and then on top of all this my ex-husband Simaa'n [her first one] became very cruel and violent ... he used to hit me badly.

When the violence continued, my uncle's wife came and told me that they couldn't stand the social scandal his violence was causing them anymore. They called my grandmother and she came and picked me up, and she wanted to help me to return to Haifa. She promised to take care of my three children and asked me to go back to my own parents in Haifa, so we [i.e., herself and her grandmother] went to Alma Al Shueb village in southern Lebanon. My cousin promised to help me cross the border. When we were beside the border, they started shooting and my cousin told me that he had four kids and couldn't help me cross anymore. He wanted to go back to the village. I refused to go back, and wanted to continue on. I wanted to go back home, to my home in Haifa. I did not care about the shootings, or the risk of being caught or killed. I promised myself never again to accept humiliation. He showed me the way, he pointed out the mountain, and the road, and explained to me exactly what I should expect. And I knew I was a very intelligent woman, so I remembered all the information, repeated it to him to make sure I understood the route. Then, he left me, and I remained alone ... I cried so much. I was only fifteen years old. But then, I prayed and prayed, and cried more. [My mother started crying when she was telling me about her fear for being alone in the mountains. Not knowing what was to be her destiny, I also started crying with her.] I slept a bit under the tree, and woke up so scared ... and started walking as my cousin had directed. He told me that there are lots of apple trees on the way, and warned me never to touch the apples, for they [the Zionists] had placed many ambushes on the road, and they knew that many Palestinians were trying to cross the borders to go back home and that they would be hungry. I walked and walked, was very hungry and thirsty, but did not touch any food along the road, until I reached El-Bassah. Then I stopped beside a tree, my hair was nice and short – for I just had a haircut in Beirut – so with my short hair, and after I combed my hair, added some lipstick so as to look Western if they caught me, I felt better. I also knew some Hebrew words, such as Shalom, and Ma Nishma. I walked in the street as if I was not afraid and took the bus to Nahariyah. When I reached Nahariyah, I was so tired, scared, and thirsty. I suddenly saw a water pipe that was broken, so I drank from the water. I looked around me and heard the voice of Palestinian men speaking Arabic – so I asked them to help me and show me my way to the bus that went to Haifa. They helped me and showed me my way from Nahariyah to Haifa. I reached Haifa, and knew God gave me the power, because he knew I suffered from injustice, that I was oppressed. God gave me the power, for God always gives the oppressed more power.

I heard stories such as this one, in fragments, for stretches at a time, and so aggressively silenced at others. Repeated, picked up by memory's logic again and begun anew. Time becomes elastic under occupation, and the colonization of the land, in the past, present, and future, and these often merge, cohere for a moment, and again disentangle into separate threads. One hears one's own life in the stories of others; there seems an infinite continuum of memories and experiences. Sometimes you lose track of which memory is your own and which belongs to someone else. My mother's ordeals of living in exile so often mirror my own – her constant yearning to return to an imagined 'home' when life away becomes unpredictable and unbearable.

My mother had a very strong Christian belief that she could talk directly to God, and she also believed that 'the Lord' would respond to her directly as well. This was also consistent with Arab Muslim tradition in Palestine, which viewed the world through a belief in God's ultimate justice and sense of rightness. My mother used her spirituality as a counter-discourse to the injustices she perceived and experienced around her. Her faith provided her with the ability to live through the hardships of everyday life, to build her ethical standards and her convictions in the struggle. This included raising us, her children who were born more than ten years after the Nakba following upon her love affair with and marriage to my late father, and also economically supporting and emotionally encouraging my father to educate himself and become a lawyer. Her tradition of praying, her spirituality, her interpretation of Jesus as the saviour, the equalizer, the liberator, appropriated her hopes for justice and achievement of rightness.

While remembering my mother's ordeal, I understood anew the unique ways in which women have been involved in the Palestinian struggle. I appreciate more clearly the effect of the Nakba on her own personal life, the fact that she tried to live in exile but could not take the daily violence and humiliation, and understand her persistence in wanting to return 'home' even without her children. She was told and was convinced that her children would be better off with their grandmother than with her – although she repeatedly mentioned how she so often refused to think about or openly discuss the Nakba, because it was the reason for her separation from her children and of her children's deprivation of the love and care of their mother.

To leave that space called home and so to exist without boundaries, all the while trying with nothing left to build new kinds of homes, and then having to respond to the innate urge to return to the lost home, all this transforms such exilic locations into a site of struggle. Coming *back* home was no less traumatic, for home itself was turned into exile – and that exacerbated the sense of loss, estrangement, and alienation. Indeed, the meaning of the Palestinian home, our home, changed the constructions of meanings and acts in the lives of Palestinian women and men. The violence of colonization on women turned home – whether at home proper or in exile – into a 'nowhere' home. The lost home, whether within home space or without it, transformed the Palestinian home for us women into not just a home or place, but also into a psychological, social, and political location that enables and promotes the constant discovery of new modes of resistance to re-create home. For us women, the loss of the home and the constant hegemonic attack on even one's memories carried with it the anaemic sense of our ability to see where we are, who we are, who we can become, and more. Turning Palestinian women into refugees at home made them engage with actual political struggle both within and outside Palestinian society in order to assert their critical presence.

Yet, these women like my mother were and are freedom fighters who have lived through exile and occupation, and they provided us with both an example and a legacy of the fight that is before us. My mother's history makes me remember the words of Edward Said when, while discussing exile, he said;

> exile can produce rancour and regret, as well as a sharpened vision. What has been left behind may either be mourned, or it can be used to provide a different set of lenses. Since almost by definition exile and memory go together, it is what one remembers of the past and how one remembers it that determines how one sees the future.
>
> (Said 2002: xxxv)

My own memories of my childhood necessarily seem more direct or clear, but they echo so many of the thematic concerns of my mother's stories, of her history. As a child who grew up in Haifa during the 1960s, I was forbidden to even utter the word 'Palestine', to learn about my history, or carry my flag, nor did I feel free in my own home. I was born in a house that used to be a Church – Al Mukhales, the Saviour's Church, on a street of the same name. At one point, my late father had to take down the cross that was on top of the house, because the Jewish Israelis used to spit every time they saw it. The Israelis also changed the street name to a Hebrew one. They decided to put the new name on our house. My memories of being called 'dirty Arab' in our own land never left me and during the 1960s, the verbal manifestation of the militarism that surrounded us was reflected in such racial epithets. Even today, my home in the Old City of Jerusalem is akin to the one in Esaweyyeh where the pervasive militarization campaign escalates into material destruction, manifesting our 'dirtiness' in the violence enacted upon us rather than in mere verbal epithets. As my experience at the checkpoint illustrates, we continue, as had our mothers and as particularly exemplified by Um Ahmad, by reappropriating our oppression and aligning our oppositional energies and powers to create new patterns of survival, to form what Chela Sandoval has called a 'hermeneutics of love' (Sandoval 2000: 180). This same energy and the set of meanings it carries is operant because war and conflict zones allow and constitute a state of exception – a space in which 'law' in the traditional sense is completely postponed, and citizens, particularly women, are reduced to the frugality of their excluded and naked lives. Even so, the very state of exception, as I have been arguing all along, allows for possibilities.

Thus not surprisingly, the colonialist policy that has always operated through a masculinist, hegemonic machinery that has supported and continues to support the Israeli state failed to hinder the rise of Palestinian feminism, given that many Palestinian women questioned the morality and authority of supposedly 'universal' imperial powers. Palestinian women had given up hope that the world at large would ever intervene on their behalf. As a result, the case of the Palestinian people caused my critical and feminist consciousness to grow. My own instinctive claims as a child for treatment as a human person always refused marginalization as 'the Other' that was imposed upon me. I understood the biases with which Palestinians were portrayed as a people by the media and, closer to home, the derision with which our Jewish neighbours treated us. Both would lead me as an adult to question the politics of knowledge production and devote a great deal of my scholarly energies to questioning the epistemologies of the powerful that are always circulated as self-evident 'truths'.

Questioning the 'truth' was an integral part of our family life, and we each did it in our own way. For my mother and my mother-in-law, it was more an issue of faith, of trust in God, of being baffled by the injustice of a supposedly just world that never gave us a hand to better our lives. As a family, we were taught to query and also to try to understand the reasons behind our oppression, of why were we deprived of our own history. But eventually such questioning led to awesome silences: I remember well my mother's refusal to share her hardships with me (interestingly enough, she has done so lately, remembering those early years of silence). Even my father, who was a prominent lawyer in Haifa, would go silent when questions arose concerning the sources of our oppression, and my mother-in-law, my Nene as we always called her, a woman who survived the Armenian genocide but lost all her family members to it, also felt that silence was a better language. She talked about the massacre, but not about her family being victimized and slaughtered during it; she talked about her school and education, but not about being a student without parents. She participated in all the memorials, enduring a great emotional anguish that refused to be translated into words except during limited, face-to-face occasions. My family's silence led me to think many questions. This perpetual questioning of life, of justice (or the lack thereof), inquiring about issues of equality and fairness, all haunted me as a child, as a young woman, and now as a mother myself of three young women, and as a feminist, activist, and teacher. But unlike my parents, I have not remained silent in the face of atrocities.

When I married, I felt and understood the love of my mother-in-law, Mary Kevorkian, dear Nene, for the Palestinian people and their constant struggle for freedom. She believed in the Palestinian leadership, and often refused to listen to my criticisms against some of their internal policies, particularly their attitudes towards gender violence. Nene's sometimes-blind support was based on her own need to unequivocally support the oppressed, given the oppression of her own nation during the Armenian genocide. Nene shared her wisdom with me, particularly sharing her own ordeal as a young girl who had lost her family and ended up being raised in an orphanage in Beirut. She shared with me her love story, of her love for my late father-in-law, and about the way she travelled and eventually came to Jerusalem. She was very proud of the fact that she was an educated woman, trained as a nurse, and that she had the ability to support herself economically – and later even to support her family as the only nurse in the neighbourhood. Nene's stories were not necessarily important for their specificity, rather, they were remembrances that foregrounded the need to fight oppression, the need to fight for justice; to hear the unheard and make visible the hidden. One of the foundational themes of her stories was what she would call the story about 'Eyes and No Eyes'. The story tells of two people who were looking at shops and houses as they were walking down a street. One said: 'Did you see the two people who were killing each other, the blood on the street?' His friend answered: 'No, I did not see any of those things; all I saw were the shop windows that looked so nice.' Nene would say: 'This is the case with the Palestinians. This is the case with the Armenians who have suffered genocide. No one has acknowledged their victimization, no one has apparently seen it. It is eyes and no eyes. Some people choose not to see what is apparent.'

Nene's account of the selective vision of human beings is reflected in the work of T. Minh-ha Trinh who quotes an Indian witch:

> They see no life
> When they look
> They see only objects.
> ....They fear
> They fear the world.
> They destroy what they fear.
> They fear themselves.
> ....Stolen rivers and mountains
> The stolen land will eat their hearts.
>
> (Trinh 1989: 132)

Given the effect of colonization, a colonization that aimed to look at us but not see us, yet fearing us nonetheless, and given the discursive traditions of my family and my formative years, it is not surprising that the plight of women in conflict areas and war zones and the politics that contextualize them have absorbed my life since childhood. My two mothers, my biological mother and my mother-in-law, are the product of the Palestinian Nakba (in the case of my mother) and the Armenian genocide (in the case of my mother-in-law). My two mothers have influenced, though sometimes in an incomplete, vicarious and informal manner, my interest in and analytical approach towards women's issues – particularly the effects of gender violence. For me, the hegemonic politics of denial surrounding both the Armenian genocide and the Palestinian Nakba and its aftermath provide the psychic geography for my explorations. In the same way, these events were the subjects of my mother's imagination, recollections, stories, and ideology, providing the parameters of their conception of culture, their thinking on 'home', and their religious beliefs. It is important to note that this psychic terrain has always been represented elegiacally, attaining congruence with displacement, dispossession, and exile.

The most influential women in my life have always tried to hide the sense of dissonance that comes from their being in exile – in the case of Palestinian women, ironically, having been in exile *at home*. The sense of dislocation, fear, and disorientation always required on their part a tremendous expenditure of energy to re-create a sense of 'home'. As dialogue with the Palestinian women I have met and learned from over the years – including conversations with my two mothers – has revealed the struggle to establish a counter-discourse, to construct alternative spaces of safety and challenge the system without increasing their geo-political and socio-cultural losses. They created a territory, both physical and psychological, to replace the lost one, but they never wanted to replace the power, memories, and love the old territory held for them and which over the years they have embodied. My Palestinian and Armenian mothers and my extended family of Palestinian women search for a workable present while functioning in a state that addresses both the past and a corresponding loss of that past and/as history. Their exilic status kept them on guard and constantly sceptical, but also made them create and re-create alternative spaces and communities from out of their memories and private subjectivities which they had always managed to preserve.

My mothers, as they carried within them their causes, their social justice projects, provided me with examples of listening to the exilic visions and insights of women. Over the many years that I have been working in the region, I have heard many voices of Palestinian women. My project, the sharing of those voices in this book, has shown me the terrible trans-formation that my mothers' hopes have gone through: what was perceived by my mothers as hopeful world-liberating movements have degraded into a miserable imprisonment, a 'peace process' that never ends and a daily fight for survival. By living in the area, by the constant reappointment of spaces, new meanings, of boundaries, I was also able to learn how my mothers and the many women I worked with realigned their realities while creating different kinds of patterns that permitted their entry at different points. While listening to the women around me, I have come to recognize the universality of their, of our, suffering, a suffering that transcends the local and so unmasks the effect of political conflict on subaltern women everywhere. I have also come to recognize the energies revolving around the process of aligning and realigning and the way this generates opposi-tional politics and discourses that produce new conjectural possibilities, as in my own experience with Um Ahmad in Esaweyyeh.

The many ways that Palestinian women have reacted when violated and abused reveals a constant disruption of the militaristic technologies and strategies that oppose our survival strategies. Hopefully, this book has provided the reader with a view of the possible ways one can initiate a critical practice of criticism that would allow a disruption of the theoret-ical orthodoxies that exist with regard to women's voices and the manner in which we listen to them. While the voices that permeate this book are of women who reside in conflict zones and militarized spaces and so are struggling for their survival, the depiction of their voices reflects the intention of this book to directly confront those who hold hegemonic power and continue to implement colonizing policies – and thus remind them of their obligation to stop violence against women and understand the plight of women living in militarized zones, spaces that I have called elsewhere in the book weaponized spaces. It is important to recognize that while these women are beholden to those who have power over them (sometimes the power of life or death), their narratives within this book are material evidence of their refusal to accept the over-determined configurations of hegemonic masculinities that attempt to exclude and oppress them. These are voices of women who – each according to her ability – have rejected the dreary failure of the world to stop the abuses inflicted upon them, choosing instead to deny the hopelessness of their reality through action, singing, screaming, loving, the education of themselves and their families, and support for peers. In many instances, the narratives of these women are aligned with the dynamics of the Palestinian cause itself: the ways in which it is a struggle against oppression, ideological terrorism, cultural determinism, religious fundamentalism, national domination, and economic tyranny.

Through presenting these voices, I aimed to emphasize the agency of the women amidst their struggles and not just or simply their 'victimization'. Although the 'voice' of Palestinian women is pluri-vocal and presents a multiplicity of views, this voices shares a common ground in accentuating the inseparability of the private and the public, the personal and the political, and the confluence of gender, class, race, and culture in the processes of marginalization and struggle for liberation. In the remaining sections of this chapter, I share some of the possible directions that our myriad oppositional strategies might take amidst a state of exile at 'home'.

A STATE OF DISPLACED IN-BETWEENNESS

> Borders are set up to define the places that are safe and unsafe ... A border is a dividing line, a narrow strip along a steep edge. A borderland is a vague and undermined place created by the emotional residue of an unnatural boundary. It is in a constant state of transition. The prohibited and forbidden are its inhabitants.
>
> (Gloria Anzaldúa 1987)

For women, states of exile, and for Palestinian women in particular the state of exile at home – what I have called elsewhere a state of

201

in-betweenness, of liminality – not only challenges any state of belonging that one might be able to imagine in the midst of struggles but also brings to the fore the recognition that such betweenness is racialized, sexualized, and genderized. Women's efforts to create an alternative home when they are already at 'home' results in a re-conceptualization of this 'home' as a place of safety where women become the central sources of that safety. As revealed through the voices of the women in this book, the historical and economic legacy of Palestine transforms the activism of women into a site of both liberation and oppression as activism must be negotiated between the belief of the occupied in liberatory possibilities and the internal patriarchal structures of Palestinian society, itself a source of oppression. The encounter with occupation and colonization situates women in what I am here calling a state of *Shatat*, 'expulsion' – in-betweenness – of exile while at home.

This unique state of exile situates women within a material and psychic temporality that constantly reminds them that their inclusion is limited depending on their adherence to 'the rules'. As the previous chapters have illustrated, one cannot study the *betweenness* of such exile without examining the national struggle (as discussed in Chapter 3), weaponization and sexual politics (Chapter 4), and geo-political policies (Chapter 5), all of which are salient components of that exile. Thus, the struggles of women and my own struggles as a feminist, activist, and scholar necessarily incorporate issues expressed at the local, regional, national, and transnational levels. Attempts to situate myself within the complex dynamics of the region prompted my exploration of the construction of local masculinities and its effects on women, even when these women were celebrating their creation of national or cultural identities along with Palestinian men in the face of adversity. This perpetual duality provokes a recasting of previous analytical frames employed to understand Palestinian resistance, for it is situated – both physically and psychically, as I have argued throughout this book – within the context of an occupied and militarized space/place, replete with strategies of the masculine and hyper-masculine – and of emasculation as well.

The analysis of women's resistance and agency in this book leads us to the realization that both the dynamic and the expression of this resistance and agency can only be understood if we examine the ways in which women come to negotiate the various masculinities that enfold them both locally and globally. This negotiation is part of their ontological 'betweenness'. Women's daily negotiations between the home, the homeland, the global, and the historical, along with the endurance of immediate everyday challenges, produces women who are in many ways 'free' *in* their enslavement and who are liberated in ways that remain unaccounted for by Western Empire. These women create their own meaning and build agency, sometimes literally from the nothingness around them; all the while being cognizant of their roots and history, they offering counter-discourses, counter-spaces, and counter-narratives. This kind of activism and agency problematizes Western feminism's concepts of the politics of representation, particularly as such politics aim to include the 'Other woman'. I believe it is time for the West to come to acknowledge its own limitations in confrontation with a new kind of feminism. As a Palestinian woman, as the Other, the marginal, the different, and the minority, we are always already constructed within exclusionary strategies that ironically normalize our exilic status as the failure to resist the internal (and internalized) hyper-masculine impositions of the 'Arab male'. The complex negotiations that Palestinian women engage in, as reflected in this book through women's voices themselves, should therefore illuminate *our own processes of knowledge production and the kinds of feminisms that are possible in such contexts.*

Thus, methodologically, it is imperative to bring together the political, economic, and historical legacies that obtain in the region, and further to scrutinize the politics of colonization and representation in order to examine the possible re-creation of oppressive genealogies within post-modern feminist practice itself. It seems to me that it is not enough to always try to locate these problems outside of our own political, theoretical, and scholarly practices. It is imperative to learn how, when, and why to restrict our complicity with the re-creation of exiled women by begetting occupied women. We must examine the humanist and individualist preconceptions employed in much contemporary Western feminism in order to reach an understanding of the ways in which 'Other' women in conflicted regions must negotiate such humanist ideals. Practices based upon such belief were part of the negotiation of that which resulted as the present. Perhaps most importantly, the examination of the political and feminist practices of Palestinian women illustrates how they take into consideration the perpetuation of global inequalities, inducing local discriminatory practices.

Drawing from women's stories and narratives that are 'located' differently – both materially and metaphorically – and focusing on the voices of Palestinian women reveals the ways in which their exilic status formed out of the betweenness that I have been describing does not address or partake of the 'universalities' of women's victimization. Instead, the voices of these women emphasize the particular victimization of Palestinian women and the neglected agency that arises out of the ashes of that victimization. The voices of these women continually suggest that we look at the confluence of history, economy, politics, gender, sexuality, social practices, culture, and more. In addition, my critical aim in this book is to draw our attention to the importance of acknowledging how Palestinian women negotiate their betweenness: a mode of negotiation that creates resistance and gives power to the powerless and also calls for revisionist epistemologies allowing for a feminist analysis and understanding of these exilic negotiations that would be more inclusive than Western feminism has hitherto allowed. Their voices have shown us in unequivocal terms the links between colonization, militarization, inequality, and patriarchy. Perhaps that is not so surprising. However, these voices also reveal the integral ties between 'home' as exilic and the negotiation of borders and boundaries between the global, the local, and 'home', raising for us the possibility of a theory of resistance in a region where resistance is always already understood as masculine.

Furthermore, the sexualization of the dynamics of this resistance needs to be read through multiple lenses at once. Such an undertaking, while enhancing the scope of feminist inquiry, would also illuminate in productive ways the limits of gender as an exclusive category of analysis. Despite the continual dislocation of women's subjectivity in the region, we learn that beyond the 'woman' there is a person who is constantly caught at the crossroads and who encounters the realities of colonization, military occupation, nationalism, sexuality, and spatial/racial dislocations as so many sharp-edged weapons. By listening to these voices, I have made a discovery that is now critical to how I see the world: for these women, living in these states of betweenness, as exiles at home, has also created a sense of solace and a space of their own making in the midst of their frustrations and despair. The constant quest for more optimistic possibilities, their own styles of coping and surviving, has enabled them to twist the political grammar of the hegemonic world and has allowed them to question our normative understanding of the possibilities for resistance of the oppressed.

When masculinist powers struggle in war and conflict zones, women there end up at the limits of several layers of the struggle. Women are often used by men as an integral part of *their* struggle. Men argue that women need protection while they rename the territory as the 'motherland', and this is sometimes invoked as the very reasons for the struggle; but at the same time women are outsiders. Women's voices in this book illustrate the ways in which they are constantly working and walking on the edges, facing the many risks such a walk might entail. In many cases, they walk while carrying or denying their own pain. Living *on* the border and being constructed *as* the border prompts the questioning of the spatial characteristics of the boundary and the associated risk of turning such spaces into both home and exile. As Said stated:

> In a secular and contingent world, homes are always provisional. Borders and barriers which enclose us within the safety of familiar territory can also become prisons, and are often defended beyond reason or necessity. Exiles cross borders, break barriers of thought and experience.
>
> (cited in Mae 1995: 4)

Walking on the edge, simultaneously living a safe and unsafe life, has transformed women's lives and bodies into transgressive spaces. Women simultaneously became and become exilic and alien subjects while developing into insiders' representative of 'indigenousness'. Walking on the edge also creates and re-creates challenges and talks back to various structures of oppression while creating new structures of resistance that constantly negotiate the limits of their lives and transform the forbidden and the non-acceptable into new-spaces, into counter-spaces, spaces of liminality for survivors – or perhaps counter-spaces for survival. Palestinian women's passage, their daily border crossings – from being frontliners, 'security threats', mothers of martyrs, icons of the nation, and protectors of the society into the weakest members of that society and so requiring protection or deserving punishment if 'transgressing the limits' – has transformed their bodies and lives into a colonial weapon, a marker of colonization and military oppression. The liminality in women's spaces and their ability to protect on the one hand and to 'terrorize', weaken, attack and/or tarnish the 'colonial honour' of the militarizing forces on the other turns their journeys into relentless and brutal campaigns. Their passages places them in a constant state of liminality and danger, yet a state where, in some cases, they manage to be and feel free of social and structural constraints and political oppression while formulating new paths and arranging new alternatives. This explains their agency, their power to open up new possibilities and unlimited modes of coping and resisting. However, this power also allows for the simultaneous breaking down of some of the barriers endangering their status, as it amends their state of betweenness into one with an elevated risk that increases, indeed feeds, their vulnerability to violence.

For Palestinian women, the contested existence of such a state of betweenness carries with it both internal and external realms of their existence, encouraging transgression and the search for a mode of survival in the midst of chaos. Palestinian women continue to challenge existing gender roles, raising taboo issues that have previously been neglected. Some women, in their search for safety, have ended up crossing over into danger zones in a state of betweenness. Hence, life in this state provides women a panoramic view of the socio-political scene, a view that was in some cases destructive, confining, and damaging – regardless of the degree to which it enabled possibilities and liberated deeply embedded problems in terms of their gender, sexual, political, class, and ethnic identities.

Whatever works of resistance women take, whether through disobedience, adaptation, hidden acts of resistance, or violent retaliation, all such actions contribute to their political protest against existing militarized and weaponized spaces. Their permanent state of liminality contributes to a feeling of displacement in their own homes and of exile in their own community. Their exilic status has made them constantly examine their surroundings (be these genderized, sexualized, or racialized), negotiate its dangers, and construct their own counter-discourses and counter-spaces. The exilic state is apparent when talking about women's weaponized bodies, for in such cases the body, their very womb, is land, hearth, and home, simultaneously emitting strength, fragility, and vulnerability.

CHOOSING THE MARGIN AS A SITE OF RESISTANCE

Women's voices quoted throughout this book raise fundamental questions and convey a clear ethical value. The primary question that women constantly raised when confronting violence is how to successfully position themselves against oppressive powers. This query is accompanied by our modes of resistance and the assertion that in such contexts resistance is an ethical rule, a moral value, and non-negotiable survival strategy for women. Challenges to the internal system also serve to prevent the slaughter of everything in and around them, be this damage to their own bodies, future, language, culture, politics, and more. However, the question remains: how do we as feminists set ourselves against power when settler-colonial philosophy/economy/physics operating through the law of the jungle is controlling the world? How do we position ourselves against power after the replacement of the old imperialism by corporate colonial imperialism and occupation?

I would believe in globalization if it was fair. I would trust in the international court of justice if it would serve me as it serves hegemonic power holders; however, the reality is that it has not. Women's voices in this book show us that what is happening in Palestine, what is happening to women in conflict zones, what is happening to poor oppressed women everywhere – in Palestine, Iraq, Afghanistan, the Sudan, Rwanda, and so on – is sexed, raced, and classed. What is happening is outside the realm of public knowledge. The women's voices in this book illustrate that by speaking against hegemonic powers and that through acts of resistance people can survive. However, people become tired of just surviving, of living on the fence, and by *being* the fence. It is hard to be the source of security while our sexuality and power are considered a source of insecurity and threat. How do we confront militarism, sexism, racism, and classism? How do we confront Empire? How do we attain political change in the context of an increase in hegemonic power and oppression? Moreover, how do we tell our Palestinian activist brothers more generally to never separate their political activism and their values?

The voices of the women in this volume challenge Empire through a form of resistance that refuses both silence and silencing, such refusal being a mode of coping and surviving. I have demonstrated the effect of hidden and apparent violence, have tried to speak back, educate, analyse, and share. Challenging Empire's new theology of freedom and its desire to 'save the world' is creating additional hardships for women in conflict zones. As a Palestinian feminist, I am willing to continue resisting and I will continue sharing, discussing, analysing, and searching for ways to expand public understanding regarding women and violence against them. I will keep increasing the number of those who can look at their way of looking and so improve their ways of hearing. The struggle is necessary and the price is required, but the state of betweenness endured by Palestinian women has serious consequences and requires serious reflection.

Pushing against oppressive boundaries, struggling against racism, classism, and sex domination requires constant movement against the realities of choices within very inhuman local and global power relations. Pushing against the colonizing mentalities of the 'war against terror' and against those who are advancing policies that 'bring freedom and democracy' to the Otherized requires the creation of new revolutionary spaces and cultures that value the power of women's voices of *and* silences around Knowing. However, how can we understand their too-often unseen and unacknowledged memories, voices, histories, and activism amidst suffering? How can I ensure that everyone will remember the many Um Ahmads who have created new homes and new locations and spaces of safety and love – homes in the nowhere of the street stolen through militarized violence? How can we find a language that crystallizes the very meaning of home – when it is militarized?

I believe that through the combined collective efforts of activists, revolutionaries, and organizations we can create new alternatives. When in this chapter I shared some of my own personal experiences, I aimed to equally share my limitations as well as my strength, illustrating my own state of betweenness and exile. The sharing of knowledge and experiences allows for an analysis of the contradictions that mould our lives and prompts critical thinking, all the while striving for a decolonized mind. The narratives of Palestinian women who have been engaged in the struggle for change offered many insights. We have each suffered when making choices, choices that have tried to transgress boundaries and so acquire knowledge, but at the same time, we have been concerned for our communities so often at the primary level of pure survival. The Palestinian women whose voices are recorded in this book all challenged sexist colonial policy though their own individual struggle while re-inventing their own coping strategies and acts of resistance.

As with so many of our colonized, raced, classed, and sexualized sisters (and subaltern brothers), I have learned that while we cannot control representations of us, we can – as many Palestinian women have done – critically intervene and challenge them. Images we make are a different matter. As bell hooks contends in her *Black Looks: Race and Representation*, 'We would consider crucial both the kind of image we produce and the way we critically write and talk about images. And most important, we would rise to the challenge to speak that which has not been spoken' (1992: 4). Moreover, continuing to engage in political activism requires that we critically attend to images in hook's fashion both within and outside militarized spaces, in this case the Palestinian community, while asserting our right to critical analyses. Our refusal to accept the role of either the exotic or the exilic Other both outside and inside Palestinian society necessitates the creation of spaces of radical openness within the location, space, and culture of domination.

In concluding this book, I would like to first convey to the readers a very strong message all of us, as Palestinian women and men – and as women living in conflict zones – learned from Ghassan Kanafani's letter to his friend Mustafa, a letter that relates the ordeal of Nadia, his niece and late brother's injured daughter. By reproducing Nadia's story, I aim to stress the inseparability of the private and the public, the personal and the political; to emphasize agency and victimization, and the intersections between marginalized groups; to bring forward gender, class, culture, and the national struggle for liberation. In so doing, I share with the reader what I have learned from the various women with whom I have worked, including the most prominent women in my life.

LETTER FROM GAZA BY GHASSAN KANAFANI

Dear Mustafa,

I have now received your letter, in which you tell me that you've done everything necessary to enable me to stay with you in Sacramento. I've also received news that I have been accepted in the department of Civil Engineering in the University of California. I must thank you for everything, my friend. But it'll strike you as rather odd when I proclaim this news to you – and make no doubt about it, I feel no hesitation at all, in fact I am pretty well positive that I have never seen things so clearly as I do now. No, my friend, I have changed my mind. I won't follow you to 'the land where there is greenery, water and lovely faces' as you wrote. No, I'll stay here, and I won't ever leave.

I am really upset that our lives won't continue to follow the same course, Mustafa. For I can almost hear you reminding me of our vow to go on together, and of the way we used to shout: 'We'll get rich!' But there's nothing I can do, my friend. Yes, I still remember the day when I stood in the hall of Cairo airport, pressing your hand and staring at the frenzied motor [i.e., of the airplane]. At that moment everything was rotating in time with the ear-splitting motor, and you stood in front of me, your round face silent.

Your face hasn't changed from the way it used to be when you were growing up in the Shajiya quarter of Gaza, apart from those slight wrinkles. We grew up together, understanding each other completely and we promised to go on together till the end. But ...

'There's a quarter of an hour left before the plane takes off. Don't look into space like that. Listen! You'll go to Kuwait next year, and you'll save enough from your salary to uproot you from Gaza and transplant you to California. We started off together and we must carry on.'

At that moment I was watching your rapidly moving lips. That was always your manner of speaking, without commas or full stops. But in an obscure way I felt that you were not completely happy with your flight. You couldn't give three good reasons for it. I too suffered from this

209

wrench, but the clearest thought was: why don't we abandon this Gaza and flee? Why don't we? Your situation had begun to improve, however. The Ministry of Education in Kuwait had given you a contract though it hadn't given me one. In the trough of misery where I existed, you sent me small sums of money. You wanted me to consider them as loans because you feared that I would feel slighted. You knew my family circumstances in and out; you knew that my meagre salary in the UNRWA [United Nations Relief and Works Administration] schools was inadequate to support my mother, my brother's widow and her four children.

'Listen carefully. Write to me every day ... every hour ... every minute! The plane's just leaving. Farewell! Or rather, till we meet again!'

Your cold lips brushed my cheek, you turned your face away from me towards the plane, and when you looked at me again I could see your tears.

Later the Ministry of Education in Kuwait gave me a contract. There's no need to repeat to you how my life there went in detail. I always wrote to you about everything. My life there had a gluey, vacuous quality as though I were a small oyster, lost in oppressive loneliness, slowly struggling with a future as dark as the beginning of the night, caught in a rotten routine, a spewed-out combat with time. Everything was hot and sticky. There was a slipperiness to my whole life, it was all a hankering for the end of the month.

In the middle of the year, that year, the Jews bombarded the central district of Sabha and attacked Gaza, our Gaza, with bombs and flame-throwers. That event might have made some change in my routine, but there was nothing for me to take much notice of; I was going to leave this Gaza behind me and go to California where I would live for myself, my self which had suffered so long. I hated Gaza and its inhabitants. Everything in the amputated town reminded me of failed pictures painted in grey by a sick man. Yes, I would send my mother and my brother's widow and her children a meagre sum to help them to live, but I would liberate myself from this last tie too, there in green California, far from the reek of defeat which for seven years had filled my nostrils. The sympathy which bound me to my brother's children, their mother and mine would never be enough to justify my tragedy in taking this perpendicular dive. It mustn't drag me any further down than it already had. I must flee!

You know these feelings, Mustafa, because you've really experienced them. What is this ill-defined tie we had with Gaza which blunted our enthusiasm for flight? Why didn't we analyse the matter in such a way as to give it a clear meaning? Why didn't we leave this defeat with its wounds behind us and move on to a brighter future which would give us deeper consolation? Why? We didn't exactly know.

When I went on holiday in June and assembled all my possessions, longing for the sweet departure, the start towards those little things which give life a nice, bright meaning, I found Gaza just as I had known it, closed like the introverted lining of a rusted snail-shell thrown up by the waves on the sticky, sandy shore by the slaughter-house. This Gaza was more cramped than the mind of a sleeper in the throes of a fearful nightmare, with its narrow streets which had their bulging balconies … this Gaza! But what are the obscure causes that draw a man to his family, his house, his memories, as a spring draws a small flock of mountain goats? I don't know. All I know is that I went to my mother in our house that morning. When I arrived my late brother's wife met me there and asked me, weeping, if I would do as her wounded daughter, Nadia, in Gaza hospital wished and visit her that evening. Do you know Nadia, my brother's beautiful thirteen-year-old daughter?

That evening I bought a pound of apples and set out for the hospital to visit Nadia. I knew that there was something about it that my mother and my sister-in-law were hiding from me, something which their tongues could not utter, something strange which I could not put my finger on. I loved Nadia from habit, the same habit that made me love all that generation which had been so brought up on defeat and displace-ment that it had come to think that a happy life was a kind of social deviation.

What happened at that moment? I don't know. I entered the white room very calm. Ill children have something of saintliness, and how much more so if the child is ill as result of cruel, painful wounds. Nadia was lying on her bed, her back propped up on a big pillow over which her hair was spread like a thick pelt. There was profound silence in her wide eyes and a tear always shining in the depths of her black pupils. Her face was calm and still but eloquent as the face of a tortured prophet might be. Nadia was still a child, but she seemed more than a child, much more, and older than a child, much older.

'Nadia!'

I've no idea whether I was the one who said it, or whether it was someone else behind me. But she raised her eyes to me and I felt them dissolve me like a piece of sugar that had fallen into a hot cup of tea.

Together with her slight smile I heard her voice. 'Uncle! Have you just come from Kuwait?'

Her voice broke in her throat, and she raised herself with the help of her hands and stretched out her neck towards me. I patted her back and sat down near her.

'Nadia! I've brought you presents from Kuwait, lots of presents. I'll wait till you can leave your bed, completely well and healed, and you'll come to my house and I'll give them to you. I've bought you the red trousers you wrote and asked me for. Yes, I've bought them.'

It was a lie, born of the tense situation, but as I uttered it I felt that I was speaking the truth for the first time. Nadia trembled as though she had an

211

electric shock and lowered her head in a terrible silence. I felt her tears wetting the back of my hand.

'Say something, Nadia! Don't you want the red trousers?' She lifted her gaze to me and made as if to speak, but then she stopped, gritted her teeth and I heard her voice again, coming from faraway.

'Uncle!'

She stretched out her hand, lifted the white coverlet with her fingers and pointed to her leg, amputated from the top of the thigh.

My friend ... Never shall I forget Nadia's leg, amputated from the top of the thigh. No! Nor shall I forget the grief which had moulded her face and merged into its traits forever. I went out of the hospital in Gaza that day, my hand clutched in silent derision on the two pounds I had brought with me to give Nadia. The blazing sun filled the streets with the colour of blood. And Gaza was brand new, Mustafa! You and I never saw it like this. The stone piled up at the beginning of the Shajiya quarter where we lived had a meaning, and they seemed to have been put there for no other reason but to explain it. This Gaza in which we had lived and with whose good people we had spent seven years of defeat was something new. It seemed to me just a beginning. I don't know why I thought it was just a beginning. I imagined that the main street that I walked along on the way back home was only the beginning of a long, long road leading to Safad. Everything in this Gaza throbbed with sadness which was not confined to weeping. It was a challenge: more than that it was something like reclamation of the amputated leg!

I went out into the streets of Gaza, streets filled with blinding sunlight. They told me that Nadia had lost her leg when she threw herself on top of her little brothers and sisters to protect them from the bombs and flames that had fastened their claws into the house. Nadia could have saved herself; she could have run away, rescued her leg. But she didn't.

Why?

No, my friend, I won't come to Sacramento, and I've no regrets. No, and nor will I finish what we began together in childhood. This obscure feeling that you had as you left Gaza, this small feeling must grow into a giant deep within you. It must expand, you must seek it in order to find yourself, here among the ugly debris of defeat.

I won't come to you. But you, return to us! Come back, to learn from Nadia's leg, amputated from the top of the thigh, what life is and what existence is worth.

Come back, my friend! We are all waiting for you.

(Kanafani 1980)

What I found compelling about Nadia is that her story reveals the epistemology of empowerment. The Nadias – and the Palestinian women I learned from and who shared their voices – were born into a war zone between exotic and exilic Otherization. Despite being displaced and violated, they possessed first-hand power and knowledge of living under military occupation while experiencing mobility despite the confinement. We all travel on amputated legs as well through the multiplicity of borders and boundaries we must negotiate. Palestinian women facing constant violence have almost always been identified with power, agency, and inner strength, but were also characterized elegiacally by dispossession, exile, and displacement. Nadia's deep conviction in her right to fight for her rights and her self-sacrifice despite the hegemonic claims (like the fight of the other women quoted in this book) created a counter-space, a counter-discourse, a counter-location. The power of the hegemonic monster did not prevent her from taking a risk with little thought of herself, of contributing to the survival of her kin. Women in this book, as the many Nadias, the many mothers (such as my two mothers), and the many Um Mahmoods looked for justice and tried to replace the loss, to create a home in the rubble of 'the-used-to-be-a-home', to create and re-re-create a new vision, home, space, and love. Their lived context, their spaces of love and resistance, kept women always on guard, asking questions, checking options, being sceptical of every single thing all the while speaking truth to power. The creation and re-creation of a new search for justice, of a new counter-location, of counter-spaces and a counter-community to this that was lost brought about what I defined as a state of betweenness, a state of dislocation while relocating – to the degree that in some cases women reached a state of exile while living at the centre, yet with an ability to create, conceptualize, and re-conceptualize alternatives improvised amidst suffering and loss. Women in Palestine, women who suffer from the violence of living in conflict zones, created a margin of safety, and indeed chose the margin, that state of betweenness as a site of resistance, while being always at risk of having to face additional suffering. Living in such a state gave them the power to see both sides, live the inside and the outside, while being able to acknowledge the power of the margin in building resistance. Such daily resistance is the one that presents despair, transcends loss, and strengthens their sense of self; they are acts and activism that re-appropriate and utilize spaces of suffering, loss, and pain as political acts of struggle and resistance.

The question remains: how long can women in conflict zones live in a state of *betweenness*, locked between the West and the non-West, public and private, male and female, reason and emotion, and home and exile, while left unacknowledged and unrecognized? To paraphrase Um-Ahmad, when will the rain come?

REFERENCES

Abdel-Halim, A. 1998. 'Attack with a Friendly Weapon', in M. Turshen and C. Twagiramariya (eds), *What Women do in Wartime: Gender and Conflict in Africa*, 85–100. New York: Zed Books.

Abdo, N. 1991. 'Women of the Intifada: Gender, Class and National Liberation'. *Race and Class* 32: 19–34.

1999. 'Gender and Politics Under the Palestinian Authority'. *Journal of Palestine Studies* 28(2): 38–51.

Abdo, N. and R. Lentin (eds) 2002. *Women and the Politics of Military Confrontation*. New York: Berghahn.

Abdulhadi, F. 2006. *The Roles of Palestinian Women in the 1930s: The Political Participation of Palestinian Women*. Ramallah: Palestinian Women's Research and Documentation Center/UNESCO.

Abdulhadi, R. 1998. 'The Palestinian Women's Autonomous Movement: Emergence, Dynamics, and Challenges'. *Gender and Society*. Special Issue: Gender and Social Movements, Part 1, 12(6): 649–73. Available online, at: www.jstor.org/stable/190511.

Abu Ali, K. 1974. *Introduction to Women's Reality and Her Experience in the Palestinian Evolution*. Beirut: General Union of Palestinian Women (GUPW).

Abu-Baker, K., N. Shalhoub-Kevorkian, S. Awaidah, and E. Dabit 2005. *Women and War in Palestine*. Jerusalem: Women's Studies Center (WSC).

Abu-Lughod, L. 1990. 'Romance of Resistance: Tracing Transformations of Power Through Bedouin Women'. *American Ethnologist* 17: 41–55.

1998. 'Feminist Longings and Postcolonial Conditions', in L. Abu-Lughod (ed.), *Remaking Women: Feminism and Modernity in the Middle East*, 3–32. Princeton: Princeton University Press.

2002. 'Do Muslim Women Really Need Saving? Anthropological Reflections on Cultural Relativism and Its Others'. *American Anthropologist* 104(3): 783–90.

Abu-Odeh, L. 2000. 'Crimes of Honor and the Construction of Gender in Arab Society', in P. Ilkkaracan (ed.), *Women and Sexuality in Muslim Society*, 363–80. Istanbul: Women for Women's Human Rights (WWHR).

Abu Sitta, S. 2000. *The Palestinian Nakba 1948: The Register of Depopulated Localities in Palestine*. London: Palestine Return Centre.

Accad, E. 1990. *Sexuality and War: Literary Masks of the Middle East*. New York: New York University Press.

Adalian, R.P. 1991. 'The Armenian Genocide: Context and Legacy'. *Social Education: The Official Journal of the National Council for the Social Studies* 55(2): 99–104.

Adelman, M. 2003. 'The Military, Militarism, and the Militarization of Domestic Violence'. *Violence Against Women* 9(9): 1118–52.

Agamben, G. 1998. *Homo Sacer: Sovereign Power and Bare Life*. Stanford: Stanford University Press.

2005. *State of Exception*. Chicago: University of Chicago Press.

Albanese, P. 1996. 'Leaders and Breeders: The Archaization of Gender Relations in Croatia', in M. Spencer and B. Wejnert (eds), *Research on Russia and Eastern Europe: Women in Post-Communism*, 185–200. Greenwich, CT: JAI.

Alexander, M.J. and C.T. Mohanty 1997. 'Introduction: Genealogies, Legacies, Movements', in M.J. Alexander and C.T. Mohanty (eds), *Feminist Genealogies, Colonial Legacies, Democratic Futures*, xiii–xlii. New York: Routledge.

Al-Haq, 1988. *Punishing a Nation: Human Rights Violations During the Palestinian Uprising December 1987 – December 1988*. Ramallah, West Bank: Al-Haq.

2004. 'Four Years Since the Beginning of the Intifada: Violations of Human Rights in the Occupied Palestinian Territories. Briefing Paper'. Available online, at: http://asp.alhaq.org/zalhaq/site/books/files/intifada04_report.pdf.

Al-Khalili, G. 1977. *The Palestinian Women and the Revolution*. Acre: Dar al-Aswar.

Allen, B. 1996. *Rape Warfare: The Hidden Genocide in Bosnia-Herzegovina and Croatia*. Minneapolis: University of Minnesota Press.

Al-Rais, N. 2000. *Al Qada'a Fi Falastin Wama'uqat Tataworeh* [The Justice System in Palestine and Obstacles to its Development]. Ramallah, West Bank: Al-Haq (in Arabic).

Al Sarraj, E. n.d. 'Why We have Become Suicide Bombers: Understanding Palestinian Terror'. Mission Islam. Available online, at: www.missionislam.com/conissues/palestine.htm.

Anderson, B. 1991. *Imagined Communities: Reflections on the Origins and Rise of Nationalism*. London: Verso.

Anthias, F. and N. Yuval-Davis 1992. *Radicalized Boundaries: Race, Nation, Gender, Colour, and Class and the Anti-Racist Struggle*. London: Routledge.

Anzaldúa, G. 1987. *Borderlands/La Frontera: The New Mestiza*. San Francisco: Aunt Lute.

Arendt, H. 1951. *The Origins of Totalitarianism*. New York: Harcourt Brace Jovanovich.

Augustin, E. (ed.) 1994. *Palestinian Women: Identity and Experience*. London: Zed Books.

215

Avnery, U. 2001. 'Barak, After All'. *Gush Shalom*. Available online, at: http://zope.gush-shalom.org/home/en/channels/avnery/archives_article130.

BBC. 2003. Available online, at http://news.bbc.co.uk/2/hi/middle_east/2986962.stm.

Benhabib, S. 1995. 'Feminism and Postmodernism', in S. Benhabib, J. Butler, D. Cornell, and N. Fraser (eds), *Feminist Contentions: A Philosophical Exchange*, 17–34. New York: Routledge.

Bhabha, H.K. 1990. 'Introduction', in H.K. Bhabha (ed.), *Nation and Narration*, 3–4. London: Routledge.

1994. *The Location of Culture*. London: Routledge.

Bisharat, E.G. 1989. *Palestinian Lawyers and Israeli Rule*. Austin: University of Texas Press.

Boric, R. 1997. 'Against the War: Women Organizing Across the National Divide in the Countries of the Former Yugoslavia', in L. Ronit (ed.), *Gender and Catastrophe*, 36–49. London: Zed Books.

B'Tselem (Israeli Information Center for Human Rights in the Occupied Territories) 2004. 'Facing the Abyss: The Isolation of Sheikh Sa'ad Village – Before and After the Separation Barrier'. Available online, at: www.btselem.org/English/Publications/Summaries/200402_Sheikh_Saed.asp.

2005a. 'Punitive Demolitions of Palestinian Homes'. Available online, at: www.btselem.org/English/Punitive_Demolitions/Statistics.asp.

2005b. 'Demolitions of Palestinian Homes for Lack of Permit'. Available online, at: www.btselem.org/English/Planning_and_Building/Statistics.asp.

2005c. 'Demolitions of Palestinian Homes for Military Necessity'. Available online, at: www.btselem.org/English/Razing/Statistics.asp.

2005d. 'Separation Barrier Statistics'. Available online, at: www.btselem.org/english/Separation_Barrier/Statistics.asp.

2005e. 'Land Expropriation in the West Bank'. Available online, at: www.btselem.org/English/Jerusalem/Land_Expropriation_Statistics.asp.

Butalia, U. 1997. 'A Question of Silence: Partition, Women and the State', in L. Ronit (ed.), *Gender and Catastrophe*, 92–109. London: Zed Books.

(ed.) 2002. *Speaking Peace: Women's Voices from Kashmir*. New Delhi: Kali for Women.

Butler, J. 1993. *Bodies that Matter: On the Discursive Limits of 'Sex'*. New York: Routledge.

Carapico, S. 2000. 'NGOs, INGOs, GO-NGOs and DO-NGOs: Making Sense of Non-Governmental Organizations'. *Middle East Report* 214: 12–15.

Chatterjee, P. 1986. *Nationalist Thought and the Colonial World: A Derivative Discourse*. London: Zed Books.

Chesler, P. 1972. *Women and Madness*. New York: Avon.

Chomsky, N. 1984. *The Fateful Triangle: The United States, Israel, and the Palestinians*. Montréal: Black Rose.

1991. 'Introduction', in R. Sayigh, *Palestinians: From Peasants to Revolutionaries*, 1–4. London: Zed Press.

Cixous, H. 1980. 'The Laugh of the Medusa', in E. Marks and I. de Courtivron (eds), *The New French Feminisms*, 245–64. Amherst: University of Massachusetts Press.

1986. 'Sorties', in H. Cixous and C. Clément (eds), *The Newly Born Woman*, 63–130. Minneapolis: University of Minnesota Press.

Cooke, M. 1988. *War's Other Voices: Women Writers on the Lebanese Civil War*. Gender, Culture, and Politics in the Middle East. Cambridge: Cambridge University Press.

Dadeghi-Fassaei, S. and K. Kendall. 2002. 'Iranian Women's Pathways to Imprisonment'. *Women's Studies International Forum* 24(6): 701–10.

Dalmage, H.M. 2000, *Tripping on the Color Line: Black-White Multiracial Families in a Racially Divided World*. New Brunswick: Rutgers University Press.

Daly, K. 1994. *Gender, Crime, and Punishment*. New Haven: Yale University Press.

Dara'awi, D. and M. Zhaika 2000. *Mahkamat Amn Al-Dawla: Bayn Al-Darura Wa'l-Mashrueiyah* [The State Security Court: Between Necessity and Legality]. Ramallah: Al Damir (in Arabic).

Daragmmi, A. 1991. *The Women's Movement in Palestine: 1903–1990*. Jerusalem: Dia'a Office for Studies.

Darwish, M. 2002. *Ha'alat Hisar. State of Siege: Poems*. Beirut: Riad El-Rayyes Books S.A.R.I.

Derrida, J. 1998. *Of Grammatology*. Baltimore: Johns Hopkins University Press.

Dowler, L. 1997. 'The Mother of all Warriors: Women in West Belfast', in L. Ronit (ed.), *Gender and Catastrophe*. London: Zed Books.

1998. '"And They Think I'm Just a Nice Old Lady": Women and War in Belfast, Northern Ireland'. *Gender, Place and Culture* 5(2): 159–76.

Dufour, J. 2007. 'The Worldwide Network of US Military Bases: The Global Deployment of US Military Personnel'. *Global Research*. Available online, at: www.globalresearch.ca.

Dugard, J. 2004. 'The Question of the Violation of Human Rights in the Occupied Arab Territories, Including Palestine'. Available online, at: http://domino.un.org/unispal.nsf/a39191b210be1d6085256da90053dee5/631c8deb907650e985256e6000520f3b!OpenDocument.

Elfstrom, B. and A. Malmgren 2005. 'Palestinian Children Behind Bars'. Report from the International Commission of Jurists, Swedish section, 12–20 December 2004, submitted 31 March 2005. Available online, at: www.dci-pal.org/english/doc/reports/2005/apr03.pdf.

El-Sadaawi, N. 1980. *The Hidden Face of Eve: Women in the Arab World*. London: Zed Press.

Enloe, C. 1983. *Does Khaki Become You? The Militarization of Women's Lives*. London: Pandora Press.

1990. *Bananas, Beaches and Bases: Making Feminist Sense of International Politics*. Berkeley and Los Angeles: University of California Press.

2000. *Maneuvers: The International Politics of Militarizing Women's Lives*. Berkeley and Los Angeles: University of California Press.

Fanon, F. 1963. *The Wretched of the Earth*. New York: Grove.

Finkelstein, N. 1995. *Image and Reality of the Israel-Palestine Conflict*. London: Verso.

Flapan, S. 1987. *The Birth of Israel: Myths and Realities*. London: Croom Helm.

Fleischmann, E. 2003. *The Nation and Its 'New' Women: The Palestinian Women's Movement, 1920–1948*. Berkeley and Los Angeles: University of California Press.

Fogelson, R.D. 1989. 'The Ethnohistory of Events and Nonevents'. *Ethnohistory* 31(4): 255–63.

Foucault, M. 1975. *Discipline and Punish: The Birth of the Prison*. New York: Random House.

1980. 'Two Lectures', in C. Gordon (ed.), *Power/Knowledge: Selected Interviews and Other Writings 1972–1977*. New York: Pantheon.

1998. *The Will to Knowledge: The History of Sexuality Volume One*. R. Hurley (trans.). London: Penguin.

2003. *Society Must Be Defended: Lectures at the College de France, 1975–6*. London: Allen Lane.

Gaidzakian, O. 1889. *Illustrated Armenia and the Armenians*. Boston: B.H. Aznive.

Ghanem, A., N. Rouhana, and O. Yiftachel 1998. 'Questioning "Ethnic Democracy": A Response to Sammy Smooha'. *Israel Studies* 3: 253–67.

Ghanem, H. 2003. 'Between Fence and Gender: Borders and Their Effect on Establishing National Gendered Identity'. Paper presented at the Israeli Anthropological Association Annual Conference, 28–29 May, Neve Ilan.

Giacaman, R., I. Jad, and P. Johnson 1996. 'For the Common Good? Gender and Social Citizenship in Palestine'. *Middle East Report* 198: 11–16.

Gibran, K. 1995. *Sand and Foam: A Book of Aphorisms*. New York: A. Knopf.

Golan G. 1997. 'Militarization and Gender: The Israeli Experience'. *Women's Studies International Forum* 20(5–6): 581–6.

Goldblatt, B. and S. Meintjes 1998. 'South African Women Demand the Truth', in M. Turshen and C. Twagiramariya (eds), *What Women Do in Wartime: Gender and Conflict in Africa*, 27–61. London: Zed Books.

Goldstein, J. 2001. *War and Gender*. Cambridge: Cambridge University Press.

Grewal I. 1998. 'On the New Global Feminism and the Family of Nations', in E. Shohat (ed.), *Talking Visions: Multicultural Feminism in a Transnational Age*, 501–30. Cambridge, MA: MIT Press.

Grewal, I. and C. Kaplan 1994. *Scattered Hegemonies: Postmodernity and Transnational Feminist Practices*. Minneapolis: University of Minnesota Press.

Hadawi, S. 1979. *Bitter Harvest: Palestine Between 1914–1979*. Rev. Delmar, NY: Caravan.

Hague Euan, R. 1997. 'Power and Masculinity: The Construction of Gender and National Identities in the War in Bosnia-Herzgovina', in L. Ronit (ed.), *Gender and Catastrophe*, 50–63. London: Zed Books.

Hale, S. 2002. 'Liberated, but not Free: Women in Post-War Eritrea', in S. Meintjes, A. Pillay, and M. Turshen (eds.), *Aftermath: Women in Post-War Reconstruction*, 122–41. New York: Zed Books.

Hammami, R. 1990. 'Women, the Hijab and the Intifada'. *Middle East Report* 164–5: 24–28, 71, 78.

2000. 'Palestinian NGOs Since Oslo: From NGO Politics to Social Movements?'. *Middle East Report* 214: 16–19, 27, 48.

Hasso, F.S. 2000. 'Modernity and Gender in Arab Accounts of the 1948 and 1967 Defeats'. *International Journal of Middle East Studies* 32(4): 491–510.

Hastings, J. 2002. 'Silencing State-Sponsored Rape In and Beyond a Transnational Guatemalan Community'. *Violence Against Women* 8(10): 1153–81.

Hatem, M. 1993. 'Toward a Critique of Modernization: Narrative in Middle East Women's Studies'. *Arab Studies Quarterly* 15(2): 117–22.

Heng, G. 1997. 'A Great Way to Fly: Nationalism, the State, and the Varieties of Third-World Feminism', in M.J. Alexander and C.T. Mohanty (eds), *Feminist Genealogies, Colonial Legacies, Democratic Futures*, 30–46. New York: Routledge.

Higonnet, M.B. 1993. 'Not So Quiet in No-Woman's-Land', in M. Cooke and A. Woollacott (eds), *Gendering War Talk*, 205–26. Princeton: Princeton University Press.

hooks, b. 1992. *Black Looks: Race and Representation*. Cambridge, MA: South End.

1995. *Killing Rage: Ending Racism*. New York: Holt.

Human Rights Council, UN General Assembly 2007. 'The Issue of Palestinian Pregnant Women Giving Birth at Israeli Checkpoints: Report of the High Commissioner for Human Rights'. A/HRC/4/57 23 February. Available online, at: http://domino.un.org/UNISPAL.NSF/99818751a6a4c9c68525 60690077ef61/c3f001363757e664852572a400774d62!OpenDocument.

Ilkkaracan, P. (ed.) 2000. *Women and Sexuality in Muslim Societies*. Istanbul: Women for Women's Human Rights (WWHR).

2002. 'Women, Sexuality and Social Change in the Middle East and the Maghreb'. *Social Research* 69(3): 753–79.

INCITE: Women of Color Against Violence 2007. *The Revolution Will Not Be Funded: Beyond the Non-Profit Industrial Complex*. Boston: South End.

Institute of Law, Birzeit University 2006. 'Informal Justice System: The Rule of Law and Dispute Settlement in Palestine'. The National Report on the Results of the Field Research. Institute of Law, Birzeit University, Birzeit.

Jacobs, J. 1996. *Edge of Empire: Postcolonialism and the City*. New York: Routledge.

Jad, I. 2003. *Gender Myths and Feminist Fables: Repositioning Gender in Development Policy and Practice*. Prepared for the international workshop 'Feminist Fables and Gender Myths: Repositioning Gender in Development Policy and Practice'. Sussex: Institute of Development Studies.

Jayawardena, K. 1986. *Feminism and Nationalism in the Third World*. London: Zed Books.

Kanafani, G. 1980. *'The 1936–39 Revolt in Palestine' and 'Letter from Gaza'*. London: Tricontinental Society.

Kandiyoti, D. 1991. *Women, Islam and the State*. Philadelphia: Temple University Press.

1992. 'Women, Islam and the State: A Comparative Approach', in J.R. Cole (ed.), *Comparing Muslim Societies: Knowledge and the State in a World Civilization*, 237–60. Ann Arbor: University of Michigan Press.

Kaplan, C., N. Alarcón, and M. Moallem (eds) 1999. *Between Woman and Nation: Nationalisms, Transnational Feminisms, and the State*. Durham, NC: Duke University Press.

Khalidi, R. 2004. *Resurrecting Empire: Western Footprints and America's Perilous Path in the Middle East*. Boston: Beacon.

Kimmerling, B. 1983. *Zionism and Territory: The Socio-territorial Dimensions of Zionist Politics*. Berkeley: Institute of International Studies.

Kimmerling, B. and J. Migdal. 2003. *Palestinians: The Making of People*. New York: Free Press.

Kuttab, E. and N.A. 'Awwad 2004. 'The Palestinian Women's Movement'. *Ru'ya Ukhra* 11(34): 27–37 (in Arabic).

Lavie, A. and M. Gorali 2003. 'I Saw Fit to Remove Her from the World'. *Ha'aretz* 29 October.

Layoun, M. 1994. 'The Female Body and Transnational Reproduction, or, Rape by Any Other Name', in I. Grewal and G. Kaplan (eds), *Scattered Hegemonies: Postmodernity and Transnational Feminist Practices*, 63–75. Minneapolis: University of Minnesota Press.

Lentin, R. (ed.) 1997. *Gender and Catastrophe*. London: Zed Books.

2004. 'Israeli Racial State and Feminist Resistance'. *Sociological Research Online* 9(3). Available online, at: www.socresonline.org.uk/9/3/lentin.html.

Levine, P. 1998. 'Battle Colors: Race, Sex, and Colonial Soldiery in World War I'. *Journal of Women's History* 9(4): 104–31.

Levy, G. 2003. 'Twilight Zone: Birth and Death at the Checkpoint'. *Ha'aretz* 12 September.

Liu, L. 1994. 'The Female Body and Nationalist Discourse: The Field of Life and Death Revisited', in I. Grewal and G. Kaplan (eds), *Scattered Hegemonies: Postmodernity and Transnational Feminist Practices*, 37–62. Minneapolis: University of Minnesota Press.

Lynd, S., S. Bahour, and A. Lynd (eds) 1994. *Homeland: Oral Histories of Palestine and Palestinians*. New York: Olive Branch.

Machel, G. 2001. *The Impact of War on Children*. New York: UNICEF and UNIFEM.

Mae, H. 1995. *Borders, Boundaries, and Frames: Cultural Criticism and Cultural Studies*. New York: Routledge.

Masalha, N. 1992. *The Expulsion of the Palestinians: The Concept of 'Transfer' in Zionist Political Thought 1882–1948*. Beirut: Institute for Palestine Studies.

McClintock, A. 1995. *Imperial Leather: Race, Gender and Sexuality in the Colonial Contest*. Routledge: London.

McKay, S. 1998. 'The Effects of Armed Conflict on Girls and Women'. *Peace and Conflict: Journal of Peace Psychology* 4(4): 381–92.

Mehta, K. 2002. 'This Happened in Kashmir', in U. Butalia (ed.), *Speaking Peace: Women's Voices from Kashmir*, 1–41. New Delhi: Kali for Women.

Mernissi, F. 1975. *Beyond the Veil: Male-Female Dynamics in Muslim Society*. New York: Schenkman.

1982. 'Virginity and Patriarchy'. *Women's Studies International Forum* 5(2): 183–91.

Merry, S.E. 2003. 'Rights Talk and the Experience of Law: Implementing Women's Human Rights to Protection from Violence'. *Human Rights Quarterly* 25: 343–81.

2006. *Human Rights and Gender Violence: Translating Law into Local Justice*. London: University of Chicago Press.

Michael, B. 2003. 'Barbed-wire Screen, Smoke Screen'. *Yediot Ahronot* 31 October.

Mies, M. 1986. *Patriarchy and Accumulation on a World Scale: Women in the International Division of Labour*. London: Zed Books.

Miller, D. and L.T. Miller. 1999. *Survivors: An Oral History of the Armenian Genocide*. Berkeley and Los Angeles: University of California Press.

Minow, M. 1993. 'Surviving Victim Talk'. *UCLA Law Review* 40: 1411–45.

Moghannam, M. 1937. *The Arab Women and the Palestinian Problem*. London: Herbert Joseph.

Mohanram, R. 1999. *Black Body: Women, Colonialism, and Space*. Minneapolis: University of Minnesota Press.

Mohanty, C.T. 1991. 'Under Western Eyes', in C.T. Mohanty, A. Russo, and L. Torres (eds), *Third World Women and the Politics of Feminism*, 51–80. Bloomington: Indiana University Press.

2003. *Feminism Without Borders: Decolonizing Theory, Practicing Solidarity*. Durham, NC: Duke University Press.

Mojab, S. 1997. 'Women and the Gulf War: Critique of Feminist Responses', in D. Sharpley-Whiting and R.T. White (eds), *Spoils of War: Women of Color, Cultures, and Revolutions*, 59–82. New York: Rowman and Littlefield.

Morris, B. 2001. *Righteous Victims: A History of the Zionist-Arab Conflict, 1881–1999*. New York: Vintage.

2004. *The Birth of the Palestinian Refugee Problem Revisited.* Cambridge: Cambridge University Press.

Nader, L. 1989. 'Orientalism, Occidentalism and the Control of Women'. *Cultural Dynamics* 11(3): 323–35.

Nandy, A. (ed.) 1998. *Science, Hegemony and Violence: A Requiem for Modernity.* Delhi: Oxford University Press.

Nazal, R. 2005. 'A Feminist Reading of the Palestinian Local Elections in Its First Stage'. Al-Hewar Al-Motamaden website. Available online, at: www.ahewar.org/debat/show.art.asp?aid=32839.

Nazzal, N. 1978. *The Palestinian Exodus from Galilee, 1948.* Beirut: Institute for Palestine Studies.

Odeh, A. 2005. *Ahlam Bil Hurrreyya* [Dreams of Freedom]. Beirut: Al Muassasah al Arabeyyah Lil Dirasat Wal Nasher (in Arabic).

Office for the Coordination of Humanitarian Affairs (OCHA), United Nations 2003. 'New Wall Projections'. Available online, at: domino.un.org/unispal.nsf.

2007. 'The Humanitarian Impact on Palestinians of Israeli Settlements and Other Infrastructure in the West Bank'. Available online, at: www.ochaopt.org/documents/TheHumanitarianImpactOfIsraeliInfrastructureTheWest Bank_full.pdf.

Oldenburg, V. T. 2002. *Dowry Murder: The Imperial Origins of a Cultural Crime.* Oxford: Oxford University Press.

Palestinian Environmental NGOs Network (PENGON) (eds) 2003. *The Wall in Palestine: Facts, Testimonies, Analysis and Call to Action.* Jerusalem: PENGON.

Pappe, I. 1994. *The Making of the Arab-Israeli Conflict 1947–1951.* London: I.B. Tauris.

2001. 'The Tantura Massacre, 22–23 May 1948'. *Journal of Palestine Studies* 119: 5–18.

2007. *The Ethnic Cleansing of Palestine.* Oxford: Oneworld.

Peteet, J. 1991. *Gender in Crisis: Women and the Palestinian Resistance Movement.* New York: Columbia University Press.

1997. 'Icons and Militants: Mothering in the Danger Zone'. *Signs* 23(1): 103–29.

2005. *Landscape of Hope and Despair: Palestinian Refugee Camps. Ethnography of Political Violence.* Philadelphia: University of Pennsylvania Press.

Qassoum, M. 2002. 'Imperial Agendas, "Civil Society" and Global Manipulation Intifada'. *Between the Lines* 3(19): 9–12.

Razack, S. 1998. *Looking White People in the Eye: Gender, Race, and Culture in Courtrooms and Classrooms.* Toronto: University of Toronto Press.

2002. 'When Place Becomes Race'. In S. Razack (ed.), *Race, Space and the Law: Unmapping a White Settler Society,* 1–20. Toronto: Between the Lines.

2007. 'The Sharia Law Debate in Ontario: The Modernity/Premodernity Distinction in Legal Efforts to Protect Women from Culture'. *Feminist Legal Studies* 15: 3–32.

Remnick, D. 2007. 'The Seventh Day: Why the Six-Day War is Still Being Fought'. *New Yorker* 28 May. Available online, at: www.newyorker.com/archive.

Roberts, M.L. 2002. *Disruptive Acts: The New Woman in Fin-de-Siècle France*. Chicago: University of Chicago Press.

Roiphe, K. 1994. *The Morning After: Sex, Fear, and Feminism on Campus*. Boston: Little, Brown.

Rouhana, N. 1997. *Palestinian Citizens in an Ethnic Jewish State: Identities and Conflict*. New Haven: Yale University Press.

Roy, A. 2003. *War Talk*. Cambridge, MA: South End.

    2004. 'Uprising'. 13 October. Berkeley: Radio KPFK.

Roy, S. 1995. *The Gaza Strip: The Political Economy of De-Development*. Washington, DC: Institute for Palestine Studies.

Rozario, S. 1977. 'Disasters and Bangladeshi Women', in R. Lentin (ed.), *Gender and Catastrophe*, 255–65. New York: Zed Books.

Sabbagh, S. 1996. *Arab Women: Between Defiance and Restraint*. Northampton, MA: Olive Branch.

    1998. 'Introduction', in S. Sabbagh (ed.), *Palestinian Women of Gaza and the West Bank*, 1–40. Bloomington: Indiana University Press.

Sahgal, G. and N. Yuval Davis 1992. *Refusing Holy Orders: Women and Fundamentalism in Britain*. London: Virago.

Said, E. 1979. *Orientalism*. New York: Vintage.

    1980. *The Question of Palestine*. London: Routledge and Kegan Paul.

    1983. *The Word, the Text, and the Critic*. Cambridge: Harvard University Press.

    1984. 'The Mind of Winter: Reflections on Life in Exile'. *Harpers* 269: 49–55.

    2002. *Reflections on Exile and Other Essays*. Cambridge, MA: Harvard University Press.

Said, E. and C. Hitchens (eds) 2001. *Blaming the Victims: Spurious Scholarship and the Palestinian Question*. London: Verso.

Saigol, R. 2000. 'Militarization, Nation and Gender: Women's Bodies as Arenas of Violent Conflict', in P. Ilkkaracan (ed.), *Women and Sexuality in Muslim Societies*, 107–120. Istanbul: Kadinin Insan Halklari Projesi/Women for Women's Human Rights (WWHR).

Sanasarian, E. 1989. 'Gender Distinction in the Genocidal Process: A Preliminary Study of the Armenian Case'. *Holocaust and Genocide Studies* 4(4): 449–61.

Sandoval, C. 2000. *Methodology of the Oppressed*. London: University of Minnesota Press.

Sayigh, R. 1979. *Palestinians: From Peasants to Revolutionaries*. London: Zed Press.

    1981. 'Encounters with Palestinian Women Under Occupation'. *Journal of Palestine Studies* 10(4): 3–26.

    1983. 'Women in Struggle: Palestine'. *Third World Quarterly* 5(4): 880–6.

1994. *Too Many Enemies: The Palestinian Experience in Lebanon.* London: Zed Books.

1996. 'Researching Gender in a Palestinian Camp: Political, Theoretical and Methodological Issues', in D. Kandiyoti (ed.), *Gendering the Middle East: Emerging Perspectives.* Syracuse: Syracuse University Press.

1998. 'Gender, Sexuality, and Class in National Narrations: Palestinian Camp Women Tell Their Lives'. *Frontliners* 19(2): 166–85.

Schneider, E. 2000. *Battered Women and Feminist Lawmaking.* New Haven: Yale University Press.

Sered, S. 2000. *What Makes Women Sick? Maternity, Modesty, and Militarism in Israeli Society.* Hanover, NH: Brandeis University Press.

Shadmi, E. 1993. 'Occupation, Violence, and Women in Israeli Society'. *News From Within* 9: 20–3. Available online, at: http://newsvote.bbc.co.uk/mpapps.

Shaheed, F. 1998. 'Engagement of Culture, Customs and Law: Women's Lives and Activism', in F. Shaheed, S. A. Warraich, C. Balchin, and A. Gazdar (eds), *Shaping Women's Lives: Laws, Practices and Strategies in Pakistan,* 61–80. Lahore: Shirkat Gah, Women's Resource Centre.

Shalhoub-Kevorkian, N. 1994. 'Fear of Sexual Harassment: Palestinian Adolescent Girls in the Intifada', in E. Augustin (ed.), *Palestinian Women: Identity and Experience,* 171–9. London: Zed Books.

1995. 'The Faith of Girls and Women During Political Struggles: The Hidden Casualties' (unpublished).

1998a. 'Crime of War, Culture, and Children's Rights: The Case Study of Female Palestinian Detainees Under Israeli Military Occupation', in G. Douglas and L. Sebba (eds), *Children's Rights and Traditional Values,* 228–48. Dartmouth: Dartmouth Press.

1998b. 'Reactions to a Case of Female Child Sexual Abuse in Palestinian Society: Protection, Silencing, Deterrence, or Punishment'. *Plilim* 7: 161–95 (in Hebrew).

1999a. 'Towards a Cultural Definition of Rape: Dilemmas in Dealing with Rape Victims in Palestinian Society'. *Women Studies International Forum* 22(2): 157–73.

1999b. 'The Politics of Disclosing Female Sexual Abuse: A Case Study of Palestinian Society'. *Child Abuse and Neglect* 23: 1275–93.

2000. 'Blocking Her Exclusion: A Contextually Sensitive Model of Intervention for Handling Female Abuse'. *Social Service Review* 74(4): 620–34.

2001. *'Qat'l Al-Nisa'a Fi Al-Mujtama'a Al-Falastini'* [Femicide in Palestinian Society]. Jerusalem: UNIFEM and Women's Center for Legal Aid and Counseling (WCLAC) (in Arabic).

2002. 'Femicide and the Palestinian Criminal Justice System: Seeds of Change in the Context of State Building?' *Law and Society Review* 36(3): 577–605.

2003a. 'Re-examining Femicide: Breaking the Silence and Crossing "Scientific" Borders'. *Signs* 28(2): 581–608.

2003b. 'Liberating Voices: The Political Implications of Palestinian Mothers Narrating Their Loss'. *Women's Studies International Forum* 26(5): 391–407.

2004a. 'Imposition of Virginity Testing: A Life-saver or a License to Kill?'. *Social Science and Medicine* 60: 1187–96.

2004b. 'The Hidden Casualties of War: Palestinian Women and the Second Intifada'. *Indigenous Peoples' Journal of Law, Culture and Resistance* 1(1): 67–82.

2004c. 'Militarization and Policing: Police Reactions to Violence Against Palestinian Women in Israel'. *Social Identities* 10(2): 171–94.

2005a. 'Voice Therapy for Women Aligned with Political Prisoners: A Case Study of Trauma Among Palestinian Women in the Second Intifada'. *Social Service Review* 79(2): 322–43.

2005b. 'Disclosure of Child Abuse in Conflict Areas'. *Violence Against Women* 11(10): 1263–91.

2005c. 'Counter-Spaces as Resistance in Conflict Zones: Palestinian Women Recreating a Home'. *Journal of Feminist Family Therapy: An International Forum* 17(3–4): 109–41.

2006. 'Negotiating the Present, Historicizing the Future: Palestinian Children Speak About the Israeli Separation Wall'. *American Behavioral Scientist Journal* 49(8): 1101–34.

2007a. *Facing the Wall: Palestinian Children and Adolescents Speak About the Israeli Separation Wall*. Jerusalem: World Vision.

2007b. 'Israeli Policies of House Demolitions: and the Struggle for Memory, Land, and Identity: A Feminist Perspective'. *Balsam* 383: 60–2 (in Arabic).

2007c. *Gender and the Militarization of Education in Palestine*. Jerusalem: Women's Studies Center (WSC).

2008. 'The Gendered Nature of Education Under Siege: A Palestinian Feminist Perspective'. *International Journal of Lifelong Education* 27(2): 179–200.

Shavit, A. 2004. 'Survival of the Fittest? An Interview with Benny Morris'. *Ha'aretz* 9 January. Available online, at: www.logosjournal.com/morris.htm.

Shehadeh, R. 1998. 'Land and Occupation: A Legal Review'. *Palestine-Israel Journal* 4(2): 25–30.

Siapno, J. 2001. 'Gender, Nationalism and the Ambiguity of Female Agency in Aceh, Indonesia, and East Timor', in M.R. Waller and J. Rycenga (eds), *Frontline Feminisms: Women, War, and Resistance*, 275–95. New York and London: Garland.

Slyomovics, S. 2007. 'The Rape of Qula: Destroyed Palestinian Village', in A. H. Sa'di and L. Abu-Lughod (eds), *Nakba, Palestine, 1948 and the Claims of Memory*, 27–51. New York: Columbia University Press.

Sousa Santos, B. de. 2002. *Toward a New Legal Common Sense: Law, Globalization, and Emancipation*. London: Butterworths LexisNexis.

Spivak, G.K. 1985. 'Can the Subaltern Speak? Speculations on Widow Sacrifice'. *Wedge* 7–8: 120–30.

Strang, H. and J. Braithwait (eds) 2002. *Restorative Justice and Family Violence*. Cambridge: Cambridge University Press.

Strauss, A. and J. Corbin. 1990. *Basics of Qualitative Research: Grounded Theory Procedures and Techniques*. Newbury Park: Sage.

Sullivan, T.Z. 1998. 'Eluding the Feminist, Overthrowing the Modern? Transformations in Twentieth-Century Iran', in L. Abu-Lughod (ed.), *Remaking Women: Feminism and Modernity in the Middle East*, 215–42. Princeton: Princeton University Press.

Thorhill, T. 1992. *Making Women Talk: The Interrogation of Palestinian Women*. London: Lawyers for Palestinian Human Rights.

Trinh, T.M.-H. 1989. *Woman, Native, Other: Writing Post-Coloniality and Feminism*. Bloomington: Indiana University Press.

Turshen, M. and C. Twagiramariya (eds) 1998. *What Women Do in Wartime: Gender and Conflict in Africa*. London: Zed Books.

Volpp, L. 2000. 'Blaming Culture for Bad Behavior'. *Yale Journal of Law and the Humanities* 12: 89–117.

——— 2001. 'Feminism Versus Multiculturalism'. *Columbia Law Review* 101: 1101–218.

Waller, M.R. and J. Rycenga (eds) 2001. *Frontline Feminisms: Women, War and Resistance*. New York: Routledge.

Warnock, K. 1990. *Land Before Honour: Palestinian Women in the Occupied Territories*. New York: Monthly Review.

Williams, P. 1999. 'Inflecting Critical Race Theory'. *Feminist Legal Studies* 7(2): 111–32.

Wing, A.K. 1994. 'Customs, Religion, and Rights: The Future Legal Status of Palestinian Women'. *Harvard International Law Journal* 35(1): 149–200.

——— 2000. *Global Critical Race Feminism: An International Reader*. New York: New York University Press.

Wolf, N. 1994. *Fire with Fire: The New Female Power and How to Use It*. New York: Random House.

Yuval-Davis, N. and F. Anthias (eds) 1989. *Woman-nation-state*. Houndmills: Macmillan.

Zureik, E. 1978. *The Palestinians in Israel: A Study in Internal Colonialism*. London: PKP.

INDEX

UNCCP (UN Conciliation Commission for Palestine), 162
UNRPR (UN Relief for Palestinian Refugees), 162
UNRWA (UN Relief and Works Agency for Palestinian Refugees in the Near East), 162
urf (customary law), 141

VAW (violence against women), *see* violence against women (VAW)
veil
 as iconic signifier of Otherness, 57–58
 as resistance, 92
 as way of coping, 59, *see also* Hijab
 forced removal, 92
'victim feminism', 46–47
victim status, 46–48
violence against women (VAW)
 and wounded masculinity, 104–105
 as cultural, 51
 narratives, 41–44
 political conflicts and, 60–62
 response to, 143–149
 theoretical context, 44–49
'virginity'
 concept of, 137–138, *see also* IVT (imposed virginity testing)

WCLAC (Women's Center for Legal Aid and Counselling), 15, 22–23, 24, 25
weaponization
 definitions, 114
 genealogy of, 112–117, 127–142
 of the body, 117–123, 126
Wing, A. K., 69–70
Wisam, 41
Wolf, Naomi, *Fire with Fire*, 46
Women, Islam and the State (Kandiyoti), 98
women's agency
 and PA (Palestinian Authority), 96–97
 and totalizing theories, 52–54
 definitions, 50
Women's Center for Legal Aid and Counselling (WCLAC), 15, 22–23, 24, 25
women's history, lack of, 13–14
World Vision (WV), 23
WSC (Women's Studies Center–Jerusalem), 23, 25
WV (World Vision), 23

Yaalon, Moshe, 5
yitsalahou, 113
Yusra, 17
Yuval-Davis, Nira, 122, 133

zaherat al fordat, 180
Zidan, Aiysha Jima, 112–113

Printed in Great Britain
by Amazon